# Dress Casual

# Dress Casual

## HOW COLLEGE STUDENTS REDEFINED
## AMERICAN STYLE

### Deirdre Clemente

*The University of North Carolina Press / Chapel Hill*

The paper in this book meets the guidelines for permanence and durability
of the Committee on Production Guidelines for Book Longevity of the Council
on Library Resources. The University of North Carolina Press has been a
member of the Green Press Initiative since 2003.

Complete cataloging information for this title is available
from the Library of Congress.
978-1-4696-1407-6 (cloth: alk. paper)
978-1-4696-1408-3 (ebook)

18  17  16  15  14    5  4  3  2  1

*For the Lison sisters and the McMahon sisters*

# Contents

# Illustrations

# Acknowledgments

I never met him, but I know Chalmers Alexander (Princeton, Class of 1932). Agnes Edwards (Berkeley, Class of 1921), annoys me, and I definitely would hang out with Nancy Murray (Radcliffe, Class of 1946). I would have borrowed Nancy's clothes (the green dress she wore to the MIT prom, maybe?), and, as a testimony to our friendship, I would have swapped rations tickets so she could get the ski boots she wanted.

I hope that Chalmers, Agnes, and Nancy would think I got it right.

This book began at Carnegie Mellon University, where I learned how to write about history from a first-rate faculty and a cohort of graduate students. Scott Sandage always saw the bigger picture when I struggled to take my gaze from the minutia, and *Dress Casual* is the direct result of our many conversations in coffee shops around Pittsburgh. Professors Steve Schlossman, David Hounshell, and Lisa Tetrault asked questions and gave advice—some of which I didn't want to hear. Colleague Michelle Mock and colleague and dear friend Carrie Hagan listened for six long years and shared their vast knowledge of twentieth-century women's history.

Along the path from research to revisions and now to book, I've benefited from the generosity of other historians. Jim Axtell and I missed each other by ten minutes at a rainy "Reunions" on the Princeton campus in 2005. We still haven't met, but his guidance and advice has profoundly shaped the content of this book. Daniel Horowitz, Kelly Schrum, Lawrence Glickman, Jacqueline Dowd Hall, Nancy Cott, and Mary C. Kelley shared their thoughts on the project at various stages of its development. I am grateful to my colleagues in the history department at UNLV, including Andy Kirk and David Tanenhaus, and the dean of the College of Liberal Arts, Chris Hudgins, who made sure I had the resources I needed to finish this book. The editorial team at UNC Press held my hand and patted me on the back. Mark Simpson-Vos backed the project from our first meeting, and his faith in me and my work has been much appreciated.

The research for this project was funded by Carnegie Mellon, the Friends of Princeton Library, Schlesinger Library at the Radcliffe Institute for Advanced Study at Harvard University, and the University Nevada Las Vegas. University archivist were incredibly helpful, including the one and only Dan Linke (Princeton), Sarah Hutcheon (Schlesinger Library), Lee Stout, Jackie Esposito, and Paul Dzyak (Penn State), Kathryn Neal (Berkeley), Eric Esau and Sarah Hartwell (Dartmouth), and Karen Cannell, Juliet Jacobson, Melissa Marra, and Tanya Melendez (Fashion Institute of Technology). Many thanks to Courtney Keel and Emily Ruby at the Heinz History Center in Pittsburgh and the remarkable Erin Goseer Mitchell, who shared her stories and her photos of life at Spelman College in the 1950s. I am indebted to my research assistant, Katie Sabo, who steered the ship when it was going off course.

My mother, Claudia Clemente, endured a very cold January in Georgia to help me research dress codes at Spelman—only one instance in a long line of extraordinary support. We got lost on the way to the archives every day and had a million laughs. My first year in graduate school, I fell in love with a Metallica-T-shirt-wearing, Iron City Beer–drinking, difficult-question-asking Irishman. I married him, and we have some long-legged daughters together. They give me reason to hurry up and get home.

For fishing at Stone Valley, paying off credit cards, and teaching me how to be a scholar, my father, Frank Clemente, gets the last word: thanks.

# Introduction

What are you wearing? Whether it is jeans and sneakers or khakis with a sports coat, chances are college kids made it cool.

The modern American wardrobe was born on the college campus in the first half of the twentieth century. Its creators were the knickers-clad members of Princeton's Cottage Club, the women of the University of California's "Committee to Wear Pants to Dinner," and the sweatshirted students of Penn State. Collegians such as Dick Eberhart (Dartmouth, Class of 1926) and Erin Goseer (Spelman, Class of 1955) cherry-picked a collection of functional garments and wove together a manner of dress that was initially suited to campus life, became a default for grown-ups on weekends and vacations, and is now worn to worship on Sundays and to the office on days other than Friday. Dick prized a shearling-lined, leather bomber jacket perfect for New Hampshire winters, and he paired it with tweed knickers. Erin wore a loose-fitting, pleated skirt with her broken-in saddle shoes—but the conservative deans at her college insisted she wear stockings instead of ankle socks. Whenever possible, students ignored the old guard's meddling. In 1938, the *Radcliffe News* told freshmen, "Every store in the country has joined with *Harper's*, *Vogue*, and *Mademoiselle* to present college fashions," but their take was what really mattered: "*We* want to tell you." In four pages they did: "you can never have too many" sweaters; don't bother wearing a hat; beat-up sports shoes are "at the head of the list for tearing over Cambridge cobblestones."[1]

Dubbed "casual" by journalists, the fashion industry, and the students themselves, this style varied by campus, by decade, and, most significantly, by individual. Yet casual style uniformly stressed comfort and practicality—two words that have gotten little respect in the history of fashion but have transformed how people in the United States and, eventually, in many

1

cultures around the world now live our everyday lives.[2] To dress casual is quintessentially to dress as an American and to live, or to dream of living, fast and loose and carefree. Casual clothing "has done much to democratize America," declared a fashion executive in 1975. "Through clothes a person can 'feel American' at every price level, at the same time, anywhere across the country."[3] This is why you are wearing what you are wearing: because American college students began to dress down in the middle part of the twentieth century, gradually blurring the visual markers of class, region, race, gender, and age. Faded jeans, a soft shirt, and shoes that are open toed by design or neglect make for a wardrobe that can be high-end, low-end, or second hand without tagging the wearer as rich or poor, old or young, powerful or oppressed, or anything else, really, except American (or trying to be). The story of how this happened—of how casual style took over and changed America by a seemingly simple change of clothes—demonstrates a seismic shift in how, why, and where collective taste is forged.

The American middle class supplied the manpower to make casual style a cultural standard in only half of a century. Neither those higher nor those lower on the socioeconomic food chain had the critical mass to do it. As historian Burton Bledstein notes, in the early twentieth century, college became the "testing grounds" for "an energetic middle class," and campus life provided them all with a working wardrobe.[4] As millions of collegians stepped off of campus and into American society, they took their comfortable clothes with them. Even those who didn't attend college embraced casual dress, calling it "the greatest act of liberation you've seen in recent years."[5] Across the socioeconomic spectrum, the casual clothing popularized by middle-class collegians and identified with the middle class more generally became the standard of dress for all Americans. In his 1950 treatise *The Lonely Crowd*, sociologist David Riesman wrote that middle class Americans wore casual clothes because they have a "fear of being high hat." He believed that "one can wear gaudy shirts but not stiff ones."[6] Even the loftiest among us took to casual. A 1952 Penn State student wondered if everyone's interest in dressing down had "something to do with President Truman's 'Oh, so bright and loud' sport shirts."[7] But men across America didn't buy those shirts because the president did. Rather, the president bought the shirts because *they* did. *He* wanted to look like *them*. Today, T-shirts, sweaters, jeans, sports shoes, and the occasional sweatpants make "middle classness" available to anyone who chooses to put them on. Ninety percent of Americans self-identify as middle class, so that's a lot of jersey.[8]

The shift from collared to comfortable came amid the kind of sweeping social change that is detailed in History 102 textbooks and Ken Burns documentaries: two waves of American feminism, one Depression, two world wars, six decades of civil rights, and the movement of millions of families into the suburbs where thousands of shopping malls awaited them. The historical context for casual style is immense. Everything from war shortages and man-made fibers to cowboy movies and comic books influenced the trajectory of casual clothing. So did the near revolutions in *how* and *why* we bought clothing: the consolidation of the ready-to-wear industry; the arrival of mass media, in particular film and magazines; and the evolution of department stores from displayers of hodgepodge products to efficient institutions of capitalism. Between 1935 and 1959, personal consumption per person increased by 87 percent.[9] By 1960, clothing production and distribution was the third-largest industry in the country, behind the steel and food industries. Just a decade earlier, the clothing industry had been the eighth.[10] In the words of a fashion industry insider, the clothing we bought in 1965, "like all that typifies our time," was unmistakably "informal."[11]

Scratchy film footage of city street scenes and sepia photographs only crack the surface of how formally we dressed at the turn of the twentieth century. Men wore bowler hats, bowties, buttoned vests, pegged pants, and ankle boots, but underneath these clothes were one-piece suits of knitted underwear—wool, most often, but cotton if the weather permitted. Suspenders held up pants, and stringlike mechanisms called garters cinched onto a man's calves, and metal clips attached to them fastened on the tops of socks to keep them from slouching. Such was life before elastic. Shirt collars were heavily starched and detachable because most men only had a few shirts and multiple collars allowed for the illusion of cleanliness every day. There was no such thing as wash and wear. We can see from a picture of a woman in 1890 that she is wearing a bustle—nobody's rear end sticks out like that. What we don't see are the buckles, lacings, and multiple layers of fabric that made dressing—and undressing—a time-consuming chore and something to be done in private. Skirts went down to the ground, stockings up to the thigh, and heads and hands were covered.

The modern viewer struggles to fully understand the physicality and social significance of these garments. Modesty was—and had long been—part of it, but dressing up is called dressing *up* for a reason. Not everybody had the means or occasion for such elaborate dressing, but if you wanted social standing, you had better try. Whether it was successfully achieved or mimicked with what you had available, formal dress was the cultural standard. Little more than sixty years later, garters, hats, gloves, hard collars, corsets, petticoats, tailcoats, and waistcoats were relics of a restrained past. Casual style fundamentally changed the relationship between our clothing and our bodies. Sportswear was the foundation of the collegiate wardrobe, and shorts and T-shirts freed appendages that had been hidden for centuries.[12] Initially, gym clothes as street clothes rattled the sensibilities of the unconvinced. Clothing that was relegated to athletics in 1910 was worn to the student lounge in the 1930s, to class in the 1940s, and to the dining hall in the 1950s. By the 1960s, nearly everyone under the age of sixty owned a sweatshirt. Men wore briefs and women wore bras—most of the time. Americans dressed not only to suit class affiliations and aspirations but also for a mélange of ever-shifting political, cultural, sexual, racial, and ethnic identities. This book is about how cultural standards are forged, challenged, and then recast.

Although modern Americans (including scholars) are habituated to give the credit to Hollywood, Madison Avenue, and even Parisian couturiers, college students were the primary players in the creation and widespread adoption of casual style. The garments collegians chose were not all born on campus. Many were taken there. Tweed sports jackets came from the golf course in an era when the elite "set the pace for all matters of fashion," as economist Thorstein Veblen put it in 1900.[13] But "trickle-down" fashion dissemination does not explain how workmen's jeans became the pants of choice for millions of middle-class collegians in the 1940s, and neither does the complex system of signs and signifiers that semiologists offer up to codify these kinds of appropriation.[14] More useful is sociologist Herbert Blumer's "collective selection," the forging of group opinion that happens when "people [are] thrown into areas of common interaction and, having similar runs of experience, develop common tastes."[15] Campus life provided such experiences, and, as the case studies in this book attest, the variables of "campus life" dictated the nature and scope of the adoption of casual style. In their letters, diaries, newspaper editorials, humor magazines, and student handbooks, the men and women of Princeton, Radcliffe, Penn State, California, Spelman, and Morehouse tell us how and why they chose comfortable clothing.

Unlike tweed-clad country clubbers or dungaree-wearing ditch diggers, middle-class collegians had the cultural muscle and demographic power to command the mass production of comfortable clothing. The strength of collegians was their numbers, and the allure of their clothing was its versatility. In little more than half a century, collegians grew from an esoteric enclave to a nationwide bevy of raccoon-coated Charleston dancers, to a team of dungaree-wearing war workers and khaki-clad GIs, to an eclectic group as diverse as the clothing they wore. In 1900 only 4 percent of eighteen- to twenty-one-year-olds attended college; 8 percent did so by 1920; 16 percent, by 1940; and 30 percent, by 1950. In 1970, nearly half of this demographic attended college. The ranks of women skyrocketed from 85,000 in 1900 to more than 800,000 five decades later.[16] Upper-class and upper-middle-class students made up the initial rush to higher education, but by the 1950s, that had drastically changed. "Who goes to Penn State?" a promotional pamphlet for the university asked in 1955: the "sons and daughters" of "artists, grocers, engineers, doctors, and salesmen—the country's artisans, business men and professional people."[17] Casual style meant lumberjack coats for some, cardigan sweaters for others, and well-worn shoes for most. In 1924, a Princetonian remarked, "Princeton students undoubtedly would be horrified to realize that flannel shirts and sweaters were worn by the undergraduates of Western universities."[18] While the actual incarnations of casual style varied, its modus operandi did not. Cal men wore flannel shirts with sweaters, and Princeton men chose dirty, white bucks paired with navy blue blazers. Both were dressed casually because both favored freedom over formality.

Casual style was not prescribed but self-selected. Cal women warned freshmen, "under no circumstances allow mother or dear auntie to take you on a shopping tour in which she picks out what she thinks a college girl should wear."[19] Time and again, collegians' comfortable and practical clothing put them at odds with their conservative mothers, fashion writers, and administrative deans, who accepted that "it's collegiate to be casual" but clarified, "That doesn't mean slipshod!"[20] Accusations of "sloppy" grew increasingly louder as the century progressed. The dean of students at Michigan State College made national news in 1948 when he said, "Sloppy clothes indicate loose morals." An angry Radcliffe freshman admitted that she had "never dressed so messily in all my life," but insisted that "my morals are the same as they were."[21] From the mouth of a college babe, here was a question we still ask: Has America become a nation of moral and physical slugs? And an answer: the coming of casual is not a story of decline. To paint it as such prioritizes one set of cultural standards over another and whitewashes the historical contexts that created casual style. So, no. That was one Cliffie's answer, and it is also mine.

Understanding when and how different groups of collegians took to casual style is far more useful for gauging social change than is shaking a finger at the yoga-panted among us. Dressing down became democratic in its accessibility, but rich, white men got to do it first. Race, class, and gender determined who wore casual clothing, how early in the century they wore it, and often, what form it took. Whether a school was in the country or the city, on the East Coast or the West Coast, in the North or South also directly informed the adoption of casual dress, as did the inclinations of school administrators. At the all-black Spelman and Morehouse Colleges in Atlanta, administrators created strict regulations to uphold the schools' conservative, Christian image. The colleges educated students from across the socioeconomic spectrum, and a large share came from southern, middle-class families. Due to a lack of historical sources, details of life at Spelman and the less-documented Morehouse are largely gleaned from official sources such as the student handbooks written by Spelman president Lucy Tapely.[22] Tapley's draconian dress codes made campus life, in the words of Langston Hughes, "like going back to . . . Massachusetts in the days of witch-burning Puritans."[23] Fancy trimmings and materials were outlawed, and handbooks decreed that no "dress made of silk or . . . materials resembling silk" would be tolerated. As for shoes, "no color except black will be allowed."[24] For most of the period studied, the students at Spelman "expected their education to lead to economic advantage and social respect but enfolded their quest within accepted middle-class gender codes," as historian Margaret Lowe writes.[25] These gender codes, written in part by middle-class white women, continued to shape Spelman's sartorial standards even as middle-class white women abandoned such formality. For example, in 1960, Spelman's student newspaper reminded women, "Girdles are always in vogue, on and off campus." Their white counterparts at the Seven Sisters had shunned that garment nearly two decades earlier.[26]

The narrative of *Dress Casual* leaves off at a time when the clothing of African American students became, perhaps, most interesting and certainly most casual.[27] As the civil rights movement made headway on and off campus, student activists mimicked the middle-class leadership of the movement and selected conservative, formal dress. In the mid- and late 1960s, however, black students such as Barnard College's Sherry Suttles used casual dress as a way to live out new racial identities. In her freshman year, Suttles wrote to her mother in Detroit of the trouble she was having finding someone to do her hair. The hairdresser "did a lousy job," she wrote. It was hardly clean; it wasn't pressed well, either."[28] Two years later, in 1967, Suttles no longer pressed her hair but had a classmate braid it or went to Harlem to have her Afro teased out. Suttles was asked to be a "queen" for Columbia's active Alpha Phi Alpha chapter, and she attended avant-garde theater productions on black history. Suttles no longer wore ironed dresses but donned rolled-up jeans and beaded necklaces she purchased on a summer trip to the Ivory Coast. Fitting in with her white colleagues was no longer her priority. She wanted to fit in with black, politically active New Yorkers—the ones who occupied Columbia University's Hamilton Hall in 1968 to protest the alleged construction of a segregated gymnasium in Morningside Park.[29]

The many upper- and middle-class white students were in the best position to push convention, and early in the century, Princeton led the way.[30] Perhaps it was F. Scott Fitzgerald, the homogeneity of student culture, or the exalted place of sports on campus, but the press sold Princetonians as the arbiters of men's collegiate fashion—even as middle-class students at Cal and Penn State developed their own interpretations of casual style. In 1931, an article in the *Saturday Evening Post* explained, "Harvard starts almost no young men's style. Yale starts a few. But the collegiate spring styles of the United States are likely to be worn home by Princeton students for the Christmas holidays."[31] Princeton men proudly proclaimed that they "make it a custom to under- rather than over-dress," but colleagues at Harvard accused them feigned nonchalance.[32] Princetonians, they claimed, tried desperately to "affect rather an air of '*Que est-ce que le diable*,' almost of negligee, attaining it by the simple expedient of leaving a button undone, or allowing a single lock to stray bewitchingly over one's temple."[33] Whether their casual style was orchestrated or authentic, the students of Princeton in the first decades of the century were instrumental in redefining the American man as youthful, leisure-focused, and casually dressed.

At Penn State and Cal, the socioeconomic status of the students and the demands of campus life fostered casual style. The universities' emphasis on agriculture, mining, engineering, and forestry made functional garments the first choice for in-class attire. As higher education became increasingly accessible to Americans of all classes, races, and ethnicities, both schools grew exponentially. In 1960, Penn State had more than 17,000 students and Cal nearly 25,000. The modest budgets of most students curbed extravagance, and students sought to make the most of what they had. Both men and women actively repurposed outdated clothes, and they valued durability and versatility. True, Princetonians were the first to wear sportswear to class and to dinner, but their middle-class colleagues at state universities made casual style accessible and alluring to the country at large. Middle-class students freed casual clothing from its tweedy origins, and prioritized blue jeans over white flannels.

Across the board, the clothing of male collegians was less regulated, less controversial, and less hampered by convention than their sisters.' Women at elite, single-sex institutions were in an optimal situation to experiment with dress standards: little interference from school administrators; few men to naysay their campus wardrobes; and ample financial resources to buy casual clothing and "date clothes," which they wore to public functions and off campus on the weekends. Country colleges such as Wellesley, Vassar, and Smith took to jeans, pants, and shorts sooner than did the women at city schools such as Barnard and Radcliffe, where many students commuted and potential boyfriends attended neighboring schools. At Radcliffe, women were "noted more for their learning than beauty."[34] Their neighbors across the Yard portrayed the Cliffie as "a thoroughly unattractive figure" who "wandered into the library like the witch of Endor and enquired if the lost volume of Kant had been returned."[35] Cliffies back-talked Harvard men and ignored the suggestions of fashion editors.

Casual style for women meant pants, and at the Seven Sisters, administrators stood silently on the sidelines when students began to wear pants and jeans in the late 1930s. At coeducational institutions such as Penn State and Cal, the presence of men impeded the more informal trends. In 1934, a student explained that at "universities where there is the constant presence of the male to contend with, heels are a little higher, tailored dresses take the place of skirts and sweaters and hats are worn on well curled heads."[36] Following World War II, more women wanted to wear pants and jeans, and deans at both schools actively policed these garments. By the mid-1950s, however, coeds no longer begrudgingly accepted dress codes. Instead, they petitioned and protested to wear what they wanted, when they wanted. Still, many schools held onto regulations that were difficult to enforce and comically outdated. As the Free Speech Movement ignited the Cal campus in 1965, dorm women petitioned the administration to let them wear sweatshirts to the cafeteria. As the 1960s progressed, student protests for women's rights, civil rights, and human rights rendered many dress codes obsolete on campuses across the country.

The development of dress styles is dependent on its social and cultural environment, and, as sociologist Dick Hebdige advises, "we should not attempt to lift them too far from the contexts in which they are produced and worn."[37] Casual style took root and grew on the college campus, and this book considers collegians and comfortable clothes in five specific venues: popular culture, the classroom, the dorm, the dance, and the gym.

Chapter 1 traces the development of collegians as tastemakers and consumers. Early in the century, a new appreciation for youthfulness and health promoted collegians to a position of cultural authority. By the 1930s, clothing manufacturers sponsored design contests on campus and retailers partnered with magazines such as *Vanity Fair* (1913), *Esquire* (1933), and *Mademoiselle* (1935) to poll readers and sell clothes. Despite efforts to understand them, collegians remained aloof.[38] Chapter 2 pinpoints when and where casual style was worn—and by whom. This chapter focuses on two garments in two areas of the campus: suits in the classroom for men and pants in the cafeteria for women. Chapter 3 shows how the demands of dorm life encouraged casual style. Here, collegians learned from one another the spoken and unspoken rules of campus dress, and encountered new technologies such as laundry machines and man-made fibers. Chapters 4 and 5 examine the most formal and informal aspects of collegiate dress: prom clothes and gym garb. Chapter 4 traces the evolution of men's formalwear from tailcoats to tuxedos to the multipurpose dark suit. Women swapped elaborate collections of gowns and accessories for a single cocktail dress. Collegians divested the American wardrobe of its most impractical garments and reset the bar for "formal" far closer to casual. Chapter 5 traces the evolution of sweaters and shorts, two collegiate clothing trends that began as gym garb became standard campus attire and, ultimately, staples of casual style. Social critics merely grumbled at the garments on men, but they decried baggy sweaters and Bermuda shorts on women. Chapters 4 and 5 track the lifecycles of specific garments and integrate archival sources with material culture.

I am the daughter of a sociologist and an avid *Vogue* reader who wore red leather pants to my third-grade parent-teacher conference. I have spent a lifetime appreciating, analyzing, researching, and dissecting clothing—both figuratively and literally. As a teen I often drove an hour from my sleepy college town to an industrial city in central Pennsylvania called Altoona. The Altoona Salvation Army sold the stuff of legends— well-worn Levis (cords and jeans), shiny leather blazers àla Tony Manero in *Saturday Night Fever,* cowboy shirts, 1930s hats, and all kinds of women's undergarments that confused me but that I inherently knew were cool. If something was handmade, I usually wanted to own it. Making things is our most primal attachment to material culture. The social meanings of dress are often instantaneous, but they are always subjective. In the blink of an eye, we interpret a three-piece suit, surfer shorts, or a tight shirt over a push-up bra. Yet the intended and received meanings don't always jibe. Clothing is too imprecise to be a language. What we wear is simultaneously our most private self and our most public self. Clothing is how we cover our bodies and how we present ourselves to the world.

So clothing matters.

Casual clothing matters because it is what Americans increasingly wore as they lived out the "big picture" changes of the twentieth century: the rise of the middle class, consumerism, suburbanization, higher education, and women's and civil rights. For the first time in human history, great swathes of a population no longer considered shelter, food, and clothing as merely meeting physical needs. Rather, our homes, our diets, and our fashions made it possible for, as one scholar put it, "a great variety of people, engaged in such varied economic roles, to identify themselves as part of the middle class." Being middle class was not about one's profession or even one's income. Rather, members of the middle class were "united by shared aspirations and cultural practices," and consumption allowed nearly everyone to purchase a place in the middle.[39] We middle classers bought dining room sets and put our leftovers in Tupperware. As historians have chronicled, more and more Americans participated in the cultural rituals we deemed "middle class": going on vacation, eating in restaurants, and using a real estate agent to find the perfect middle-class home.[40] Clothing is far more overt than a new bedroom set or a subscription to *Life* magazine. Veblen has told us, "Our apparel is always in evidence," but for cultural historians, the closet has remained unopened.[41]

The clothing of the twentieth century is the clothing of the American middle class. Casual clothing provided it with what fashion theorist Gilles Liposvetsky called "a way out of the world of tradition."[42] Those who chose the way out left behind starched formality and skin-irritating undergarments. Their departure was slow but steady, and it was about more than clothes. "It's been called an American explosion," said a suburban mother in 1954, and "it is knocking down the walls of outworn and confining patterns of living." Comfortable, practical garments inspired middle-class Americans to "throw off" their "slavish conformity to the culture and fashions of the past" and "live as free Americans in a style peculiarly [their] own."[43] Pedal pushers, white Keds, ankle socks, a twin sweater set, and a headscarf? College women were the first to popularize every piece of clothing in Mrs. Suburbia's iconic ensemble. Much more than wasp-waisted dresses or grey flannel suits, casual clothing was constitutive of the American middle-class experience in the post–World War II period. For middle-class men, "casual dress," wrote Riesman, showed "that one is a good fellow not only on the golf course or on vacation but in the office and at dinner too."[44] College men pioneered the versatile wardrobe. In 1939 a trade publication wrote, "College men are changing the apparel habits of the nation. They've gone one step beyond the 'change your clothes at six' idea to say that one should be enough of an individualist to wear comfortable, colorful clothes whenever the spirit moves."[45] The cultural standards that define what can be worn and when were ultimately approved at the

PTA meetings, the Little League games, the backyard barbecues, the family-friendly beach resorts in Florida, and the countless other places where a diverse middle class created and confirmed a middle-class culture. However, the garments the middle class wore and the trend toward dressing down came from the college campus.

The clothing we put on our bodies is a lived experience, not an afterthought. What collegians wore mattered to them. On 5 April 1930, Chalmers Alexander (Princeton, Class of 1932) told his mother, "In the Spring a lot of flannels are worn here" and "displayed in windows." Get "mine as soon as possible," he wrote. "Be sure the bottoms of the trousers are 19 inches."[46] He was anxious to fit in on a campus where there are "so many fine Packards, Cadillacs, and Pierce-Arrows that you don't even notice them."[47] At the forefront of a new kind of femininity, Marjorie Cherry (Pomona, Class of 1932) thanked her mother for letting her buy "those dear little pants with their bell-bottoms" that are "just the right size and color" and made her "feel Catalina-ish." She could not wait to show off the pants and told her mother, "If Clancy doesn't take me to the beach pretty soon, I'll expire!"[48]

This book documents the daily decision made by millions of collegians to dress casual.

### CHAPTER ONE

# In the Public Eye

In the first half of the twentieth century, college students seemed to be everywhere. Their football games were followed at a national level, their dances were deemed immoral, and their hygiene habits were suspect. Journalists, social commentators, and educators dissected nearly every aspect of collegians' culture, and did so in front of a very interested American public. Songs such as 1925's "Collegiate" proclaimed the undergrad's arrival: "Trousers baggy. And our clothes look raggy. But we're rough and ready."[1] They were rough and ready—to play and to buy.

Collegians came to national attention in the 1910s, phased into a raccoon-coated phenomenon in the 1920s, and proved their collective buying power in the 1930s. Itself just a newcomer to the country's cultural landscape, the American fashion industry understood that "casual clothing which will stand up under hard wear and still continue to look well is what the co-ed wants."[2] Yet retailers, manufacturers, and fashion editors struggled to understand and meet the group's demands. Princeton was inundated with trend scouts who were looking for inspiration. In 1936, a student reporter snipped, "It's hardly worth an undergraduate's life these days to appear on the campus in presentable garb. If he does, a dapper gentleman with a camera pops out from behind some tree or other, snaps a quick photo, and the next thing the bewildered undergrad knows, he finds himself in the style magazines or in clothing advertisements."[3]

Retailers recruited students to help select and sell back-to-school styles. Magazines such as the *Saturday Evening Post* (1897), *Vanity Fair* (1913), *Esquire* (1932), and *Mademoiselle* (1935) ran advertisements, fiction, and fashion advice aimed to catch the eye of collegians—or the many others who followed their cultural lead. "College students," writes historian Paula Fass, "were fashion and fad pacesetters whose behavior, interest, and amusements caught the national imagination and were emulated by other youth." This power "turned the idea of youth into an eminently salable commodity."[4] In 1932, fashion theorist J. C. Flugel noted the influence of college youth on their parents' generation: "Maturity has willingly forgone its former dignities in return for the right of sharing in the appearance and activities of youth."[5] Illustrations by John Held and novels by F. Scott Fitzgerald delivered a deceptively homogenous collegiate experience in which everyone was white and upper middle class.

Visible cracks came to the surface after World War II, as the sheer number of collegians made even the semblance of monolithic student culture impossible. The ranks of college students swelled from 1.5 million in 1940 to 3.7 million in 1960.[6] These new recruits came from across the socioeconomic spectrum, but the bulk of them were solidly middle class. With time, students became increasingly disenchanted with the status quo. Historian of student culture Helen Lefkowitz Horowitz writes of the 1960s, "Traditional college life had lost its appeal to many. Schools suspended college rituals due to lack of interest." Clothing made to "distinguish between the sexes, and enhance status, gave way to revealing, 'natural,' androgenized looks democratized by denim."[7] A more diverse collegiate demographic and an increasingly powerful teenage market complicated the fashion industry's attempts to understand youth's tastes. In many ways, as historian Thomas Frank has explained, "The conceptual position of youthfulness became as great an element of the marketing picture as youth itself."[8] In 1969, the editor of *Mademoiselle* told fashion industry insiders, "For the first time in history, there is freedom of fashion choice . . . the mature and the young can establish her own identity, express her own individuality, and, as never before, do her own thing."[9] "Lifestyle," with its celebration of personal choice, guided consumption. As fashion executives, publicity agents, and department store buyers learned, one size no longer fit all.

What and how an individual student bought depended on circumstance, individual tastes, and most significantly, personal finance. Radcliffe freshman and clotheshorse Nancy Murray (Class of 1946) wrote of her relationship with spending: "Money is liquid and flows gaily in the wrong direction—to other pockets than my own."[10] Princeton's Chalmers Alexander (Class of 1932) received weekly boxes of his maid's oatmeal-raisin cookies and his mother's latest offerings for his wardrobe. His purchasing instructions were exacting, and many packages were exchanged between his home in Jackson, Mississippi, and his dorm room in New Jersey. Despite his seemingly affluent background, the tightly wound Chalmers methodically documented daily expenses. During the Depression, the family's financial situation was dire, and Chalmers moved to Edwards Hall, a dorm he described as "old and shaggy and the lowest ranking dormitory on campus (a lot of boys who are working their way through)." The move was difficult, and he admitted to his parents, "I naturally would prefer not moving there just as you'd prefer not moving to South Jackson."[11] The decision to buy or not to buy was ultimately a personal one.[12]

### "A Kind of 'Exhibit X'": Collegians Come to the Fore

The number of college-going youth grew from nearly 240,000 in 1900 to 600,000 in 1920—a 150 percent increase that repositioned collegians on America's cultural landscape.[13] Ready-to-wear clothing manufacturers and retailers realized that collegians' dress standards were markedly different from those of their parents. College men sought clothing that proclaimed their alliance to the campus's all-important sports culture. These men wanted comfortable, practical clothing that could be worn from the golf course to the dining hall to the classroom with few social repercussions. Magazines such as the *Saturday Evening Post* and *Collier's* brought images of J. C. Leyendecker's Arrow Collar Man and tales of gridiron battles into American homes and lives. Manufacturers such as Brooks Brothers stepped in to supply the demand. For college women, however, this distinctly new genre of dress called "sportswear" met with raised eyebrows from social critics. While college women were identified as potential consumers, the retailers, manufacturers, and magazine editors of the 1910s were slow to pursue them.

In the first years of the twentieth century, a cultural interest in youthfulness brought collegians to the attention of the American public as never before. Historian Bill Osgerby argues that the growing emphasis on age stratification was a result of changing demographics and labor markets interfacing with "developments in the fields of legislation, family organization and education to mark out young people as a distinct group associated with particular social needs and cultural characteristics."[14] In the early decades, a new masculinity emerged that stood "in stark contrast to Victorian ideals of masculinity that had prized diligence, thrift and self control." As witnessed in the educational writings of G. Stanley Hall, the Rough Rider rhetoric of Theodore Roosevelt, and the naturalist novels of Frank Norris, the male "body itself became a vital component of manhood: strength, appearance," writes historian E. Anthony Rotundo, and "athletic skill mattered more than in previous centuries."[15] The emphasis on youth's physical wellness was, in the words of one Princeton educator, about "more than

Figure 1.1. An avid shopper even during wartime, Nancy Murray (Radcliffe, Class of 1946) wrote to her parents in September of 1942, "Money is liquid and flows gaily in the wrong direction—to other pockets than my own." Here, she wears saddle shoes, a man's work shirt, and dungaree jeans (note the heavy seams and patch pockets). This kind of clothing was first worn in the 1930s on elite women's campuses in the Northeast but became standard campus wear for women during World War II. Murray's letters home chronicled her buying and beautifying regimen. She wrote of a new and costly perm, a lost earring, and a cocktail dress that was too long. Courtesy of the Schlesinger Library, Radcliffe Institute, Harvard University.

health and strength." Joseph E. Raycroft, the head of the university's Hygiene and Physical Education Department, told alumni in 1915 that by staying fit, the American man was "getting a training in emotional control and an ability to adapt himself successfully to changing conditions that give poise and confidence." These experiences, said Raycroft, were "the most effective ways of educating and developing the real man that lies back of his intellectual processes."[16] Well-funded institutions had elaborate facilities. The lore of Yale's gym, swimming pool, and locker rooms made it all the way to the West Coast. A Cal student who had visited New Haven in 1912 reported in his student newspaper of the private fencing, boxing, and wrestling lessons available.[17] Morehouse College was on the other end of the spectrum, and its students raised money for their own gym. At Morehouse, sports were "encouraged under restrictions that prevent danger to health and neglect to regular school duties."[18] Administrators kept a close eye on the men's exercise to ensure it aided in the "development of manly qualities and moral character."[19] Historian Martin Summers writes of the growing tension between school administrators and young black men on the campuses of Fisk and Howard. The students were "rebelling against the imposition of late-Victorian standards of morality at a time when the ascendancy of consumer culture was increasingly undermining the importance of producer values and respectability among the American middle class." "At stake," says Summers "was the [men's] desire and ability to control their own bodies, the freedom to consume and experience bodily pleasure without fear of being punished."[20]

As social critics, educators, and the students themselves reconceptualized the American man as youthful and healthful, J. C. Leyendecker gave him an enduring image in the Arrow Collar Man.[21] In the first decades of the century, Leyendecker produced illustrations for fashion companies such as Kuppenheimer and Hart, Schaffner & Marx, but his work for Arrow Collars, based in Troy, New York, proved most popular. Arrow Collars and college men were silent partners in the transition from the hard, detachable collar to the more casual, soft or rolled collar. The soft collar was first worn at Princeton around 1912 and then picked up on other campuses after World War I. Students, recent graduates, and the many others who followed collegiate fashions saw themselves in Leyendecker's creation. For example, the Penn State student in figure 1.2 sports a clean-shaven face, lightly slicked (or "watered" hair), and the all-important letterman's sweater. The Arrow Collar Man's fresh-faced appeal broke with "previous notions of masculinity that relegated grooming and fashion to the feminine sphere."[22]

Figure 1.2. The fresh-faced, athletic college man became a cultural icon in the first decades of the twentieth century. His letterman's sweater was a badge of allegiance to the campus sports culture, making it a sought-after fashion statement. Sweaters—and their less formal cousins, sweatshirts—became staples of casual style because they inspired versatility. This 1908 Penn State student and his roomate lounging on the bed behind him demonstrate the varieties of dormwear. Thick robes and wool sweaters were practical solutions to drafty dorms. Courtesy of the Penn State University Archives, Pennsylvania State University Libraries.

In the first decade of the century, magazines such as *Scribner's*, *Collier's*, and *Good Housekeeping* featured articles about white college students, but not necessarily *for* them. The magazines' readers were middle-class Americans, those who aspired to (and did) send their children to college. Hence, hopeful and prospective parents were the target audience. Many insiders believed the result of this coverage to be a "superficial glance," as one put it, made by "theoretical critics who have never lived on a college campus, but have gained their information in secondhand fashion from questionnaires or from newspaper-accounts of the youthful escapades of students." Such a portrait painted the collegian as "an enigma . . . not exactly a boy, certainly not a man, an interesting species, a kind of 'Exhibit X.'"[23] Magazines were routinely charged with miscasting collegians as pranksters or dilettantes. By the eve of World War I, publications such as the *Saturday Evening Post* and the more heady *Smart Set,* whose tagline was "A Magazine of Cleverness," had established a readership of actual undergraduates. *Vanity Fair* was the most coveted magazine by the clothing-conscious collegian. Only one year after it was launched in 1914, the Condé Nast publication ran more pages of advertisements than any other magazine. College students were front and center in the magazine's target demographic. *Vanity Fair* partnered with campus publications to provide fashion advice, running columns on pressing topics such as how to accessorize formal wear in Penn State's humor magazine *Froth* and Cal's *Pelican.* Editors told students: "Don't wear a belt with evening trousers for the simple reason that they do not hang well unless worn with braces."[24] This advice was particularly useful to the growing number of middle-class students who were relatively unaware of the nuances of formal dress.

While college men enjoyed an increasingly public profile via advertisements and magazines articles, college women had a slower rise to celebrity. Early in the century, articles from education experts helped parents pick the right college for their daughter and fictionalized accounts told of dorm antics and midnight feeding parties. Yet manufacturers were slow to market directly to white college women, so they and their mothers cobbled together wardrobes with advice from fellow students and newspapers. An article in the *New York Times* in 1906 told campus-bound women, "One of the rarest delights of the girl who is anticipating life at college is the perpetration of her first freshman trunk." All of its contents must be "just right" or she will know "the blush that comes through the knowledge of wearing clothes that are not in good taste." The author told women to write to the college secretary for advice and have their clothes made "with the social functions of your future Alma Mater in mind."[25] Each campus had its own requirements for graduation gowns or dresses for Class or Founder's Day. These requirements varied from campus to campus and were best learned from experience. Collegiate culture stressed traditions—many of which were only recently invented. Academic class provided an instant pecking order that used social pressure to force newcomers to comply. Peer pressure to adhere to the school's dress standards was particularly high at Spelman, where upper-class students took it as their personal responsibility to educate underclassmen. As Margaret Lowe argues, students did their part in carrying out the school's mission because they believed that "cleanliness and self-control linked to Christian doctrine were critical to creating respectable ladies."[26]

Early in the century, college women's fashions were identified with young women more generally and linked indirectly to campus life. Illustrator Charles Dana Gibson's "Gibson Girl" was sometimes seen sporting a tasseled graduation cap but was more often on a bicycle or with her friends at the beach. Historian Lynn Gordon writes, "By the turn of the century, women could have both higher education and social approval, symbolized by the connection between college life and the Gibson Girl, an American beauty."[27] For women, pale skin and fainting spells were out. Rosy cheeks and physical vigor were in. Despite changing cultural standards, female collegians initially struggled to balance the emerging emphasis on physical fitness with established notions of "ladylike" behavior. In the early 1890s, a Radcliffe student wrote in her daily journal, "I think more and more of my gym every day but how it would shock some of my friends if they knew of our performances."[28] Charlotte Perkins Gilman's treatise *The Dress of Women* canonized the culture buzz around women's fashion and exercise in the first decades of the century. A sociologist, Gilman believed women were crippled in physical action "solely due to the limitations of their clothes and of the conduct supposed to become them."[29] By the mid-1910s, more college women celebrated their athletic skills. Like their male classmates, college women viewed exercise as a "mental tonic" and believed that there was "nothing better than a brisk walk or skate for an hour or two to liven us up for an evening of clear-headed studying."[30] Unlike the new masculinity that stressed aggressive competition, the new femininity discouraged it, and this hindered the development of intercollegiate sports for women well into the 1930s.[31]

In the early years of the century, athleticwear for college women was bloomers, sweaters, and middies—boxy, sailor-inspired blouses that were made of washable duck cotton. Athleticwear allowed for women to "run, dive, leap, hurdle, exert themselves." Historian of sportswear Patricia Campbell Warner notes that before these garments were popularized on the college campus, "women were not permitted any of this activity, in large part, because they were not permitted to wear the clothing that made it possible."[32] As seen in figure 1.3, women's athleticwear was made of breathable and washable materials and allowed for freedom of motion because it was cut loosely. In the first decade of the century, manufacturers and retailers were reluctant to make and sell these garments to college women. Rather, "pattern companies sold designs intended to be interpreted in different ways, allowing readers to create their own definitions of what was appropriate and feminine." Sewing their own gym clothing "gave women the opportunity to experience and discuss the meaning, design,

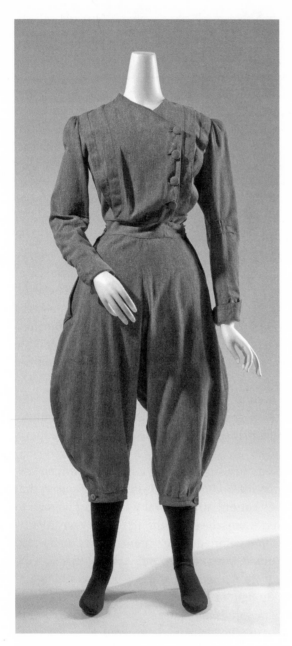

Figure 1.3. Gym suits for women were made of washable, breathable materials that were easy to care for and designed to allow for a range of movement. This 1896 suit is made of cotton twill, though many like it were made of wool because of its hydrophilic properties that whisked sweat from the skin. Companies such as Spaulding manufactured the garments that were sold to universities, who then leased or sold the suits to students. Women also made athleticwear, and home sewing provided an "opportunity to experience and discuss the meaning, design, and feel of their clothing previously left to women seen as oddballs or radicals." Shorts replaced gym suits in the 1920s and then found their way into women's wardrobes for sports and informal occasions in the 1930s. Courtesy of The Museum at FIT.

and feel of their clothing previously left to women seen as oddballs or radicals."[33] In the mid-1910s, key elements of the athleticwear worn by college women in campus gymnasiums (such as a boxy cut, open neckline, loose-fitting sleeves) became associated with a developing genre of dress known as "sportswear." Female collegians became the most ardent supporters.[34]

## "Gold in Them Thar Hills": Collegians Consolidate Their Cultural Power

The decade of the 1920s saw the arrival of a different kind of collegian. Yes, the college man still wore tweed jackets and patterned hosiery, but he abandoned garters, so his socks slouched. John Held drawings depicted pennant-waving students in raccoon-skin coats, but at Princeton in 1924 the "fur coat evil has spread to such proportions that one wonders just where it will lead," according to one dissenter. He felt the coats represented "a false standard of affluence" and warned, "A social stratum based on clothing is fatal—if we must have one, let its foundation be ability."[35] Figure 1.4 offers a vision of the 1920s collegian in a colorful bowtie and oversized raccoon coat. The clean-shaven Arrow Collar man had given way to a more ostentatious and slovenly character. As Penn State's *Froth* told freshman in 1922: "Be drunken, vain, extravagant, wear trick, sloppy clothes, [a]nd you will be the college man the fiction-reader knows."[36] Accusations of "sloppy"—leveled at both men and women—became increasingly loud as the decades progressed, but they were first heard in the 1920s.

In the 1920s, college women became a vibrant market for manufacturers and retailers, who came to realize, as one student put it: "There was gold in them thar hills."[37] By the mid-1910s, retailers began to pursue college women, whose ranks grew from 85,000 in 1900 to nearly 500,000 in 1929.[38] Amid changing standards of sexuality, a distinct breed of flappers, the "Flappera Collegiata," commanded attention. She lived in a group of her own kind along with a dorm mother, who herself had morphed from a chaperone/bodyguard in the 1910s to more of a watchful eye in the 1920s. The "Collegiata," according to an article in *Froth*, was "often found in the wild state, but she submits readily to petting," and her "hobbies are matinees, motors, and millionaires." The author estimated "that a specimen of this family consumes 218 square feet of rouge, 111 pounds of powder, 3 gallons of perfume, 432 hair-nets, and 4,766 cigarettes a year."[39] Thus college men and women became consumers in the 1920s. Manufacturers such as Brooks Brothers made college men their mainstay and others created

Figure 1.4. Perfect for the all-important "big game," raccoon coats were "almost as thick as flies" on the Princeton campus in 1924. Parodied in illustrations by John Held Jr. and copied at other schools, the craze for 'coon skins riled some students, who called it the "fur coat evil" and claimed it represented "a false standard of affluence." Despite its enduring influence on popular culture, the trend was short-lived. Chalmers Alexander was asked to sell a cousin's coat on the Princeton campus in 1930, and he claimed he would have better luck selling "a white elephant." Courtesy of The Museum at FIT.

specialized clothing lines for their specific demands. Retailers hired recent graduates as sales staff to dole out advice on campus essentials.

As historians Helen Lefkowitz Horowitz and Margaret Lowe have documented, a national student culture came to the fore in the 1920s and "linked students on any particular campus to a network of shared assumptions and joined them to their fellows in other institutions." To Horowitz, the three key tenets of this network were "youthful high spirits, insubordination, and sexuality."[40] Paula Fass argues that in the 1920s, clothing for collegians became "outwards signs of the escape from convention." Dress "gave the college man or woman a distinctive air and the group identity that enhanced a sense of personal security."[41] Comfort drove nearly every clothing trend born on the college campus after 1920. In 1925, Helen Fancher, an instructor in household arts at Cal, believed there was "a growing tendency" for undergraduates "to dress more comfortable" as the "style and dress of today are far more sensible and hygienic."[42] A national collegiate culture allowed manufacturers to mass produce the same sweater for a Bull Dog as for an Aggie. Knitwear, footwear, and sportswear makers communicated countrywide trends and regional variations through their trade magazines.[43]

Across the country, students had more and sustained contact with one another through the national media. *College Humor* magazine (1920) compiled the best of campus humor publications, which were thick with references to dress. The *New Student* (1921), the nationally distributed left-wing newspaper, published articles on politics, Prohibition, and the problems of the higher education system. Students commonly wrote of differences in campus styles in their own newspapers and magazines. At Harvard, Princeton men were mocked for their vanity. In 1926, the *Harvard Lampoon* published the "Princetonian's Dictionary," which included: "Book: Obsolete term for old torture device, since used occasionally for insomnia in the more barbarous countries. Car: An instrument for getting to New York. Clothes: Most important aspect of college. Position of 'best-dressed man' leads to lucrative testimonial writing for Ide collars and loss of amateur standing. Coat: A tribe of dead raccoons gloriously serving humanity."[44] Even as much as collegiate attire became more standardized, campus cultures retained distinctive rules particular to their university. Princeton freshman wore yellow slickers; California men were known for their dirty corduroy pants. *Vanity Fair* prescribed fashion for "Model Collegians," those "who are all recognizable products of their respective Alma Maters" and who "dress alike, act alike, talk alike." Its pages were filled with articles on appropriate attire, surveys of the latest trends, and witticisms. In 1926, a writer joked, "You would know a Yale man if you met him in Patagonia; or a Columbia man if you met him at the Ritz. You can always recognize a Princeton man—usually in the nick of time."[45] The college students at less elite institutions such as Penn State and Cal bought and wore many of the same garments as their counterparts at Princeton and Yale. However, the quality of the items differed. They might own a tweed blazer, but it was less likely to be made of imported Harris tweed.

For college women, the development of casual style depended upon their school's location and administrators' inclinations. Students at city colleges, such as Radcliffe and Barnard, dressed more formally because many were commuters who spent much of their day in the public eye. As the *Boston Post* noted, "The complaint of the commuter is that she has to look well coming in on the trains or cars no matter how she feels." For her, "heels are apt to grow higher in these cases and the full length coat, preferably fur, replaces the oxford and jacket."[46] In the 1920s, Cliffies were expected to adhere to social standards of dress when in the public eye, evidenced by the long-standing rule requiring students to wear hats when going to Harvard Square. The regulation was first instated around the turn of the century by the first dean of the college, Agnes Irwin, but the students voted, year after year, for the rule to remain in effect. Their reasoning was based on the location of their college. Vera Micheles (Class of 1925) endorsed the mandate because "nowhere in Cambridge are we distinctly separated from the rest of the world. We are living among the people of Cambridge [and] it has seemed the most courteous attitude to accept a convention that we find here."[47] Students at rural women's colleges such as Vassar and Smith were held to no such regulations, and they spearheaded the trend toward going hatless. By 1930, Cliffies voted to do the same.[48]

In the case of Spelman College, social constraints imposed by administrators resulted in a formal standard of dress more conservative than the white women at Radcliffe could have imagined. Spelman was "emphatically Christian," and administrators focused on the "development of women of character and good-will with their mental capacities trained to the highest point of usefulness."[49] In the 1920s, Spelman administrators battled changing cultural standards, and official publications encouraged students to hold fast to the previous generation's modes and morals. The *Campus Mirror* told readers: "The old-fashioned girl of today is not like the flapper of today," who was only interested in "dancing, card playing, or fancy dressing." The flapper "keeps up with every style that comes in and she is crazy about the men," but the old-fashioned girl "is quiet and believes in substantial things." Old-fashioned women may be "slow in attracting the men" but are "often the first to get married, and leave the flapper behind to take her place."[50]

Spelman insisted on simplicity in dress partly to combat what white, middle-class society identified as the African American proclivity for bright colors and gaudy ornamentation. Early in the century, students were told to shun "glittering combs, pins, barrettes, and bright ribbons, surmounting indescribable rolls and puffs."[51] In 1926, Spelman administrators summoned women to a meeting, at which "they talked of many things—specializing, perhaps, on shoes, or to be more exact, heels." The young women agreed to buy clothing that allowed them to "dress more like sensible students with cultural tastes than like lilies of the field."[52] In the late 1920s, administrators and students transformed Spelman from an institution with a primary and secondary school to a full-fledged liberal arts college. This gave rise to a more lenient administration under Florence Read, a graduate of Mount Holyoke. The women happily left behind the days when "wearing oxfords with three eyelets [was] immodest" and "white middies and blue shirts were official uniforms for official days."[53]

The 1920s defined the relationship between collegians and the fashion industry. At the national level, manufacturers took to heart the advice of industry insiders who warned, "If you don't study the college man—you'll never get his business."[54] Manufacturers understood that identifying and bringing to market new trends meant real money. Collar company George P. Ide, which, like Arrow, was based in Troy, New York, scoured campuses both for trends and for models. Their "Best Dressed Man" campaign featured students from elite schools such Princeton, Yale, and Dartmouth, but increasing those from the universities of Chicago, Pittsburgh, and Wisconsin. As more and more middle-class families sent sons to college, manufacturers came courting. Associating one's business with the students of a prominent university gave products an authenticity that was key to attracting the college crowd. A picture of Princeton representative Thomas Clarke (Class of 1928) was accompanied by the copy, "Men at Princeton express their taste in dress by being exact in details." The ad noted, "Collars, in particular, give one the opportunity to present oneself properly. Soft collars are generally accepted only when worn with sports clothes."[55] The advertisement demonstrated the disconnection between manufacturers' aims and students' preferences. By the mid-1920s, soft collars were pervasive at Princeton. Editors at the *Daily Princetonian* mocked Clarke, whose "masculine beauty" would "attract offers of marriage from millionairesses."[56] Collegians understood their power with manufacturers. The editors of Penn State's *Froth* distrusted the "so-called sartorial experts" who "scout the campuses" and "concoct new fads to transform even the more ordinary-figured student into a present-day Lord Chesterfield." The main goal was simple: to "accelerate the processions of simoleons rolling into the pockets of the clothing manufacturers."[57]

Clothing manufacturers associated themselves with trendsetting campuses to give them clout at other schools. None did it better than Brooks Brothers, whose unofficial association with Princeton was primary to its success. Brooks, established in 1818, advertised in Princeton's yearbook in 1875 and held a full page every year until the mid-1950s. Brooks courted other Ivy Leaguers. In 1915, the company moved its headquarters to 346 Madison, a locale that was conveniently close to the Harvard and Yale Clubs. The first half of the twentieth century saw tremendous growth of the New York City–based company. They opened a major store in Boston in 1928, as well as seasonal stores in Newport and Palm Beach. Merchandise was at the heart of their success. Brooks introduced a four-button version of its "Number One Sack Suit" in 1900, and it became the standard for college men across the country. In 1913, Brooks rolled out its enduringly popular three-button model, which was quickly adopted at elite Eastern schools, such as Princeton, Yale, and Columbia. There, collegians paired the suit with a shirt featuring a soft, nondetachable, button-down collar. Brooks Brothers claimed to have brought the shirt from England, where polo players favored it to keep collars from flapping in their faces. The shirt, according to Brooks Brothers, was "the single most imitated item in American clothing history." By 1920, the shirt, now called a button-down oxford, was "firmly entrenched as a fashion in Eastern colleges" and within a decade, made it to Penn State and the like in the Midwest. Additionally, Brooks Brothers pioneered the striped "rep" tie and the khakis and sports coat combo.[58]

The fiction of F. Scott Fitzgerald, who attended Princeton, forged the connection between the university and the brand in the public's consciousness. Fitzgerald, who was such a Brooks Brothers fan he had his military uniform tailored there, makes references to the company in *Tender is the Night* and *The Beautiful and Damned*, as well as in several of his short stories. He calls the firm variously River Brothers, Baker Brothers, and Brooks—names thinly veiled for those in the know. In *This Side of Paradise*, Tom Parke D'Invilliers (a character based on Princeton classmate and famed poet John Peale Bishop) gets a makeover to be "clothed by Brooks, shod by Franks." The pressure of staying in step with the styles takes its toll on D'Invilliers, who becomes disillusioned by the critical and snobbish air of Princeton. "I want to go where people aren't barred because of the color of their neckties and the roll of their coats," Tom declares. The book's main character, Amory Blaine, quickly replies, "You can't Tom. Wherever you go now you will always unconsciously apply these standards of 'having it' or 'lacking it.' For better or worse, we've stamped you. You're a Princeton type." The Princeton type wore Brooks Brothers.[59]

Brooks Brothers caught the attention of women in 1910, when its polo coats achieved campus notoriety. Vassarite Hazel Hunkins coveted a white polo coat that she intended to wear with a white imitation fur cap. She wrote to her mother in Billings, Montana, of the coat's popularity and utility: "They are wearing them so much and such a hat and coat will serve every purpose I have for evening."[60] Brooks Brothers' long-standing big seller was its crewneck pullover sweater. The trend began in the mid-1920s at the Seven Sisters and was taken national by the late 1930s. The garment's widespread success spoke to the college girl's growing cultural influence. As *Vogue* declared in 1937, "All college girls, from Smith to Stanford, are sisters under their Brooks sweaters."[61] These women shopped in men's stores and bought and wore garments produced for men. Brooks Brothers did not market directly to women until the 1970s.

In the 1920s, retailers—both local venues on the perimeter of campus and larger department stores—became more aggressive in courting the college market. To lure college men to its Oakland shop, Herman's Smart Shop had prominent campus athletes on staff, such as Irving "Brick" Marcus, a halfback for Cal's football team, and Charles Merrill, the varsity cheerleader. An ad in the school newspaper noted that the duo held an informal "football symposium" of "post mortem discussions."[62] "Style expert" Mrs. Edith Goodall, owner of the Youth Shop in Cambridge, visited Radcliffe several times a year to keep students up-to-date on trends or to help them "think most seriously about winter clothes."[63] On-campus fashion shows for both men and women allowed retailers to reach dozens of students on their own turf. Clubs, sororities, or dormitories hosted stores' onsite efforts. Retailers had their pick of student models, who were compensated with an outfit of their choice. Some shows were simply demonstrative or instructive; others sold goods. In the mid-1920s, New York's Fifth Avenue shops sent out touring fashion shows to regional colleges. The shows took place in rented meeting rooms at local hotels, and the coordinator "hired a few students to take orders, which were shipped from New York at a later date."[64]

Both on campus and off, college women from across the socioeconomic spectrum had increasing interaction with department stores. Letters home document shopping trips and purchases. Edith Culver wrote in her diary of an afternoon with Betty when they "did all the store windows and went into Filene's where . . . we had a chance to see the rest of the underwear floor which fascinates us." Culver wrote of cutting classes to meet her mother for shopping, watching in-store fashion shows, and charging her (and also a friend's) new sweater to her mother's store account.[65] Several weeks later she went to "town alone and went to a fashion show with living models in Jordan's which was very interesting."[66] Dances, alumni reunions, and homecoming festivities featured on-campus shows that were presented in conjunction with student groups and local retailers. Culver and her colleagues shopped and bought with relative independence. So did Bailey Patterson, a Radcliffe student whose diary recorded daily life in the late 1920s. A suitor gave her a "swell $12 bottle of Guerlain's Shalimar."[67] Patterson spent freely with her first paycheck. She wrote in her diary: "Yesterday morning I went shopping by myself. With the $5.81, I got myself a 'Roughies' suit for $3.95 at Lord & Taylors. It's adorable, so chic—beret, pants and shirt. Then a dress, hat and shoes at Wannamaker's for a grand total of $8.70."[68] As the 1920s came to a close, Bailey Patterson experienced it in a profoundly personal way, writing: "Honestly, skirts are getting so long that it's a dead give away as to vintage if they don't come way down, almost to the ankle."[69] Within two years, Patterson married the giver of the Guerlain, took a honeymoon to Europe, and became a mother.[70]

## "They'd Better Listen to Our Little Gang of Conformists": Collegians Come of Age

By 1930, collegians were the established tastemakers for American youth, and their ranks included upper-, middle-, and even working-class members. Their cultural influence was pervasive. A Wheaton student wrote that not "all collegiate girls are in college." Rather, "the greatest number, in fact, are found in high schools where, in their own youthful way, they ape the sweaters and saddle shoes of their older sisters."[71] College men set the pace for a larger class of men, including "young business men who are just out of college a year or two or three" who are "prone to maintain the college spirit and affect the prevailing cut and color as favored by the better dressed college man."[72] Despite ongoing input from mothers, fashion editors, and retailing executives, collegians remained, in the words of one journalist, "unmindful of disapproval" and wore "the sort of thing that is comfortable and suited to her personal needs."[73]

By the 1930s, collegians were primary in bringing to market and selling the kinds of garments that were called "casual." The word had been around since the fourteenth century, but became the term of choice for fashion editors in the 1930s when they needed to succinctly describe the increasing popularity of informal dress. By the end of the decade, the "overworked term 'casual,'" according to one fashion reporter, was "in for a well-earned rest."[74] That rest never came. Developing concurrently with the rise of casual dress was the study of retailing and marketing. These fields made the department store a dynamic place where floor layouts and sales promotions were conceived and reconceived to, in the words of marketing guru Paul Nystrom, "induce interest among prospective customers by offering one class of goods but in which the expectation is to sell them other goods."[75] Economists and sociologists formed marketing graduate programs at schools such as the Wharton School of Business and Finance and published their findings in the *Journal of Marketing* (1936). These groups studied what, why, and how Americans consumed, and collegians were key players. Home economists charted students' hosiery-buying habits and psychologists theorized lifecycles of campus clothing fads.

Anecdotal and academic research found that to sell to collegians, manufacturers, retailers, and magazine editors had to enlist them. Retailers put them to work in college shops, seasonal in-store boutiques that provided students one-stop shopping. An industry publication believed that students as salespeople "have proven invaluable in building college shop reputations and sales." The students provided "atmosphere" and have the "ability to give the potential college girl authentic clothes advice." College shop staff also brought "in their friends for customers, too."[76] Peer-driven consumption assured that the opinions of mothers and marketing executives took a back seat. Academic class provided an instant chain of hierarchy. According to *Life* magazine, "Gushing freshmen will buy anything if the right upper classmate is wearing it."[77] Seniors at Penn State told first-years: "All over the country you freshmen are jamming into college shops, overworking mamma's checkbook. What do you need? You need everything, or you think you need everything." Upperclassmen encouraged restraint and gave detailed advice.[78]

To tap directly into the market, manufacturers and retailers solicited student-created designs. In 1934, the Chicago retailer Marshall Field held a Young American Fashion Contest, a contest based on the store's "belief that in the American college and university" one can find "any number of young women with more than an average flair for fashion."[79] Through each college's newspaper, publicity office, or dean of women, the store identified interested students and then supplied them with supplementary materials, fabric samples, and dispatches from European style centers. Of applications from 254 colleges, a board of "fashion authorities" selected twenty prizewinners.[80] In the late 1930s, Campus Originals Guild, a Park Avenue–based firm, solicited clothing and accessories designed by college women in order to "discover real talent through the medium of the guild." The group paid between $10 and $25 for ideas, which they then sold to major manufacturers who were part of the guild. The item's hangtag featured the name and school of the student designer. Vassar's Mimi Dworsky (Class of 1942) designed a pair of black gloves with notes from Beethoven's Fifth Symphony stitched in white. The gloves were brought to market by Aris Gloves. Campus Original Guild also enlisted seniors to serve as a campus representative and "keep the Guild informed of [the] latest fashion news."[81]

More commonplace than student-designed garments were student-approved garments. In 1930, New York department store Stern's enlisted the help of an appointed college board made up of local students to inspect buyer-selected dresses, sweaters, luggage, shoes, and pajamas. The "approved" goods were sold in a specific and aptly decorated area of the store. As their 1931 advertisement read: "Word has already been passed along from seniors to freshmen, from deans to mothers, that no college wardrobe is really smart unless it is passed by Stern's College Board."[82] By the end of the decade, an industry source confirmed, "Advisory groups chosen from among students are almost standard practice."[83] The various prongs of the fashion industry often worked in tandem. Knitwear manufacturers Woolknits teamed up with *Mademoiselle* to use guest editors as guinea pigs. From universities as socioeconomically diverse and geographically distant as the University of Southern California and Bennington, a dozen students offered their opinions on the lengths of sweaters and knee socks, and the merits of one-piece versus two-piece swimsuits.

Collegians yielded the most power in the college shop, a student-staffed section of the ever-evolving department store. From the early 1930s through the 1950s, virtually every department store had one of these "All-American institutions," and each wooed shoppers with gimmicky marketing campaigns that included free Cokes and rumba lessons. The elaborately decorated shops popped up "all over town during the last weeks of August, like mushrooms after a rain" and disappeared with the first frost.[84] One of the first college shops opened at Stern's around the same time it implemented its college board, and other stores followed suit. Lord & Taylor, sometimes identified as the purveyor of the college shop trend, premiered a shop in 1933 when a junior executive named Helene Maddock was given a small area to sell what she called "authentic Eastern College fashions." In 1934,

Figure 1.5. Sportswear manufacturers such as Davidow created garments to be mixed and matched, such as these versatile separates from 1933. Clothing designers followed the college woman's lead and played masculine pieces (the plaid jacket and "pant skirt") off of a feminine, body-revealing garment (the fitted red sweater). Low-heeled oxford shoes, gored or pleated skirts, blazers, sports socks, and sweaters—all of which were first worn on the court or course—defined campus dress in the 1930s. Here, the illustrator paired these clothes with a delicate pump, but in real life the ensemble would have been worn with saddle shoes or white canvas tennis shoes. Courtesy of the Fashion Institute of Technology, Special Collections at Gladys Marcus Library.

Vassar student Sally Kirkland was a staffer. "There we were," she remembered, "sitting around in our little sweaters and skirts and telling those poor old buyers, 'No, that will never do' or 'why don't you get something in red velveteen?'" The buyers realized, she concluded, "they'd better listen to our little gang of conformists."[85] As with many college shop staffers, the gig launched Kirkland's career in fashion. She became a high-ranking executive at Lord & Taylor and the fashion editor of *Life* magazine.

For men, the college shop made shopping easy because it assembled needed items in one area. In 1938, a reporter for a trade magazine for menswear retailers wrote, "The College Shop has, within a comparatively short space of time, evolved into a very essential counterpart of the modern men's clothing store." Its patrons were both "a considerable army of college men" but also the "even larger army of non-college men who are influenced by what collegians favor." The shop's success was about more than meeting demand: "The college shop may be said to 'pep up' the old conservative clothing store—adding 'life' and zest to a onetime prosaic business." The reporter believed, "We are witnessing the passing of the revered 'old storekeeper' whose business wisdom was universally believed to have been gauged by the number of years to his credit." Now, "young men take the helm . . . with the spirit of youth and modernism in their blood."[86] Retailers offered items at various price points to accommodate the growing diversity of the collegiate demographic.

In the last years of the 1930s, the strategy for attracting collegians and their followers was solidified, and *Tobé Report* outlined it for retailers in 1938: Stores should assemble all college-related goods in one spot because the college shopper "will buy more than if she has to shop all over the store to assemble it," and shops should use "comfortable lounges and chairs" to "add up to a welcoming atmosphere."[87] According to *Life* magazine, retailers must know whether their market is "the classic conscious Eastern college girl or the dress-up minded Middle West coed" because "it makes a great deal of difference in actual sales." Most importantly, retailers should staff the shop with actual undergrads because a misinformed college woman "will rarely again shop in the store that gave her wrong information." The college shop capitalized on peer-driven consumption. One report of the August openings noted, "Sales of merchandise off a salesgirl's back are numerous."[88]

Fashion editors served as important allies to manufacturers and retailers. Launched in 1935, *Mademoiselle* initiated the practice of students serving as guest editors. College publicity departments submitted nominees, and the magazine selected those to come for a two-week stint in New York.

The guest editors contributed directly to the all-important August issue. Upon returning to campus, the editors sent seasonal dispatches on campus styles. The guest editors were as much for show as they were for service. In correspondence with Radcliffe's publicist, a *Mademoiselle* editor asked how photogenic the nominees were, to which the publicist responded, "Without her glasses [one of them] is a cute, perky, elf-like looking girl." The other "is a blond, quite attractive girl with a wide smile." The publicist admitted that "neither are beauties, but both are nice looking girls." Campus publicists connected the students to the fashion industry and mediated much of the interaction. In attempts to control the school's public image, Radcliffe women were forbidden from giving interviews or posing for pictures in the absence of a publicity department member. Similar regulations existed at other Seven Sisters schools.[89]

Through the mid-1930s and into the 1950s, the August issues of *Vogue* and *Harper's Bazaar* were devoted to back-to-school styles. Students took the advice as they saw fit. An opinionated Radcliffe student wrote of the trends: "If you read fashion magazines as much as I (and I bet you do), doubtless those cunning jerkins, feminine pinafores, checked vests and wrap around skirts have caught your eye too." She warned that these were precisely the kinds of trends that a collegian should "forget about," because they were too formal and too quickly outdated.[90] At Spelman, students were more reverent. The *Campus Mirror* wrote, "If milady's fashions are to be up-to-date, she must not miss those latest issues of *Harper's Bazaar* and *Vogue*."[91] The paper commonly reprinted advice from *Vogue's Book of Etiquette*. When *Vogue* asked for a campus representative from Spelman in 1937, student Lurlene Baker became the "final authority on lines, colors, and types."[92] This partnership between Spelman and *Vogue* was indeed unique because black students were rarely asked to participate in store advisory boards or serve as staff in the college shop. Manufacturers and retailers failed to recognize these women as a viable market, worthy of direct marketing. As documented in the pages of Spelman's school newspaper, many students made their own clothes in classes and at home, while white college women increasing bought their campus wardrobes in department stores.

*Vogue* was particularly savvy about the college woman market and made good use of the contact information provided by the entrants for its Prix de Paris contest, a writing competition first introduced in 1935 that awarded the winner a yearlong stint at its Paris office. In order "to find out what they wore in their chat sessions, for rushing, week-ends, midnight-oil cramming— even in bed," the magazine "quizzed them. We probed into their private lives." The results were certainly useful for its and manufacturers' purposes.

They learned that college girls "sleep in silk, lounge in flannel," and "want about eight pairs of shoes, four or five pairs of gloves and at least five hats."[93] *Vogue*'s methods provided concrete information on trends, but they often failed to use it. Its poll of women's colleges in 1939 showed that 35 percent of students wore pants to campus, but other than the photos for the story, none of the layouts featured slacks.[94]

*Esquire* magazine was the heir to *Vanity Fair*'s male audience, but unlike its predecessor, its audience was decidedly middle class. As Bill Osgerby notes, "In charting the minutiae of middle-class student style, *Esquire* not only acquired a cachet with the profitable marketed represented by 'Joe College.' The strategy also afforded the magazine an aura of youthful dynamism."[95] The *Radcliffe News* covered the magazine's launch in 1933. "Men have broken into a realm previously considered exclusive to women," it reported, but, the author wondered, "Are the men merely asserting their rights, or are they becoming effeminate?"[96] Cliffies hoped that Harvard men, known widely for their slouchy hats, would heed *Esquire*'s advice that the "basic campus wardrobe is one that is casual but never sloppy, unrestrained but always in good taste."[97] The men did not. *Esquire* also studied its demographic closely. To gauge purchasing habits, the magazine paired up with student publications, such as Princeton's *Nassau Sovereign*, to conduct a survey of men's wardrobes. They confirmed that Princetonians owned more sweaters than sports coats.

Despite collegians' direct involvement in what was being sold and promoted, a fundamental tension remained between the demands of students and the opinions of fashion editors, retailing executives, and store buyers. Retailer Irving Joseph of Evanston, Illinois, claimed his formula for reaching students was "simple": "We never try to sell the girls any special style or type which we might be inclined to think they should like."[98] In practice, few department stores resisted the urge to influence student choice. In 1938, Boston-based department store Slattery's held a "Clothes Conference" at which local college women offered their opinions on buyer-selected garments. The *Radcliffe News* covered the event and noted, "The store buyer was discouraged because members of the Conference would have nothing of the elaborate afternoon date dress" she had selected. The paper told of a run-in between Emily Hill (Class of 1939) and the buyer: "Theoretically they had the run of the store to choose from, but you wore what was thrust upon you." Despite Hill's insistence on a certain gown, the buyer "produced an ultra new model with hoop skirts 'which simply must be shown.'" Hill was the only student who fit into the gown and "modeled the hoop-skirt evening gown to a full house."[99]

The "sloppy joe"—an oversized, wide-gauge knit cardigan sweater that was "smartest when it is about four sizes too large"—demonstrates the disconnection between students and the fashion industry.[100] Boyfriends reviled the sweater because it concealed women's bodies and encouraged an "emphasis on everything being 'sloppily baggy.'"[101] The sweater's introduction in the late 1930s was "the biggest success item in College Shops everywhere." Some stores sold more than a hundred sloppy joes a day. College women who insisted on comfort exalted loose-fitting clothing that was deemed sloppy by the old guard, whose objections were about more than aesthetics or even profit. Not only did the baggy sweater obscure curves, but it also allowed a woman to forgo a girdle—an indication of "loose morals."[102] The lack of foundation garments directly informed the fit of the clothing. One survey of college women noted that "since girls don't wear girdles, they don't like to have stuff that hugs their hips, so knitted dresses and suits weren't first choice."[103] The knitwear, hosiery, and lingerie industries cowered in the face of college women, who preferred a natural silhouette. They "do not like extremely cut brassieres" but prefer "a rounder, more moderate type" in "fine handkerchief linen.[104] Mothers and administrators encouraged the girdle's continued use. At a fashion show sponsored by *Mademoiselle* and Radcliffe, the college's publicity department issued a memo that clarified: "every girl who wished to model must wear a girdle."[105] In the 1940s, women at Wellesley, Vassar, and Smith all but abandoned the garment, and in the next decade, many of their sisters would do the same. Neither comfortable nor practical, hosiery, girdles, and other accessories of modesty, such as hats and gloves, were relegated to the back of the collegian's closet—if they made it there at all.

### "Casual-Minded Customers of Almost Any Age": Collegians Diversify Their Ranks

In the 1940s, the casual style worn by collegians became the provenance of Americans at large. Sweaters, oxford shoes, and even pants were "clothes not for college girls only" but considered "good basics that would fit almost any American scheme of life today."[106] The diversification of the market prompted retailers to abandon the gimmicky promotions they favored in the early years of the decade for more subtle tactics. Back-to-school events of the 1950s had broad appeal, and, while themed around the college campus, the styles presented were "college-y but not too rah-rah."[107] Fashion editors commonly pushed a more conservative wardrobe than students actually wanted. A student reported to the women of Cal the latest offerings of fashion editors: "Between you and me, lovely as these clothes are, the average girl with the average budget is going to pass them by. And that is because they are too dignified . . . too sophisticated."[108] The uniformity in dress that marked the college campus in the first half of the twentieth century disintegrated in the wake of World War II and vanished by the 1960s. Lord & Taylor executive Jeanne Eddy told her peers who were courting the youth market, "There is no longer one way to dress. It's the era of individuality."[109]

Early in the 1940s, marketing and publicity executives used gimmicks and promotions to create a shopping environment that encouraged, as one Penn Stater put it, "getting clothes-drunk."[110] The college shop was at the pinnacle of its power. Each retail store aimed to create a shop with "distinctive settings and merchandise exclusively their's [sic]."[111] Men's college shops were more commonly called "university shops," a title that spoke of the gendered nature of higher education. Women went to college; men went to university. Men's shops featured faux ivy, oversized golf clubs, and stained glass windows but lacked the elaborate décor and promotional events associated with college women's retail areas in the 1940s. For women, college shops offered Coke bars, fashion shows, and rumba lessons. Gimmicks ranged from the comical (such as a "giant-sized wooden cart marked 'back to college' and drawn by an amusing [cardboard] donkey") to the practical (such as a knitting shop with "yarns matched to the plaids and wools in the ready-to-wear stock."[112] Every season, retailers reinvented their shops, and acknowledged: "It's not always the easiest to do this with a new approach each year."[113]

The war proved an inspiration for creative promotion. Franklin Simon's College Canteen in 1942 featured a milk bar that catered to "college girls who were now war workers and have really made their wardrobe practical." The bar served raw carrots and celery and featured red milk cans as stools. Saks Fifth Avenue also picked up on the college girl/war worker theme and showed blown-up pictures of the students practicing Morse code, fixing engines, and caring for wounded soldiers. The war did more than provide decorating motifs. It provided a venue where young American women wore unrestrictive clothing and were called patriotic for it. *Women's Wear Daily* reported, "War work is important at most colleges. Blue jeans are much favored for it. Slacks are also worn and some coveralls."[114] Pants and jeans were no longer relegated to remote women's colleges or coeds painting theater sets. Penn State reported that "slacks of any loud color with a tailored jacket are perfect togs for accelerated program activities."[115] Accelerated programs fast-tracked students through a revised curriculum and required compulsory physical education. Cal fashion editors noted, "Mannish slacks in red, white, and blue are all the rage."[116] College shops provided shoppers with goods and the know-how of when and where to wear them. Saks Fifth Avenue put its 1942 college shop employees in "blue denim overalls embroidered with their own name and their college in red."[117]

Jeans were considered acceptable garb for wartime campus life. However, when the war ended and men returned to coed campuses, deans of women created new dress codes that limited when and where pants and jeans could be worn. Such rules did not exist on mixed-sex campuses before the war because the garments had not achieved widespread popularity. Jeans were worn on many single-sex campuses in the Northeast since the early 1930s with little to no comment from administrators. Significant variations existed from one campus to another on the popularity of and policy toward jeans. Factors influencing these standards included not only the presence of men but also geography, religious affiliation, and political leanings of students and administrators.

Despite war restrictions such as L-85, which limited materials available for civilian clothing, collegians still bought. The *Boot and Shoe Recorder* wrote in August 1942, "College promotions, particularly for coeds, certainly hasn't [*sic*] been retarded by the war this fall" and "remains one of the few 'normal' markets even for women."[118] *Tobé* reported of the 1942 college shop openings, "While there are evidences of L-85's influences, it does not by any means predominate."[119] In the winter of 1942, Radcliffe's Nancy Murray wrote to her well-to-do mother in Scarsdale, New York: "Is it true that shoes of size 4 and under are not rationed? If so, I can get a pair of Bass Norwegian moccasins." Savvy students swapped ration tickets to get what they needed and practiced conservation to prolong the life of their garments.[120] Many thrifty college women believed, as one Spelman women wrote, "The biggest thing a college student can do in the all-out war effort is to play a part in the campaign to prevent waste."[121] Patriotism combined with a lack of funds kept many middle-class students from buying elaborate back-to-school wardrobes. A fashion editor asked the women of Berkeley, "Have you got any A.I. [Anti-Inflation] clothes in your closet? Because if you haven't it seems you are not doing right either by your country or yourself." She admitted that she was "no economist," but remodeling "A.I." clothes rather than spending money on back-to-school garb "made sense . . . so that our dollars can go into war bonds—or savings instead."[122] Campuses with home economics programs offered workshops on making over last year's fashions. At Penn State, faculty members supervised students "who are interested in their appearance and who wish to make the most of what they have."[123]

As the 1940s progressed, students became increasingly independent as consumers. Nancy Murray's parents paid for most of her purchases, and she occasionally asked them to mail moccasins and an evening wrap from home. They were rarely involved in the decision-making. In September 1943, Murray charged a dress to her mother's account at Boston department store Filene's and allowed a friend to charge a sweater.[124] Similarly, when Murray and her friend Prez decided to get hair permanents, she promised her mother the new hairstyle would be "nothing extreme" and she would have "none of these 5 dollar permanents which burn off the hair." She asked her parents, "Did you say something about footing the bill for that?" When Murray's boyfriend Paul offered to front her the money, she told her mother to "send only as much as you can because I can pay Paul via installments." In the end, Murray got the perm for $15 from Charles at the Ritz, which was "such a snazzy place, I think it's worth [it]." Prez took the plunge as well.[125]

Collegians' enhanced power as consumers gave them the confidence to ignore convention. Such flouting of the rules met with contempt and accusations of sloppiness. At Cal, women "nominated for oblivion" men in T-shirts, which were deemed "fine for tennis but slightly informal for campus wear."[126] An editor at Harvard, an institution known for its students' relaxed, even rumpled attire, wrote, "Women gripe about the two types of men most common in American colleges; the utter conformist, and the sloppy person who wants only comfort in his clothes." The latter "dress in sweatshirts and jeans whenever they can get away with it." Always looking for a chance to slight their counterparts across the Yard, the student noted: "In this manner, they unconsciously copy their feminine counterparts."[127] At Carnegie Tech, a returning soldier wrote to the editor of the school newspaper that he "had a belly full" of seeing a "very miserable assortment of people dressed in ill-fitting rags." He complained that women at Tech "go around looking no better than those unfortunate Europeans" and warned that the girl he dated "will have to look pretty neat."[128] Baggy sweaters and droopy socks were often cited sources of disdain, but pants received the most criticism.

Boyfriends, retailers, and magazine editors worked in tandem to encourage a more "feminine" campus wardrobe. In 1948, Bonwit Teller, *Mademoiselle*, and Radcliffe's literary magazine *Signature* held a benefit for the Free University of Berlin called "A Course in Social Psychology." The event featured women from ten regional colleges, selected from more than

250 applicants. The premise of the show was that plaid-skirted upperclass-men would give jeans-clad freshmen lessons on dressing for the first day of classes, the Harvard football game, and a late-night study session. Female collegians selected and modeled the outfits, and the review board graded the ensembles. The men "failed" masculine styles, but "passed" skirts, dresses, angora sweaters, and stockings instead of anklets. One jury member "was violently against wool socks and sneakers" and labeled suits "underly feminine." Boston College's Ed Galotti thought that jeans "look better on a man."[129] Despite the advice and opinions of others, college women continued to wear pants and jeans with, what one Harvard student called, "a quiet contempt."[130]

To appeal to a wider audience, manufacturers, retailers, and magazine editors broadened their marketing efforts. In 1938, *Vogue* called itself "the college girl's *vade mecum*" (manual), but in 1946 it proclaimed, "This year, the College Issue isn't College-Only anymore. This issue is for college girls and their out-of-school contemporaries." The magazine offered up a twenty-five-page spread for "all the Smart Girls who have suddenly become young-people-of-importance as far as fall fashion is concerned."[131] *Tobé* told retailers that because college clothes were "designed for and bought by young-minded casual customers of almost *any* age and pursuit the trick is to get this idea across implicitly while promoting college explicitly."[132] The department store Russeks reported that "the girl striving for a sheepskin has left her whimsies behind her and . . . the career girl is a bit more casual about her clothes. Thus, both meet on a more or less common ground." Their shop was themed "College-Career Shop."[133]

In 1954, Macy's concluded that because "college and career girls have about identical needs and tastes," they opened "twin shops" that separated merchandise by sizes: the shops catered "to sizes from 8 to 20 and from 5 to 17 respectively."[134] Junior sizes were numbered unevenly (11, 13, 15) and featured a cut "that complements collegianne measurements."[135] The junior size, which came to the fore in the 1930s, thrived in the college shops among the young and not-so-young with short waists and petite proportions. B. Altman reported that 70 percent of its college shop merchandise was junior-sized.[136] "Junior is a size, not an age" was the unofficial slogan of the trend, which had gone from being "the step-child of the clothes market" to "the Cinderella" in the course of two decades.[137] Junior sizes received more floor space because "many stores have realized they can increase their sale of junior wear by grouping junior sizes of all types of apparel in a single department."[138] Despite the appeal of the size, its styles were often accused of being, as one Bergdorf Goodman survey reported, "too baby-doll, too youthful, too frilly, too lacking in sophistication."[139] Distinguishing between junior as a size and as a style was a source of confusion for both retailers and the public alike.

In the 1950s, Americans at large took to casual style, which was also being promoted by American designers such as Claire McCardell, Tina Leser, and Bonnie Cashin.[140] The college campus was specifically identified with casual dress. August's "Back-to-School" push became more about promoting seasonal sportswear than student-approved styles. In 1951, *Tobé* acknowledged what "everyone has long realized": "the college angle was largely the spark plug that started off the fall sportswear business." The declaration, said *Tobé*, was "the first time that has been officially acknowledged in public."[141] In the 1950s, retailers paired down their events and promoted merchandise rather than events or themes. In 1957, the simplicity of the shops met with rave reviews from *Tobé*. "The story told by New York's college shops," it reported, was "not a forced story" and had "no extraneous gimmicks to detract from the merchandise itself." Instead the clothing "is allowed to and does speak for itself." Stores, such as Ohrbach's, had "little or no 'shop' atmosphere" and "no special sales help as a college board." In the late 1950s, the high-end New York stores such as Lord & Taylor and Saks Fifth Avenue held press showings of their styles but "skipped customer fashion shows" and instead offered "informal modeling, which seems to be the newest thought in many other cities too."[142] Meier & Frank of Portland, Oregon, had a series of four Monday night forums where models in the shop's top-selling garments milled about and onlookers enjoyed free refreshments. Filene's of Boston sent models clad in the latest styles through their popular store restaurant. There were no student saleswomen in matching uniforms, cardboard donkeys, or rumba lessons.

■ Oxford shoes, button-down oxford shirts, jeans, T-shirts, Bermuda shorts, sweaters, sweatshirts, clam diggers, sports coats, and garterless socks: by the 1960s, collegians' wardrobes were no longer their own. Americans were buying casual clothing and wearing it as they pleased. "Casual wear is creeping into everyday business life," reported a syndicated business writer covering the downturn in the men's suit industry.[143] In 1960, Bloomingdales noted that 90 percent of their college shop patronage came not from students but from working women and young matrons.[144] Many college women did not even shop there but preferred to cherry-pick their clothes from various departments. In 1967, Trudi Kellerman, a freshman at Southern Connecticut College, noted, "I like more of the things in college shops this year, but I shop all over the store."[145] As advisory boards gave way to specialized research firms and retailers abandoned college shops for more inclusive fall promotional campaigns, the fashion industry finally came to realize what a vice president of Bonwit Teller tried to tell them in 1948: college girls don't "want to be put in a monkey cage."[146]

Developing concurrently with the mass acceptance of casual style, the growing cultural power of the American high-schooler demanded teen-specific marketing. Teen girls got their own permanent sections in department stores and seasonal shops that sold swimwear or winter coats. They were invited to participate in focus groups and had their own age-appropriate magazines, such as *Calling All Girls* (1941) and *Seventeen* (1944). In 1962, an editor of *Seventeen* told fashion and cosmetics executives, "America's teenage population is front page news." While teen girls comprised only 10 percent of the total female population, they spent 20 percent of the apparel and footwear dollars and nearly 25 percent of the total cosmetics and toiletries dollar, which surpassed $450 million that year.[147]

Collegians changed, too. The cracks in a deceptively monolithic collegiate culture became schisms in the 1960s, as the ranks of students grew from nearly 3.7 million in 1950 to more than 8 million strong in 1970.[148] Campus clothing styles stressed individuality, rustic construction, and do-it-yourself-ary. Buying and wearing the same ensemble as the girl in the next dorm room over was not cool. Prescribed "looks" from the fashion system were not cool either, and many students took great pains to disassociate themselves with mainstream clothing trends.

■ Casual style was born, nurtured, and came of age in the first half of the twentieth century. American youth became increasingly self-aware and more savvy buyers as the century progressed. Middies and rubber-soled oxfords turned to sloppy joes and tennis shoes and then to sweatshirts and mukluks. Retailers, fashion editors, and marketing executives knew firsthand the power of collegians as consumers but still struggled to understand, meet, and predict their demands. Little could be done to slow the rising tide of casual style. Collegians' buying power was simply too strong, and they had converted too many noncollegians to the cause. In 1958, the *New York Times*'s "College Togs Extend Past Campus" explained that the "gray-haired matron," "the 13-year-old who was sizing up Bermuda shorts," and "women of all ages" were "in search of the kind of easy . . . clothes that are identified with campus life."[149] The fashion industry saw the writing on the wall: middle-class Americans wanted to dress casual, and stores had the responsibility to deliver. Retailers placed clam-digger pants and polo shirts in the juniors department and in the boutiques that courted more mature buyers. As retailers adapted their offerings, social critics still tried to tease out the difference between casual and sloppy. Throughout the country, journalists, reformers, and religious leaders called collegians' clothing "sloppy" and associated it with loose morals. In 1962, one journalist surmised, "Perhaps if the modern students, male and female, were not so sloppy in dress and in manner, their minds would not be so devoted even on weekends to illicit sex and taverns and motels."[150] The best hope for those who wished to halt the adoption of "sloppy" clothes was to take the battle to campus. Administrators proved valuable but undependable allies.

# On the Campus

Casual style was born of practicality. Students chose low-heeled oxfords for long walks across the quad and cardigan sweaters to stay warm in drafty buildings. One Vassar student foretold the fashion future: "If dormitory temperatures next year are as low as they were this past winter, jackets will be important."[1] The geography of each campus demanded different concessions. For her freshman year in 1917, Cal student Agnes Edwards lived in a boardinghouse on the edge of town. She complained to her mother about the long walk to campus: "The whole town is the hilliest thing I ever saw." In the first weeks of school, Berkeley's unpaved streets and rough terrain prompted Edwards to spend $5 on a new pair of shoes that were "good and stout" and "look almost like boy's shoes." She wrote, "I got an extra pair of laces and a ticket for ten full shines with it."[2] To the outside world, fads such as the 1935 craze for earmuffs gave collegiate clothing an air of capriciousness; administrators grumbled about being "afflicted every season with a fad or two."[3] Yet the long march toward casual style redefined the way we choose and the way we wear clothing. This profound shift was most visible in two areas of primary importance on every college campus: the classroom and the cafeteria. Here, versatility and comfort came to the fore as men stopped wearing suits and women started wearing slacks.

When and where casual clothing thrived sheds light on the gendered nature of higher education. The new, casual standard of dress for men met with commentary but little action from administrators. In the words of one Michigan university president, he considered "no restrictions or rules" for "types of clothing (even to the extent of knickers halfway to the ankles)."[4] At Princeton two decades later, a dean clarified this the hands-off approach: Dress was "not in the Administration's realm."[5] Unlike their peers at Morehouse, Princeton administrators had little need or interest in regulating student attire. In 1963, Dean of Students Bill Lippincott admitted to the *Daily Princetonian*, "The administration has been and is still seeking ways to improve the dress habits of students, short of attempting to accomplish this by edict." However, he knew that "an official edict promulgated by the university would be a much less desirable means of accomplishing the goal than a spontaneous change brought about by the students themselves."[6] Unsurprisingly, his hopes for the return of suits in class and ties in the cafeteria never came to fruition.

Administrators of women made attempts—some successful, some not—to control casual attire on campus. Their efforts ranged from outlawing specific garments to regulating (with the help of dorm supervisors and students) times and places that such garments could be worn. Most often administrators stood at the sidelines and piped in pleas for a more conservative dress standard. The creation of dress codes was often a dynamic process. For example, a list of regulations for Cal women in 1952 was written by the students but edited by the dean. The students submitted: "Slacks and peddle [*sic*] pushers may be worn only when the occasion calls for it." The administration added the line: "This means not in the Library."[7] Deans struggled to maintain the boundaries of when and where casual dress could be worn.

College men wore their casual style to the classroom. There, under the unbatting eye of the administration, men replaced the once-standard suit with the sports coat and pants combination—a duo that was pioneered by Ivy Leaguers in the 1910s and picked up on other campuses in the following decades. The "odd jacket"—a term for a jacket worn with nonmatching pants—and the sports blazer were less physically restrictive and more versatile than the suit. College men wore odd jackets with corduroys and sweaters with shined-up brogues or dirty saddle oxfords. Men's shunning of the suit began in the late 1910s, culminated in the 1920s, and had far-reaching implications in the 1930s. In 1937, the editors of Cal's student newspaper made their preference clear: "No single item in a man's wardrobe offers more service and comfort than the sports coat."[8] An on-campus survey at Penn State found that "the trend in male campus wear is toward informality and comfort." Of the 323 male students who passed the surveyors in the course of an hour, 52 percent wore "assorted clothing," 40 percent wore sports coats and slacks, and 8 percent wore suits, though some were worn without ties.[9] Two World Wars, remarkable developments in clothing and textile manufacturing, and an acquired appreciation for what Bill Osgerby called, "youthful hedonism, heterosexual pleasure, and the 'ethic of fun'" all drastically changed what men wanted to wear.[10] The decision to dress casual was an individual man's choice, made in the context of a specific campus culture.

Women's administrators wrestled to control these choices. Their approach varied significantly from one era and institution to the next. At staid Spelman, well into the 1930s, administrators had required that white gloves be worn to town. Students themselves understood the need for the rules. One Spelman woman wrote, "I had always expected to acquire a certain polish from college life. . . . I looked forward to having charm, good manners, and a well developed code of morals."[11] In the 1960s, Spelman students became vocal about the "excessive number of regulations" created and imposed by administrators.[12] Conversely, higher-ups at women's colleges in the Northeast allowed the students to vote each year on the dress codes, believing that they could and should police themselves. Radcliffe women decided collectively what they could wear, where they could entertain dorm guests, and when they had to come home from a date. Whether issued by student government or higher-ups, dress codes at elite schools were often ignored. In 1940, a Wellesley student explained that slacks were officially banned, but "everyone wears them anyway and nobody bothers to enforce the rule."[13]

The inequities of "his" and "hers" clothing regulations were most visible at coeducational institutions where deans, faculty, dorm supervisors, and cafeteria administrators told college women what they could wear and when.[14] The cafeteria became contested ground as collegians demanded the right to don jeans, shorts, and even headscarves to the dinner table. The cafeteria was a public space, and administrators of both men and women defended it as one of the last vestiges of formality on campus. In the 1950s and 1960s, dorm councils and individual students circulated petitions, penned letters to the editor, and met with deans to gain control of their own social space. They won their victories piecemeal. The student movements of the 1960s cast a long shadow, and our public consciousness lumps together the many forms of protest and activism into "unrest." Early in the decade, college women actively sought the freedom to wear Bermudas to Sunday brunch. In the second half of the 1960s, they found other causes: reproductive rights, gender equality, civil liberties.

### "A Sports Coat Is a Practical Necessity": Sports Coats in the Classroom

Since its appearance in the courts of England and France in the late sixteenth century, the suit has dominated menswear.[15] In the first decade of the twentieth century, the well-dressed college man needed several. The *Harvard Crimson* advised students traveling abroad—for "even a short business trip"—to take a formal dinner suit and a top hat, "three or four sacque suits," and casual suits for hiking and sports.[16] Sack suits were the college man's sartorial staple. Bankers, shopkeepers, and civil servants popularized the sack suit in the 1860s, but the models marketed to college men in the early 1900s featured shorter jackets with broad, unpadded shoulders and tapered (also called "peg-topped") trousers. These "college suits" or "college models" endorsed an emerging masculinity that stressed athleticism and body consciousness. In 1910, a trade magazine for the menswear industry wrote of the college man's sack suit: "Both the wide, athletic shoulder and the peg-top or semi-peg-top trousers originated with college youth and are affected by the younger element, and ultimately in a measure by all men."[17] From early in the century, the college man's influence extended beyond the campus.

For the classroom, a casual alternative to the sack suit was the Norfolk, which paired a belted, patch-pocketed jacket with knickers. The Duke of Norfolk first wore the jacket with matching or nonmatching pants while hunting on his country estate in the 1860s. The jacket's gusseted sleeves and vented back allowed for a full range of motion and became a favorite of hunters and golfers. Men at Oxford and Cambridge took to the style as everyday wear. In 1901, a report on campus dress at Princeton confirmed that Norfolk jackets "have been popular for some time." "Those who have calves, and some alas who have not" wore the suit. Calves, previously hidden under trouser legs, met with much commentary. The *Princeton Alumni Weekly* advised those who were not endowed with muscular calves to wear a high, laced boot because they were "a great help in giving the illusion of reality."[18] The Norfolk was made of tweed, a woolen weave whose roughness—in the words of one student supporter—lends itself "beautifully to the informal effect desired in sports clothes."[19] For its warmth, durability, and casual connotations, tweed became the fabric of choice for collegians' sports coats. Since the mid-nineteenth century, tweed was the "characteristic cloth of the hardy sportsman, whose sartorial appearance was modern, yet indicative of unquestionable manly worth."[20]

In the 1920s, the college man traded in sack and Norfolk suits for a blazer or sports coat worn with flannel pants—a change documented in figure 2.1, where Princetonians in blazers sit next to colleagues from the old guard who are still wearing full suits and hard collars. By the end of the 1920, many manufacturers marketed the same or similar products to collegians across the country, hired Madison Avenue agencies to create advertising

Figure 2.1. Members of Princeton's Dial Club in 1912 wore everything from three-piece suits with hard collars to "odd jackets"—the term for sport coats when worn with nonmatching pants. The variety of footwear affirms the uneven pace at which casual style infiltrated campuses in the 1910s. Some men sported black ankle boots; others had on brogues. Several members wore the forerunner to sneakers, white canvas (or leather) high tops with flat, suede soles. As the decade progressed, white bucks and two-toned saddle shoes became de rigueur on the Princeton campus, and the shoes were worn to near dilapidation. Courtesy of Princeton University Library.

campaigns, and partnered with retailers to lure college men to their wares. Student-written humor magazines and serialized fiction in mainstream magazines detailed what collegians nationwide were wearing. The college man's public stature as a tastemaker and an avid consumer had broader implications on the culture at large. Historian Bill Osgerby writes, "During the 1920s and 1930s the mores and fashions of collegiate youth culture heralded the rise of a middle-class masculinity formed around consumerist desire and youthful hedonism."[21]

As collegians consolidated their collective power as consumers, they began to voice their demands. Men returning from World War I refused to return to stiff collars and fitted vests. The design of their service uniforms prioritized practicality and comfort, and now, so did they. Collegians favored rolled collars that made the wearer look "less rigid." The government replaced cumbersome military breeches with full-length pants because soldiers considered them more comfortable, warmer, and easier to put on.[22] Military leaders believed less restrictive uniforms were "a gain in comfort" and promised doubters that "discipline will probably not suffer."[23] The army also developed footwear to replace the single-soled Russet Marching Shoe worn by the military early in the century, which proved too delicate for trench conditions. The Pershing and Victory shoes were designed to withstand long marches and offer warmth on cold nights. Thick-soled, durable shoes became collegians' calling card in the 1920s.

During and immediately after the war, students were unable to purchase new clothes, and so their garments either wore out or went out of style. When the clothing stocks were restored, students bought sportswear.[24] Sweaters, flannel pants and shirts, corduroys, plus-four knickers, white bucks, and sneakers were worn for active participation in sports but also for everyday campus wear to class. Collegians defied the mandates of groups such as the National Association of Retail Clothiers (NARC), who, in 1923, "strongly advocated the confinement of sports attire strictly to its respective realm and further declared that its use as street dress was not in good form."[25] One example of sportswear-turned-streetwear was the blazer, which was first worn in the mid-1830s as part of a British naval uniform. Commonly navy blue or blue-and-white striped, the blazer had signature brass buttons with the emblem of an anchor. British crew teams borrowed the blazer and incorporated it into their team uniform. Princeton rowers wore the garment by the turn of the century, and other athletes soon wore team blazers with pride. The team blazer was the forerunner of the letterman's sweater. The navy blazer and white flannel pants ensemble had distinct associations with yachting and, consequently, was worn only during the spring and summer months. Since the early 1900s, Princeton graduates wore the blazer and flannel pants duo on commencement day, and it became closely associated with the university. In *This Side of Paradise*, Amory Blaine observes the ensemble in its campus context on his first day at Princeton: "Several times he could have sworn that men turned to look at him critically. He wondered vaguely if there was something the matter with his clothes. . . . He felt unnecessarily stiff and awkward among these white-flannelled, bare-headed youths who must be juniors and seniors, judging by the *savoir faire* with which they strolled."[26]

The tweed or corduroy sports coat, which assumed a primary importance to the male undergraduate's wardrobe in the 1920s, was also a Princeton-born trend. As *Life* magazine noted: "The contrasting jacket and trousers are practically a Princeton uniform." The magazine acknowledged that, because "Princeton undergraduates are the prototype of Hollywood's conception of how the well-dressed college boy should look . . . tailors and haberdashers watch Princeton students closely."[27] For all the heralding of Princeton as a style center, the real push for sartorial freedom came from places like Penn State, where suits in the classroom gave way to not just sports coats but sweaters and collared shirts.

In the early 1930s, young men began to step away from the suit. An advertisement for Rose Brothers of Seventh Avenue in a 1932 issue of *National Retail Clothier* trumpeted the prevalence of the sports coat and khakis trend. The sports coat combination "again proves sensationally popular for 1932!" the ad declared. "Every store throughout the country is pushing the ensemble! Pushing it with greater zeal!"[28] In the 1930s, the sports coat replaced the suit as classroom attire at the majority of universities across the country. In 1934, an editor at Penn State predicted of classroom wear: "When Spring again makes a young man fancy, he will be so in informal attire. There will be no wane in the popularity of the sport coat."[29] Cal men knew "sweaters are peachy for daytime and for most anytime on campus, for that matter, but a sports coat is a practical necessity if you are at all serious about your appearance." While many men considered the sports coat a casual alternative to the suit, at Cal, where dress standards were notoriously informal, it was worn to class, but mostly it was reserved for "those special occasions."[30] For everyday wear, Cal men preferred lumberjack jackets in bright checks and plaids.

Collegians chose the sports coat over the suit and wore it to class, to dinner, and on a date. Grumblings about a general decline in dress standards were common among faculty and administrators throughout of the period studied. At Cal, the dean of men complained in a memo to the university president, the men attended meals dressed like "applicants for a free Thanksgiving dinner gather[ed] before a Salvation Army Hall." Their dress, manners, and general demeanor was "a disgrace."[31] Some even threatened action. A rumor at Washington and Jefferson College whispered of a faculty-penned rule that required a tie for class, because "during the last several months a marked spread of carelessness among the students in their dress . . . has grown in great proportions." Following up on the rumor, the student newspaper reported that the faculty had expressed their interest in men paying more attention to neatness but decided to forgo any official policy.[32]

"Official policy" on dress for men was rare. Stanford's 1940 student handbook, for example, told men, "Around the campus on school days you will wear almost anything you want."[33] Even at Morehouse, where men wore suits and ties on campus well into the 1960s, dress standards were tacit rather than written. Morehouse administrators believed that students who were neatly and conservatively dressed helped to gain respectability in the eyes of white America. The college wanted to make sure that "correct personal habits are inculcated" and thus required "cleanliness and neatness," but higher-ups regulated student behavior, not appearance. By controlling behavior, administrators tried to ensure "the development of manly qualities and moral character."[34] Administrators prohibited the "use of intoxicating liquors and tobacco" and encouraged sports "under restrictions that prevent danger to health and neglect to regular school duties." Rather than mandate dress codes, administrators led by example. At Morehouse, wrote the biographers of its president, Benjamin Mays, "professors weren't only interested in teaching their curriculum. They sought to pass on to students social graces, how to dress, how to speak correctly, how to show respect."[35] Students wearing suits and ties to class demonstrated respect for their professors and the institution. When student leader Lonnie King showed up at campus events and public appearances in shabby clothing, President Mays had his personal tailor make a suit and overcoat for the young man. Years later, Mays remembered the student's pride when he wore the ensemble.[36] Morehouse administrators actively crafted a conservative image of its students for the American public.

At both Spelman and Morehouse, administrators and faculty worked hard to counteract what they saw as "the proneness of the Negro for pomp and display."[37] Students, said one Morehouse commencement speaker, "must worry more about the style of our brain and not so much about the style of clothing."[38] Morehouse aimed to inculcate moral fortitude and avoidance of luxuries. In 1931, President John Hope told Morehouse students to "be deeply interested in public welfare" and warned them not to get sidetracked by indulgence. He cautioned them about two common pitfalls: "food and clothes."[39] Many students agreed and thought that keeping up with fashion trends was a waste of time, inspired by evils such as "love of change, extreme individuality, [and] commercial interest." School literature and student-penned articles urged readers to remember that "the keynote to good dressing is appropriate dressing" and "being well dressed often means knowing what to leave off."[40]

Princeton and Morehouse encouraged homogeneity in dress, but the socioeconomic diversity of Penn State and Cal allowed for an array of options for "the aspiring sartorialist." The "future farmers" on "Ag Hill" were known to "step forth in a pair of old Army shoes, overalls, and a straw hat, chewing a bit of hay to give the proper atmosphere." One could spot the education major by his "pair of horn-rimmed glasses, and a dumb look." Those in liberal arts were the most fashion-minded, said the report. "Following the custom of previous years," these men "appear garbed in a pair of well-worn sports shoes, old flannel pants, and an unpressed coat."[41] The curriculum at Penn State and Cal demanded functional attire to survey land, dig a ditch, or milk a cow. One student wrote, "For that lab, it doesn't take much imagination to figure what would be appropriate. Write home for that old dirty pair of dungarees, and that torn high school football jersey."[42] Many students worked their way through school, and clothing was a valuable possession. An editorial in Cal's student newspaper rebuked the ripping of clothing in interclass brawls, because for students with limited budgets, "any destruction to clothing is regarded as a real loss."[43] Elaborate wardrobes were not the norm.

Cal men remained aloof to many eastern college trends. As demonstrated by the sweaters, work shirts, jeans, and corduroys in figure 2.2, Cal men collectively had a more diverse wardrobe than those in a homogenous student culture, such as that of Princeton. Their interpretation of casual style for the classroom included sweaters worn with or without sports coats and dirty corduroy pants, whose "convenience and suitability" made them a wardrobe mainstay.[44] Dirty cords were a campus tradition and worn only by juniors and seniors. Their prevalence evoked the ire of administrators. In 1925, president W. W. Campbell expressed "his delight in seeing that many of the numerous pairs of cords worn by upperclassman on the campus had been cleaned or washed during vacation interim." A public backlash came from the men, who believed, "a clean pair of cords is almost as bad as a new pair." A letter to the editor from "E. J. D." believed that washing cords "whiffed away all the studied carelessness and sloppiness." Clean cords were an insult to a man's autonomy because they "always signified that the wearer has been overcome by outside forces, probably his parents or friends, and has been compelled to submit to the humiliation of having them cleaned."[45] The president did not mention them again, but Cal women did—and often.

Women at Penn State who shared classes and social activities were vocal in their dislike of men's campus clothes. In the early 1940s, the Association of Women Students published an advice book on appropriate attire for campus. *College Customs and Co-Ediquette at Penn State* stressed that "cleanliness and neatness are of first importance." Men were reminded that "a crease and a clean shirt" are fundamental to "making a good impression." The level of formality recommended for their colleagues was far higher than the men could have stomached. The editors told their

Figure 2.2. This photograph taken at Cal's Sather Gate captures the diversity of men's dress on campus in the mid-1920s. Students lifted patterned sweaters and hose from golfwear and newsboy caps from the working classes. Several students wear cuffed jeans with a sport coat or sweater. The student looking at the camera has on corduroy pants, a nationally recognized favorite of California campuses such as Cal and Stanford. Much to the chagrin of women, the men wore the corduroys for months on end without washing because they believed "a clean pair of cords is almost as bad as a new pair." Courtesy of the University of California Archives.

classmates, "Even if the only time you ever wore a tie at home was when the family dragged you off to church, remember that you're a college boy now; it's a good idea to wear one to class."[46] Their advice fell on deaf ears. In the spring of 1948, only 10 percent of Penn Staters wore ties to class.[47]

If Penn State men did not want to wear ties to class, then wearing them to the dining hall was out of the question. In the 1950s, newly instated administrative policies that required ties at dinner were met with outrage: "What folly! We feel this regulation is not only unnecessary but impractical," wrote one student group.[48] In 1955, the dean of men's ruling that ties and coats become standard dining attire for evening meals was voted on and approved by the student-led All-University Cabinet. The rule was not well received by many, including the men at Nittany Hall, which proved to be a hotbed for dissent. The rule was repealed. A half-decade struggle between the dean, campus government, and individual dorm councils, such

Figure 2.3. Because administrators hoped to instill a sense of propriety among students, the cafeteria remained a contested space on campus. Women were forbidden from wearing jeans, Bermuda shorts, hair curlers, head scarves, sleeveless shirts, and sweatshirts. Men had far fewer regulations. One administrator at Cal reported that male students showed up to dinner looking like "applicants for a free Thanksgiving dinner gathered before a Salvation Army Hall." Their dress, manners, and general demeanor was "a disgrace." Here, students from Penn State's Nittany Hall, a hotbed of dress code violations, wear T-shirts, turtleneck sweaters, and collared shirts to lunch in 1959. Dress standards depended on the meal and the day of the week, with Sunday dinners being the most formal. Courtesy of the Penn State University Archives, Pennsylvania State University Libraries.

as the vocal Nittany Hall, went from legislating ties at dinner to banning T-shirts in the cafeteria a few years later. The men pictured in figure 2.3 confirm that T-shirts were permitted at Nittany Hall at lunchtime. The biggest problem for the administration was following through on the policies. Student Phil Austin voiced his support of the dress standards in a letter to the editor and noted, "Although the dress rule is officially still in operation, enforcement has gone to the rock pile." Austin believed "there should be no buck-passing."[49] More students were in line with Thomas Farr (Class of 1962), who said they did not wish "to be compared with Einstein, nor do they wish to be a disgrace to the University," but they had "no intention of dressing up unless there is an occasion to do so."[50]

In the 1950s, men's classroom clothing entered its next phase. The suit had been abandoned for the sports coat, which then gave way to the T-shirt worn with or without a sweatshirt. In 1957, Stanford students preferred red letterman's jackets, jeans, and white shirts, and "liberally sprinkled among these are khakis, slacks, Tee-shirts, sport shirts, and sweaters."[51] Some students considered the shift away from the sports coat to be disrespectful to their teachers. As a Princeton student reporter noted, "The faculty wear suits and odd coats to class and the undergraduate body is being discourteous to them when they appear in khakis and T shirts."[52] Other students felt they had purchased the freedom to wear what they wanted on campus. A Penn State student explained that many of his colleagues believed that "their dress should not prevent them from receiving what they have rightfully paid for."[53] As men began to don T-shirts and jeans to class, the old guard whimpered their final objections. In an article titled "Informality Pervades Campus Dress," a student reporter told of a Nassau Street clothing merchant at Princeton who "looks across the street at students in cut-off sweat shirts, and blue jeans, patched jackets and shrunken slacks" and "can only wonder what happened to Princeton."[54] The tweed sports coat and dirty bucks that seemed so informal in contrast to the four-button suit became quite formal in the shadow of the sweatshirt.

## "Comfort, Warmth and Feeling at Ease": Pants in the Cafeteria

Women wearing pants broke gender standards in place in Western culture for more than half a millennium. Since the Middle Ages, men and women wanted "to have a very clear sense of distance from the other one."[55] To a large degree, women's adoption of pants first happened on the college campus. Despite men's pleas and administrators' dictates, despite fashion editors who refused to endorse the trend, and despite raised eyebrows and open hostility, women wore pants. Men pushed the boundaries of "appropriate attire" by wearing sports coats, khakis, and sweaters to the classroom; women did so by wearing pants and jeans to the cafeteria.

The cafeteria was central to the collegian's world. Radcliffe student Nancy Murray wrote to her parents in 1943, "We have super cafeteria style too. . . . I gulp the food—I'm not the only one. You have to if you want to get any of the best food."[56] In accordance to regulations they penned themselves, Murray and her colleagues wore pants to breakfast and lunch but not dinner. A 1943 editorial in the school paper titled "Pulling in the Slack" complained of how often the problem of pants "occupies the Student

Council." The writer linked the topic to an issue more poignant than fashion: "How much are we responsible to community opinion and taste, even when we don't agree?" After several spirited meetings, the student council decided that women could wear pants anywhere in the dorm, except the living room, and to Harvard Square, but only at night. Pants were allowed in class and in public "under inclement conditions, blizzards are being regarded adequate excuse to wear dungarees."[57] Unlike their counterparts at Smith, Vassar, and Wellesley, Radcliffe women upheld a comparatively conservative dress code. More than a decade later, Radcliffe's 1957 student handbook still mandated that "slacks, blue jeans, or shorts may not be worn outside the quad at any time without a long coat."[58] Radcliffe's urban location was a key factor in maintaining these standards.

Few universities took such a liberal approach to pants in the cafeteria as did the Seven Sisters. At Spelman, students were "expected to exemplify good taste in dress at all times."[59] No shorts, jeans, or pants in the dining hall. Top-down edicts confined the garments to "occasions when activities warrant such attire"—a murky delineation that implied only when women were completely out of the public eye. Rules from a 1959–60 handbook decreed, "All Spelman students, day or dormitory, when going on or off campus are expected to wear skirts."[60] At coeducational schools such as Penn State and Cal, administrators regulated women's behavior and their clothing: a well-guarded sign-in/out system, specifications on where laundry could be dried, and designated areas to entertain male visitors—but only until 8:00 P.M. Rules for pants in the cafeteria were convoluted. A 1960 Penn State edict clarified: "Bermuda shorts, kilts, and slacks are considered suitable attire for residence hall entertaining for breakfast, lunch and Sunday supper during the semester, and for all meals during finals except Sunday noon dinner." Women could not wear pants "in administrative buildings and offices or for evening meals during the semester and Sunday noon dinner."[61]

Such clarification of when and where pants could be worn was necessary for two reasons. First, the unspoken standards of dress that made jeans taboo in certain circumstances were holding less weight than they had in the late 1940s. To eliminate any misinterpretation, the rules were spelled out. Second, female students at both Penn State and Cal began to actively protest dress codes in the mid-1950s. The students at Cal spent much energy convincing the administration that by replacing "inflexible, centralized rules with a rule of reason" the students themselves "were in a better position to suggest a particular girl's attire was inappropriate." Self-regulation of the cafeteria, they argued, made "the girls more respectful to our dress suggestions because they knew we were not simply defending an administrative rule." By the end of the 1960s, college women had fought—and won—the right to wear pants, shorts, dungarees, hair curlers, flip-flops, and sweatshirts to the cafeteria. With that battle over, dress codes were doomed.[62]

In October 1944, *Life*'s "Picture of the Week" featured two Wellesley students in jeans and untucked men's shirts (see figure 2.4). The photograph "made the nation's jaw drop and set tongues clucking round the country."[63] Accusations that the students were unfeminine and unfashionable—critiques that had long been levied at the Seven Sisters—abounded.[64] For more than half a century, deans, presidents, and faculty members presided over what the public believed to be "Adamless Edens," as one writer put it, where higher-ups "desire to turn out their pupils in their own image. And too often they succeed." Social critics made distinctions between "the increasing class of girls who merely go to college" and those who were "highly intelligent [and] go there for purely intellectual purposes." The latter group—those who went to women's colleges—spent their time "bending over books and burning the midnight oil." These women simply could not compete with the "half-educated girl," who was "going from beauty salon to beauty salon, trying a succession of Marcel waves, complexion tonics, rouges and hair tints."[65] While fashion magazines ran glossy spreads of Smith girls in tweed skirt suits and youthful, plaid pinafores, many women of the Seven Sisters and elite women's colleges favored pants, and they wore the garments with liberty. Administrators did little to intervene.

As the hubbub over the *Life* photo demonstrates, the mainstream press attempted to understand the "how" and "why" of the trendsetters at elite women's colleges. In 1944, a *New York Times* fashion writer offered answers to "Why College Girls Dress That Way." She attributed dress standards at elite women's colleges to "the desire for comfort, the locale of the school, the absence of men, the war, and last but not least, an unashamed desire to be 'different' and to slap at convention." The colleges' publicity departments scrambled to explain student dress. A spokeswoman for Smith believed the adoption of jeans was a reaction to strict dress codes at preparatory schools. Both the writer and the officials she interviewed considered dungarees as the latest "badge" of the college girl, one that would soon be replaced by another trend. They were wrong.[66]

The *Times* article brought to light two enduring and important elements of collegiate dress at the Seven Sisters: the absence of men as an influence on women's appearance and the differences between campuses. Without males, they surmised, comfort was prioritized. Another writer noted,

Figure 2.4. *Life*'s 15 October 1944 "Picture of the Week" featured two Wellesley students in frayed jeans and untucked men's shirts. The photograph "made the nation's jaw drop and set tongues clucking round the country." Women on secluded campuses such as Wellesley, Vassar, and Smith wore men's garments sooner and more often than their sisters in the city at Radcliffe or Barnard. Much of the uproar about the photo centered on the women's "unfeminine" appearance and their gall for wearing the clothes into town. Courtesy of the Associated Press.

"Intellectuals are traditionally a rather careless-looking breed. Perhaps campus sloppiness is a hangover from the days when many college girls dreamed of living on the Left Bank." What mattered, argued the writer, was not how they looked in private but how they looked in public, an occurrence that was "the most startling of all college phenomena." She assured readers, "The Monday frumps in pigtails are unrecognizable as fashion plates on Saturday." However, the writer believed that "the seemingly inevitable conclusion that women dress for men alone only partly explains the oddity of college girls' clothing." Those who shared classrooms with men also took up fads that defied convention. Oversized sweaters and worn-out shoes were commonplace at Penn State and Cal. The women, concluded the fashion writer, "want to be conspicuous—men or no men."[67]

Students at Wellesley, Smith, and Vassar took to pants in the mid-1930s and jeans later in the decade. Administrators paid little attention to either garment. At the very liberal Bennington College, women wore "dungarees" to the cafeteria, to town, and to class. The "first thing" the women did was "roll up the trouser legs half way." Students paired their jeans with men's shirts and high rubber boots, which they removed in class and "park[ed] underneath their chairs[,] and concentrate[d] on the lecture at hand in their stocking feet."[68] Wellesley's public relations department promised that pants, jeans, and men's shirts have "by no means taken the campus by storm." Jeans, the publicists stated, "have their place—for hiking or working in the college potato patch."[69] Despite these claims, women at elite women's schools such as Wellesley, Smith, and Vassar wore pants and jeans freely, and soon, others followed their lead. A fashion reporter confirmed, "Shirts with tails still worn outside [are] favored at various colleges, often with blue jeans."[70] The *Tobé Report* noted "that big college-girl furor . . . for the rolled up blue jean."[71] Even students at Radcliffe, which maintained a stricter dress code than her sisters, became very casual during finals week when "braids, dungarees, ballet slippers, moccasins, [and] big brother's old shirts" contributed to a "nonchalance" in dress on "those hectic days."[72]

The popularity of jeans and pants was a direct result of college women's war activities. In 1942, *Women's Wear Daily* reported, "War work is important at most colleges. Blue jeans are much favored for it. Slacks are also worn and some coveralls."[73] As seen in figure 2.5, hands-on courses in first aid, nursing, motor mechanics, and airplane maintenance demanded comfortable, durable clothes, and pants and jeans fit the bill. A Penn State student noted, "The war was hardly a month old when Penn State coeds, foreseeing that women might rule the world, began wearing pants."[74] The fashion industry foresaw the impact of such work clothing on the future of women's dress more generally. An insider reported to a luncheon of the Fashion Group International in November 1941, "A great many people feel that if women go into uniform for the duration of the emergency and they find these things becoming an attractive as well as comfortable and practical thing, they are going to stick with them, and there is the beginning of a whole new trend."[75] Indeed, the comfort and practicality college students found in their wartime wardrobes endeared slacks and jeans to them and other young women involved in the efforts on the home front.[76]

Wartime brought with it "a lot of talk going on everywhere about the necessity of 'cutting back.'" Students at Sweet Briar College attracted national attention when they started a campaign to get students to wear jeans in order to help conserve dress clothes for formal occasions. "We are fortunate in having a location in the country, and so could not possibly offend people in the city by such casual dress," wrote a student who felt that the woman "who is neat and clean in a skirt and sweater will be just as meticulous in jeans and a shirt." Female students often referenced their fear of offending the local communities with their casual style. Many of her

Figure 2.5. A publicity still from Barnard College shows the kinds of war work that allowed women to wear pants and jeans even on urban campuses, where students were typically more conservative in dress due to the many commuters who spent much of their day in the public eye. Here, women wear jeans, saddle shoes, tennis shoes, sweaters, and men's shirts under their work coats. College publicity departments used such stills to promote their students' involvement in the war efforts. In addition to learning new skills, students renovated their clothing to avoid purchasing new garments, sold war bonds, and knitted socks and gloves for servicemen. Courtesy of the Barnard College Archives.

colleagues agreed, but others "would feel sorry to see the whole community decked out as it prepared to build Noah's arc." Another student noted, "It is common knowledge that Sweet Briar is renowned for the pleasing appearance of its students." The women did not mandate jeans as campus wear but just allowed restrictions to be lifted so "the arc builders and those who fancy themselves as such" could don jeans "at all times during the week except for dinner."[77]

There was a significant difference between what college women wore to tend gardens or study in their dorm rooms and what they wore to evening meals. On most campuses, the cafeteria was a public space where women were expected to uphold standards of decorum that distinguished them as ladies. Expectations were not always met. A Radcliffe student noted,

"Dormitory table manners are famous, mainly because they are atrocious. What poor dormitory dweller has not performed unconsciously for her shocked parents on her first night home?"[78] Cafeteria dress regulations spelled out specific times and occasions when pants and jeans were permitted. Dress codes for breakfast and lunch were more lax than those for evening meals. A Boston newspaper reporter confirmed in 1940, "In most colleges, slacks are prohibited for dinner."[79]

The variance in when, where, and how women began to wear pants to the cafeteria speaks to both student culture and an administration's policy on monitoring women's behavior. Elite women's schools such as Bennington and the Seven Sisters had hands-off administrators who took little interest in policing their students' attire. Harvard men had more to say about Radcliffe women's appearances than the deans. Harvardians believed a Cliffie to be "a bony female wearing flat-heeled shoes, and horn-rimmed glasses, and carrying half a dozen textbooks." They considered "Wellesley girls on average prettier but dumber than Radcliffeites. Smith is ditto, but more fun to spend a week-end at."[80] Given Radcliffe's urban location, students dressed more conservatively. A Radcliffe student editor for *Mademoiselle* told readers, "An all-women campus near or in a large city—Radcliffe or Barnard for example—requires a wardrobe that puts the emphasis on citified clothes. You don't spend too much time in blue jeans or sweaters and skirts (outside of classes), so don't spend much money on them either."[81] A 1942 poll at Radcliffe revealed that only 20 percent of women said they approved of women in slacks on the street, while 40 percent said slacks should be allowed in class. Pants, in private, however, were a different matter. When asked if slacks were okay to wear at home, 90 percent said "yes."[82]

Radcliffe students voted yearly on whether or not to allow pants and jeans in the cafeteria. In the early 1940s, they instated strict regulations on cafeteria attire and outlawed the garments for most lunches and at all dinners. By the end of the 1940s, the student council pushed conservative dress standards by more implicit methods. "It is good morale to change for dinner," the 1948–49 handbook encouraged. "Wednesday night and Sunday noon you dress anyway."[83] Some students thought pants were too mannish on college women and feared the end of femininity. In the 1950s, the rules regarding jeans in the cafeteria became the provenance of each individual dining hall. Students in the residence hall voted as to whether or not they could wear jeans to Saturday or Sunday dinner. If jeans were approved, no guests were permitted at these meals. The provision demonstrated that while casual clothing was a prerogative of the students, public perception still mattered to Radcliffe women.

Such democracy was not the case at Spelman, where conservative administrators and students worked together to enforce dress codes. Early administrators' regulation of clothing was due to necessity and the need to control the school's public image. Many Spelman women showed up with little clothing. Spelman founder Harriet E. Giles wrote in her diary of a "not atypical" student who did not have any "underclothes [but] only a coarse black skirt and a calico waist." Northern churches donated barrels of clothing, and Giles routinely "spent most of the afternoon distributing clothes."[84] The necessity of dressing students prompted the development of sewing and millinery programs, which provided marketable skills and padded students' wardrobes. Early administrators, who understood the importance of their students' appearance in wooing donors, made efforts to stamp out elaborate dress. In 1912, the directors of Spelman's sister institution, Atlanta University, told new women that "silks, velvets and other expensive or showy materials or trimmings" were "considered inappropriate." Only dresses of cotton and wool were allowed. To ward off outside influence, parents were "asked not to send clothing, unless the request for it is endorsed by the preceptress."[85] Modesty was at the heart of many of Spelman's rules, whether it was the insistence on white gloves for town visits or the requirement that necklines "be high enough to avoid any appearance of immodesty."[86]

Such regulations remained intact into the 1920s. In 1920, Spelman president Lucy Tapley issued an elaborate list of dress codes to be "rigidly enforced" by teachers. "The growing tendency toward extravagance and lack of good judgment in the matter of dress is deplorable," Tapley announced. She deemed "cheap jewelry" as "injurious to health" and insisted, "Showy and immodest styles and materials will be carefully avoided by the cultured and virtuous." Skirts were "not to be too short or too narrow," and shoes were limited to black oxfords with at least four eyelets. She specified, "We shall not expect any shoes of fancy variety," and only "strong, black cotton" stockings were allowed.[87] Tapley pursued offenders, "uninviting" students who would not comply with "the spirit as well as the letter of the rules."[88] Dressing and behaving conservatively enabled Spelman's students to gain respect from white society and to carve out a social role for the educated African American woman.[89] Administrators considered fashion to be morally dangerous. As hemlines began to rise in the spring of 1917, the *Spelman Messenger* ran an editorial titled, "Do Not Let Your Daughter Wear Them." The piece promised that because of the "extreme, indecent, freakish spring style," many girls not only were "going to lose their modesty" but were going "to lose their virtue as a result of a style that is nothing less than an invitation."[90] Administrators stressed the enduring benefits of health over the fickleness of fashion. Lectures, such as "Happy's Vanity Case" that was given during 1929's Health Week, promised students that sleep, exercise, and nutrition were healthier than cosmetics.

Spelman's stringent dress codes began to relax in 1927 with the inauguration of President Florence Read, a graduate of Mount Holyoke, who aimed "to bring the college to as close an approximation of the general run of women's college in the United States as possible without alienating any outside monetary assistance."[91] To do so, she lifted the more rigid regulations. Upon her arrival, Read held a meeting with students in Howe Chapel where "dress in general was discussed."[92] She quickly became "aware of the growing impatience among the students at being regarded as benighted heathens and at being subjected to rigid discipline."[93] Under Read, students replaced their schoolmarmish, all-black oxfords with nationally popular saddle shoes. Students at Spelman were primary in enforcing dress codes. Upperclassmen monitored the clothing and conduct of underclassmen to create, in the words of one student, a "place where everyone acts a 'perfect lady.'"[94] Girdles and hats—which had been abandoned by many northern college women in the 1940s—were worn well into the 1960s. The newspaper's fashion editors gave advice on how to select the perfect hat for every occasion, for, they asked, "what accessory is more important than your hat?"[95] As always, conservatism was stressed. Administrators told freshmen to make sure that hats for Sunday service were "not too flashy as to be inappropriate for a religious service."[96]

Given the history of conservative dress at Spelman, pants in the cafeteria were verboten until the late 1960s. President Albert Manley, who came to Spelman in 1953, noted that when he arrived, "Students ate in the dining hall fully dressed with no hair curlers or jeans allowed."[97] After breakfast, women went to chapel—a requirement for all students on Mondays through Fridays. Spelman women wore pants to private events. At Christmas in 1947, students held a gift-wrapping party in their dorm, and attendees came "donned in slacks, shorts, jeans, and 'what have you.'"[98] The 1955–56 handbook told freshmen that they could bring jeans, slacks, and shorts, if they wanted. However, these were for "special occasions," such as "tennis, bicycling and the like." As shown in figure 2.6, women were permitted to wear pants and jeans on Saturday afternoons, but the handbook made clear that these were not to be worn to "the classroom . . . the library, [or] the dining hall."[99] In 1960, the College Government Handbook indicated that "slacks, pedal pushers, or Bermuda shorts may be worn to Sunday morning breakfast in the dining room." Every other meal required

Figure 2.6. In the early 1950s, Spelman women adhered to administrator-imposed dress standards during the week but were permitted to wear pants and jeans on Saturdays. Despite the well-enforced rule that they had to dress up for shopping trips into downtown Atlanta, the women sidestepped it by neglecting to sign out of the dorm or claiming they were just going to the library at nearby Atlanta University. Even on the most conservative campuses, students pushed the boundaries of when and where they could wear casual clothing. Courtesy of Erin Goseer Mitchell.

skirts. Students dressed up for Sunday dinner, and the handbook specified that that included "hose and appropriate shoes."[100]

Despite the "fear of being campus bound, or worse yet, sent home," Spelman women in the 1950s found creative ways to sidestep administrator-imposed rules that required them to wear hats, gloves, and hose on shopping excursions to downtown.[101] A sign-out system tracked the students' comings and goings, but juniors and seniors either ignored the system or wrote that their destination was the Atlanta University library. School

Figure 2.7. Erin Goseer attended Spelman College in the early 1950s, and her time there is detailed in her memoir *Born Colored: Life Before Bloody Sunday.* Goseer's mother was a talented seamstress who made most of her daughter's clothes. Goseer was able to get away with not wearing a girdle (a Spelman dress code requirement) because of her slight build. This pink nylon blouse was a gift from a family friend and fit her need for clothing that was both lightweight for Atlanta weather and easy to wash. In 1956, Goseer married Aldus Mitchell, a "Spelman Willie"—the term used for Morehouse men who spent as much time on the Spelman campus as the rules allowed. Courtesy of Erin Goseer Mitchell.

policy dictated that first-semester freshmen were to be accompanied into town by an upperclassmen, but the dress-up rule made finding a chaperone difficult. Even without their telltale white gloves, Spelman women were noticeable in downtown Atlanta. Erin Goseer (Class of 1955; see figure 2.7) writes in her memoir, *Born Colored*, of a shoe-shopping excursion to the popular Davison's department store. When the salesman asked her to try on her desired shoes in the back of the store, Goseer refused. After several attempts to get her to move, the salesman asked, "Y'all from Spelman, ain't you?" Goseer tried on the shoes in the front of the store and purchased the black patent leather and mesh, three-inch high heels. It was her "first time standing up to a white man for fair and just treatment," and she "wore the shoes the next day even taller than the extra three inches."[102]

At Penn State and Berkeley, women negotiated, petitioned, and protested for the right to wear pants and jeans to the cafeteria. Much like at other schools, students were allowed to wear the garments to certain meals on certain days. Yet, as the garments' popularity grew, and as college women became more comfortable with defying administrators' dictates, students actively sought to abolish dress codes, claiming that freedom of dress "is one of the 'little things' that makes dormitory life more enjoyable."[103] These organized campaigns were among the first instances where students worked collectively to seize complete control of their own student culture. In doing so, the women set the stage for more radical protests that came to the fore in the 1960s.

Much like other college women, the women of Penn State and Cal wore pants and occasionally jeans before World War II. Throughout the

1930s, they wore pants on bicycling trips, on boating excursions, and to the beach. The *Daily Californian* told readers, "Lazy life figures up to a good part of every girl's time, and she will be well prepared if she has a set of those excellently tailored slacks."[104] A student handbook at Penn State clarified when and where pants were appropriate: "For more informal affairs, such as hikes, picnics and hay-rides, slacks are fine. For classes, slacks are frowned upon by the men."[105]

College men at Penn State and Cal were vocal in their distaste for pants. At Penn State, criticism initially came from ex-servicemen who had spent months gazing "languishingly at the works of art drawn by Messers. Varga and Petty, and hoped someday to return to the States to do their gazing on live specimens."[106] These men banded together in December 1945 to launch the Anti-Slacks Campaign. Spearheaded by the brothers of Delta Sigma Phi, the campaign deemed pants inappropriate for all aspects of campus life, except lab classes. Men collected data at the local hangout, The Corner Room, to disprove the women's assertion that cold weather prompted them to wear pants. Their study showed that sunny days did not stop the outbreak of "slackitis." The campaign advertised in the student newspaper and posted bulletins around campus and in downtown stores. However, many businesses were reluctant to participate out of fear that angry pants-wearers would boycott. Despite the campaign's obvious failure and the onslaught of hate mail, the men vowed to continue their campaign "until the last pair of offensive slacks disappears from State College." When the fight in the student newspaper reached a standoff, men gave their girlfriends an ultimatum: "So girls, it's a choice between men or slacks. Which is it going to be?"[107] The women chose slacks for a simple reason. As one "slacker" wrote in her letter to the editor, "Comfort, warmth and feeling at ease signifies slacks to the female sex." Some women told men to put their energy into "changing a more serious and important problem." Another offered a radical solution: "I am sorry you can't compare our legs with your precious French mademoiselle, but as far as we are concerned you can re-enlist and go back to *Mademoiselle from Armentiers*."[108]

Many fashion editors echoed men's distaste for pants. One advice writer from the old guard told college women that if they must wear the dreaded pants they should "get slacks that are tailored . . . so they hold up and don't sag around the hind like most boy's pants get to doing." The writer wished the "gals really knew how cute you look in a well-cut dress." She complained, "Of course you've got to be comfortable, ah, me! Even if you have to insult the aesthetic sense of men to do it. What a pity."[109] *Vogue* told college women they should "strive for a trim, tidy wits-about-you look. You'll

Figure 2.8. Jeans took many forms on the college campus, as this picture from the University of Wisconsin in 1958 demonstrates. Earlier versions resembled painter's pants, complete with patch pockets and loose-fitting legs. As manufacturers became more savvy about the market in the 1950s, they made jeans with fitted tops and tapered legs (as seen above on the blonde woman with a white shirt and saddle shoes). However, many college women simply bought men's Levi's, wore them with a belt, and rolled up the legs. From the late 1940s, jeans were worn for outdoor events such as picnics or hiking, but on most campuses, it took nearly two decades for them to be acceptable attire for class or official school events. Courtesy of the University of Wisconsin Archives.

practically abandon blue jeans in favor of nicely tailored slacks—grey flannel or corduroy."[110] As demonstrated in figure 2.8, college women did not abandon jeans. A frank Associate Press writer told her readers across the country of the "annual big push" to "make real-life college girls look like they do in the movies." Despite the "tons of newsprint, rivers of printer's ink and millions of words" wasted on "what the well-dressed girl will wear to college," the women will wear "blue jeans, preferably patched, a frayed shirt or old sweat shirt." She warned campus visitors of the "painful scene when Betty comes leaping into the dormitory reception room to greet her fond parents looking like a soiled Huckleberry Finn."[111] College women prioritized comfort, and pants were comfortable.

Following the war, women were reluctant to return to what Pearl O. Weston, the dean of women at Penn State, called "pre-war requirements." In a 1948 letter to women at Penn State, she noted that while "the war period brought with it many innovations for women . . . this period has passed." She cited the forestry students of the Mont Alto campus who "of necessity dress very informally for class and work" and who now dressed for dinner, as did "practically all of the men's fraternities at Penn State." To get her point across, she laid down rules:

1. Make neatness and cleanliness the keynote of your appearance at all times.

2. Never appear in the dining room in raincoats, jeans, shirt hanging out, kerchiefs on head, bedroom slippers, pajamas, bathrobes, any night clothes, shorts and halter-style dresses.

3. Always appear in dresses appropriate for the occasion.

The dean noted, "Frequently, faculty and staff members are called upon to fill in application blanks for the students," and, she warned, "naturally the rating checked will be in the lower half of the scale if you are in the habit of dressing careless for class and general wear." She ended her letter with flattery and direction: "You are good looking; you do have nice clothes. By wearing them to fit the occasion, you will be putting your best foot forward."[112] The dean's letter "stirred up many new bull sessions in the dormitories" partly because she had instated new codes on pants and headscarves without consulting the Women's Student Government Association (WSGA).[113] Such blatant disregard for "the group that is supposed to make all rules and regulations governing women" resulted in a flurry of letters and an emergency meeting of the WSGA. The president of the group, Suzanne Romig, told women via the student newspaper, "The present suggestions of Dean Weston carry no penalties unless this is decided at a future Senate meeting."[114] The students soon ratified the majority of the dean's new regulations.

The back and forth between administrators and the students demonstrates the dynamic process of making and enforcing dress codes. By the 1950s, Cal administrators no longer wrote but heavily edited student-penned policies. In 1952, a posting at Cal outlined "Social Policy Suggestions." The elaborate list was written by a "representative group" and then passed to the administration for approval. Student-created rules included: "Earrings or an over abundance of jewelry should not be worn on campus or when wearing campus clothes" and "Strapless or off-shoulder dresses should not be worn on campus." They also stipulated that "jeans, levis, and other men's pants should not be worn outside the House except on picnics or hikes," which the administration clarified by adding, "They are not to be worn for coffee time."[115] These "policy suggestions" were distributed to dormitories and boardinghouses. The actual number of women in dormitories at Cal was significantly less than those in sorority or boardinghouses, in private apartments, or at home. Cal struggled to supply the demand for on-campus housing, and private enterprise stepped in to meet the always growing demand. Hence the number of women the administration was actually regulating was not even a quarter of the female population on campus.

Despite the general acceptance of pants on women in California, the dean maintained a hard line regarding their place in dorms and cafeterias. Members of dormitory boards, student councils, and sororities wrote letters to the dean to ask for more leeway. Cal women pushed for complete freedom to wear pants because:

1. [they are] more convenient for studying
2. the girls are given a choice as to what they can wear
3. there is more of a 'homey' feel
4. releasing a few rules makes the dorm a more pleasant place to live.[116]

By the end of the 1950s, most clothing regulations at Cal were gone, but the administration's hold on the cafeteria endured. Students believed "going to the cafeteria in pants" was a "convenience for those who enjoy wearing slacks to study in and to attend class." In 1965, the Committee to Wear Pants to Dinner announced the implementation of a trial period for the spring semester. Pants were to be allowed at any dinner but Sunday, when dresses were worn "out of respect for those to whom this is important."[117] The trial period was renewed. As the free speech movement raged outside the cafeteria walls, the women of Berkeley could finally wear anything they wanted to any meal in 1967.

At Penn State, women dismantled dress codes piecemeal. Areas of campus were deemed okay for pants and shorts one at a time. In 1964, the Associated Women Students (AWS) removed a clause from their rules that prohibited pants and shorts in administrative buildings. In January 1967, dress rules for Sunday dinner fell. In a newspaper editorial, one woman told her colleagues not to waste their time "rhapsodizing over the magnanimous liberal spirit which allows coeds to wear slacks." Bigger issues were at hand, she argued. The requirement that women live on campus and be subjected to any administrative regulation just went to prove that "the University's corporate attitude towards women was sick." It was pathetic, she continued, that a final eradication of dress codes "was considered a great leap forward." The students blamed the line-toers of the AWS, which had sought only to have "its collective Pollyanna curls patted approvingly by the administration."[118] A more radical Penn State coed had come to the fore.

■ In the classroom and in the cafeteria, collegians challenged and ultimately recast cultural standards that prioritized formality for public spaces. Collegians pioneered a catchall wardrobe that allowed the same thing to be worn to a club meeting as to a late-night study session. They prioritized versatility. As much as casual clothes were practical, they were also a visible rejection of outdated codes of conduct. Women wore pants and jeans to be comfortable but also to participate in a wider cultural discourse about what was "appropriate" and "inappropriate" for women to do and to wear. In the 1960s, many women dressed for a new era of social, political, and economic equality. Their demands for social change might not have packed the same punch had they done it in high heels and hip cinchers. For men, the demise of the suit gave the freedom to mix and match khakis, jeans, sweaters, sports coats, and eventually T-shirts and sweatshirts. The result was a comparatively eclectic wardrobe that enabled college men to accommodate personal needs and identities. With time, other middle-class men, followed college men's lead and stepped away from the business suit, a trend the industry caught on to in the late 1950s. "Casual wear is creeping into everyday business life," said an Associated Press reporter who noted that more sweaters and sports coats were seen in the office than every before. In the decade to follow, manufacturers of men's suits decreased their output by percentages in the double digits.[119] American youths were on the vanguard, but their married sisters, suburban mothers, weekend-loving dads, and baseball-card-collecting little brothers watched and learned. Even with the social unrest on college campuses in the 1960s, collegians' choices in casual dress had widespread implications for the American wardrobe at large.

The variations of who accepted casual style and when and where it was accepted demonstrate how our understandings of race, class, and gender are played out in our everyday lives. Ultimately, the decision to forgo a tie in favor of a turtleneck sweater or the choice *not* to change into a skirt before dinner was a profoundly personal one. College students made these choices in the context of their own surroundings—the classroom, the cafeteria, and the dorm.

·

### CHAPTER THREE

# In the Dorm

"Dormitory life," wrote the *Radcliffe News* in 1938, "is a noun that defies definition." Cigarette breaks, impromptu pranks, "bull" sessions, and midnight snacks were only part of communal living. To many dwellers, "their conversation, their shared experiences, and their mutual appreciation of each other's woes and merry moments" forged the most enduring memories of college. As one student put it, "A group of weary girls, clustered on the stairs at 12:00 or 1:00 after dates can produce the most congenial atmosphere of good fellowship known to man."[1] Since the turn of the century, the intricacies of dorm life intrigued the American public, and women provoked the lion's share of the curiosity.[2]

Aspects of collegiate culture truly baffled observers, such as a British exchange student who explained, "The desire for privacy is reared as bad form in American colleges; and the usual rule is that everybody's door must always be open for everybody to walk in or look in at random."[3] For those who lived it, such camaraderie was, as Marjorie Cherry wrote to her parents in 1928, one of "the happy habits of the dorm." She praised "the utter informality with which everyone traipses in and out other people's rooms at all hours. We don't go to bed until 1:30."[4] Diaries and letters home vividly detail the escapades and exhaustions of living with one's peers. Princetonian Chalmers Alexander and pal Ernie Rendeke dismantled a roommate's bicycle and put it between his bed sheets.[5] Nancy Murray wrote home to complain of her room's location; the constant flushing of the bathroom toilets kept her up all night. She successfully petitioned to move to another floor.[6]

Students controlled many of the day-to-day aspects of dorm life, but administrators decided when to construct new buildings and how to renovate old ones—a power that defined the very tenor of student life. Proximity to campus was the premier factor for students in deciding where to live. In that regard, universities had the market cornered, yet from the 1900s to the 1960s, nearly every university struggled to provide adequate space.[7] Penn State administrators admitted that the university's "long history of student housing has basically always been one of shortage."[8] The university required that women live on campus, which severely limited enrollment. By contrast, Cal had no such rule, and its female enrollment skyrocketed as sorority and boardinghouses and co-ops cropped up to accommodate demand. In 1915, the graduating class at Penn State contained only 15 women, but the total enrollment of women at Cal reached nearly 2,000.[9] Morehouse and Spelman lacked rooms and facilities; students lived in run-down, crowded rooms with little storage and few amenities. Before a large-scale remodeling project in 1935, Morehouse students complained of having to tiptoe "gingerly down the halls in our bare feet because we had not house slippers, fearing every moment we would snag our feet on one of the large splinters that stuck so untimely out of the worn boards of the flooring."[10] At Spelman, Morehouse, and Cal, commuters comprised between 20 and 40 percent of the student population. As sociologist Edwards Hartshorne wrote in 1943, "Students who live at home or in boarding houses clearly inhabit a different social world from that of the 'dorm' student."[11] These students fall beyond the scope of this study.

In an effort to create a more cohesive student culture, administrators at Radcliffe and Princeton constructed dormitories. Its image as a school for commuters plagued Radcliffe. In 1909, the *Boston Herald* commented, "It is often said that there is no college life at Radcliffe" because "a large percentage of students live in their own home."[12] By 1950, 70 percent of women lived on campus, and Radcliffe had successfully transformed itself into a full-fledged residential college.[13] Turn-of-the-century Princeton students lived in boardinghouses or hotels, and administrators such as Woodrow Wilson hoped that more on-campus housing would curb the school's bacchanalian atmosphere. Freshman Robb Carson reported to his parents in September 1904 that he and his brother had been evicted from the Nassau Hotel, a "result of certain carryings on, culminating in a midnight booze party, which so incensed Mr. Cook, the proprietor of the hotel, that he posted notices on the doors" and gave offenders "three hours to clear out."[14] Dormitories did little to discourage drinking, and Princeton remained the Ivy League's place to party.

In the dorm, students pioneered new standards of casual dress and learned the "official" and "unofficial" rules of what to wear. In shared lounges and private rooms, students mended, made, and maintained their wardrobes. Turn-of-the-century students welcomed packages of clean laundry and recent purchases made by well-meaning mothers. By the 1930s, however, students relied more heavily on their peers for wardrobe advice, and many washed their own clothes in dormitory laundry rooms. Durability became paramount. "Remember," a Stanford publication told new arrivals in 1951, "it is the usefulness of the clothes that you bring that counts, not the quantity."[15] Man-made fibers and chemical treatments for natural fibers made it easier for students to clean and care for their clothes. Ironing boards became relics of a more formal past. Casual style was wash and wear.

## "To Be Out of Step with the Group Is Nothing Short of a Real Tragedy": Living and Learning in the Dorm

Dorm life was fun. Radcliffe's Eleanor Stabler (Class of 1914) wrote to a friend who was interested in attending the college: "I am living in a dormitory. I like it ever so much! There are about twenty-six girls in this hall, many of them very attractive and refined." She explained that all bedrooms were single, but some were joined by a study that was shared by several women. Her room was "a very cozy little room fitted up with every luxury." Such closeness inspired camaraderie. She noted, "Every night after dinner we dance and sing in the big dining room."[16] In the dorm, Radcliffe women entertained themselves and visitors. Radcliffe's "Jolly Ups" were informal parties held in their social rooms several times a year. One student explained the tradition: "The name Jolly Up, doesn't denote any specific sort of entertainment, but that is the point—they can be anything. They are packs of fun, always something different and with men—as many as you want, just invite them."[17] The upperclassmen at Harvard warned freshmen to avoid Jolly Ups and other "Radcliffe social functions as he would the bubonic plague, unless he cares for French ices, scones, and elderly maiden chaperones."[18] Despite their feigned disinterest, Harvard men attended en masse.

Food was at the center of dorm life. In figure 3.1, Eleanor Stabler captured her dorm friends eating a midnight snack in their nightgowns. In a letter to a friend from home, she wrote: "We have very good things to eat— ice cream three times a week and orange marmalade for breakfast. Every evening at 9:30 we have crackers and milk in the 'milk room.' Besides there are jolly chafing-dish parties and afternoon teas."[19] Chafing dish parties were an easy fix for hungry students. At Penn State, one woman wrote to her parents in 1915: "If you can spare the electric stove please send it. One of the freshmen Em Kurtz just got a chafing dish and we can have regular

Figure 3.1. A midnight feed in a Radcliffe dorm room (ca. 1912) included Welsh rarebit, fudge, cookies, and glasses of milk. A period source recommended that freshmen have "at least two lounging robes, one of heavy stuff, another of lighter materials for the evening study hour." The robes should be "dressy enough to wear to the cracker and candy munching and the chocolate drinking in another's room but . . . easy enough for study and work." To accessorize, it advised, "provide some hair ribbons to go with these, for in the privacy of the study hall pigtails are allowed." Courtesy of the Schlesinger Library, Radcliffe Institute, Harvard University.

feeds if we work them both. There is a special room where we do that."[20] Administrators and parents feared fires caused by chafing dishes and stoves, and the dorms conducted fire drills to ensure residents' safety. The drills sent into the streets "girls with curl-papers, girls with cold-creamed faces, girls with pigtails, girls in pajamas with coats on, girls in night-gowns, girls just in from parties with evening gowns on." The more levelheaded students warned classmates "not to primp before coming downstairs. In the first place, it is a very rare thing for one of the firemen to be the slightest bit attractive and, in the second, it is a waste of time."[21] The chaos caused by fire drills prompted an observer at Cal, who "fully appreciated coeds" and "the scenery they provide," to wonder, "cannot fire drills be more thoughtfully scheduled, that we neighbors might not be needlessly disturbed or the girls embarrassed?"[22]

In the dorm, students shared information about drinking, dating, and sex, which were points of ongoing discussions for both men and women.

In her diary, Radcliffe student Bailey Patterson (Class of 1932) recorded details of a date, on which she "looked pretty swell" in her "new suit with the satin blouse and the black velvet hat." She wrote, "When I got home the whole second floor, with no exaggeration, came into my room to get all the dope."[23] Patterson's diary told of backseat conversations with "fast workers" who wanted to know "why women seem so mysterious to men." Wellesley student Dorothy Kneeland (Class of 1929) recalled a prank she pulled on her friend and dorm president, Mary. Upon "coming home one night from a date, [Mary] opened her compact and revealed a condom. I seized it and tacked it on the 'Lost and Found' bulletin board in the dormitory front hall." Years later, Kneeland wrote in her autobiography that the joke "still strikes me as sheer madness in view of the official temper of the times."[24] According to an academic study of college girls' "bull sessions" conducted in the early 1930s, sex and men were addressed in more than half of all the dorm room discussions documented.[25] Men discussed sex and women but were warned by official school publications that while "Cat and Hen sessions on personalities and the opposite sex are frequent," such gossiping "is rather frowned on in the best circles." Stanford men were told: "Everyone has to talk but it is better to make it among your intimate friends than everyone in the house."[26]

Students learned to be self-reliant in the dormitory. As the men of the University of Michigan told newcomers, "You will have more liberty than has probably been granted you ever before, but you will need to show your judgment in accepting this."[27] The degree of autonomy afforded to dorm dwellers varied according to the institution. Women had far more regulations than men. The reasoning was simple. As one dean of women put it: "Since women are not equal to men physically, their health must be protected; social regulations provide a means of doing this."[28] At Spelman, an undergraduate from the late 1930s complained that dorm rules were more rigid than those at home—a situation she considered to be "an insult to the student's sense of responsibility." She recalled, "In the dormitory I was to find that my freedom would be limited, and perhaps my greatest adjustment would have to be made here. There are rules and regulations that must be adhered to, regardless of individual differences or habits." The women's "every move must be accounted for; time is budgeted by the sounding of bells throughout the day."[29] The degree of regimentation loosened over the years, but Spelman dorm women had much less freedom than their peers at Radcliffe.

Cliffies prided themselves on the high degree of autonomy that self-governance ensured. In 1917, the women actively negotiated "a new set of

Chaperon Rules" that were "more liberal . . . than the old ones" and "very far ahead of similar regulations in other colleges." The success of this negotiation caused the student government to "become a big factor at the dormitories." Despite fewer regulations, students insisted that they "must never allow the dormitories to degenerate into mere boarding houses for women." They were determined not to let "the friendly atmosphere and the feeling of home . . . [be] diminished by the new system."[30] The new rules allowed women to attend functions in Cambridge with a man as long as they were home by ten, prohibited automobile rides after dark unless they were on their way home, and banned talking from windows to friends on the street. Those who broke the rules were called before the Board of Hall Presidents and were forced to enter their name in a "Black Book." Many students took the responsibility of enforcing dorm rules with the utmost seriousness. In 1921, Edith Culver reported to her parents that she and some friends had gone out for a late-night drive and "didn't get in until 1." Her neighbor, Jane, she added, "feels obliged to report it being class president," and as a result "we may lose privileges for 2 weeks!!"[31]

Self-governance encouraged getting along, and harmonious living was important to all dorm dwellers. Because, as one administrator noted, "dormitory living is a special situation requiring a restriction of individual freedoms," students were told to remember that one's roommate "shares a room with you, rather than being merely a guest in your own home. His rights to the common properties of the room should be respected."[32] Of course, policy and practice were two different things. Dartmouth's humor magazine, *Jack-O-Lantern*, issued "The Ten Commandments: Dormitory Edition." The dictates included: "I shalt not permit my roommate to study when I am in the room"; "I shalt borrow anything I may require"; "I shalt forget to return all borrowed articles"; "I shalt sing, whistle, or play the phonograph whenever I please, be it midnight or daybreak"; and "I shalt when there is nothing else to do, pound upon the walls or stamp upon the floor."[33]

In the dormitory, students learned the nuances of the campus's sartorial standards by two means: experience and observation. The demands of dormitory life required durable and comfortable clothes. This need was recognized early in the century, when a journalist advised mothers, "Clothes for the student must be conservative, sturdy and suitable." Garments for studying assumed primary importance in the dorm student's wardrobe. The article recommended two lounging robes, one of light material and another for warmth. The robes should be "dressy enough to wear to the cracker and candy munching and the chocolate drinking in

Figure 3.2. College women began to wear pajamas instead of nightowns in the late 1910s because two-piece sets were more comfortable for lounging, as demonstrated in this 1954 picture from Penn State. Student publications recommended at least two pairs—a light, cotton pair for spring and fall and a flannel set for the winter. As Americans came to accept synthetic fibers, rayon and eventually nylon pajamas provided collegians with easy-to-wash and quick-to-dry alternatives to cotton and wool. Courtesy of the Penn State University Archives, Pennsylvania State University Libraries.

another's room but . . . easy enough for study and work." These clothes fit both practical and emotional needs. After all, said the article, "the warm lounging robe, the warm slippers, and the slumber robe are usually the only things that a girl at college requires to cure a fit of the blues or the spell of homesickness."[34] The garments in figure 3.1 document the various kinds of nightclothes worn by college women in the 1910s, and figure 3.2 shows dorm clothes four decades later.

Both men and women quickly learned that bathrobes, slippers, and pajamas were necessities of dorm life. A plaid tartan flannel robe paired with soft, cushion-soled slippers made "comfortable companions in the wee hours that come quickly when you're cramming."[35] Penn State's home economics majors told new dorm students, "Slippers should have soft soles and heels. These are important in all dormitories for consideration of our neighbors who may be studying."[36] A pair of these slippers can be seen in figure 3.2. Dorm-dwelling women at Cal favored "quilted cotton bathrobes in nursery prints," which were perfect for finding "one's way to the shower" because "they defy arctic atmosphere."[37] The quilted cotton robe was not simply a matter of aesthetics; it was one of necessity. In an article titled, "War Has Caused Refashioning of Nearly All College Clothes," the *Radcliffe News* reported that government restrictions on fabric meant that lounging garments had to be made with less material and with fewer frills. The *News* wrote, "Pajama and robe combinations and other two-for-one price items are out—wool cannot be used to make sleeping or lounging clothes. College dorms will be seeing more and more quilted cottons, velveteens and cotton flannels."[38] The restrictions on weightier fabrics were unfortunate, given other wartime conditions in the dorm. Penn State students quickly learned a "warm bathrobe is an essential, especially since fuel is rationed."[39]

Experienced students knew that pajamas fit the bill for lounging in their own or other's rooms. Women began the century dressed in nightgowns, but pajamas became their preference in the early 1920s. In 1917, Cal student Agnes Edwards wrote to her mother that she "wanted pajamas for a change."[40] By 1931, the Jordan Marsh department store in Boston had an entire section devoted to pajamas. Its advertisement in Radcliffe's newspaper read, "For Around the Dorm! Pajamas are such fun." Jordan Marsh promised "everything from trim cottons at $2 to the most entrancing evening pajamas at $59.50, with beach, bridge, and dinner pajamas in between. Of course there are sleeping pajamas, as well!"[41] According to the *Daily Californian* in 1940, Cal students needed six pairs to get through their college years and could plan to spend around $12 for the lot.[42]

Pajamas were needed for campus traditions as well. Men at Cal sponsored their yearly "Pajamarino" rally to celebrate the accomplishments of the football team and showcase their own sleeping apparel. Cal women were not allowed to appear in public in their pajamas, but they could attend the rally. The men at Princeton had such a predilection for silk pajamas that a tongue-in-cheek letter to the editor of the newspaper in 1941 proposed that the students "make an iron clad rule that all men leave their jersey silk night apparel behind." In its stead, the school would provide, "a fresh pair of pajamas to each man, and behold! A near perfect state of social equality would result." Of course, even sleepwear was subject to the university's stringent sartorial hierarchy. As a freshman, Chalmers Alexander was reluctant to don luxury nightwear. He told his mother that he "wouldn't want a silk robe for Christmas–'too highbrow' for a Freshie."[43] Lowerclassmen were constantly eyeing the apparel of upperclassmen and usually avoided clothing that attracted too much attention.

Students learned by experience that comfortable clothing was the right fit for studying, lounging, and late-night snacking. In the dorm, they also learned by observation. Freshmen and sophomores took fashion cues from juniors and seniors. Appearing in showy, overly dressy or "rah rah" clothing was social suicide, and students often learned of their mistakes too late. As Cal's fashion editors told newcomers, they must avoid being that "innocent and bewildered" freshman who will "unpack with dawning misgivings from their trunk strange house dresses and make-overs, little party frocks of the sort that mother thought made them look sweet and girlish." Too often, students were misled by mothers and "misguided by enthusiasm into the way of elaboration." Rather, simplicity should be their guide: their wardrobe should include low-heeled sports shoes, plain woolen skirts, and comfortable sweaters (the kind seen in figure 2.5).[44] In the mid-1930s, the *Radcliffe News* began sending to incoming freshman an informational newsletter that outlined everything from what to pack to where to study. After a long description of wardrobe requirements, the editors advised, "If you are still in doubt wait until you come to Boston as the stores here have everything you need."[45] California students suggested the same, noting, "A glance toward Wheeler steps at about 10 A.M. some day would give an idea of what the well dressed lady Bear wears on campus."[46] Stanford men were told, "The first rule to remember is—Don't buy expensive new clothing until you get here unless you are sure of campus styles at Stanford. Many new students stock up on clothes in their home-town [and] arrive at Stanford to find they didn't buy at all what they needed."[47]

Dorm dwellers' need to fit in with their colleagues often ran in opposition to their mothers' opinions and their family's finances. Vassar student Hazel Hunkins (Class of 1913) wrote letters home to her mother in Billings, Montana, detailing her additions to her wardrobe. Her mother sent money, gifts of cloth, garments, and accessories. One letter confirmed the arrival of a package and noted, "Mother dear, you don't know how I'll prize that wonderful lace." The student also received a package from "Mrs. B" that contained an egret feather—a plume she used to adorn her hat. She told her mother, "Oh, it's so nice to have a decent hat."[48] Hunkins, who feared that her geographic origins made her clothing unfashionable, took great pains to dress like the other women in her dorm. She paid careful attention to what her dorm mates bought, and she made a point to use the same local seamstress to make her clothing. She reported home, "Florence is having 3 new dresses made, a beautiful brown shamuses [*sic*] and a lavender crepe de chine and a pink accordion plaited." Hazel told her mother, "My class day dress will be accordion plaited and my graduation [dress] white creped de chine. I've engaged Miss Atkins to make it and that means a good deal of expense."[49]

Hunkins's desire to fit in with her roommates required a wardrobe that became a financial burden to her family. Her father had died, and her mother lived on a limited income. At one point in Hazel's education, she had to secure a loan from Vassar to pay tuition. Still, Hazel routinely commissioned clothing from local seamstresses. She understood the need to cut back and did not "know where the money goes but it goes."[50] On occasion, Hazel's brother, Carl, was given the responsibility of telling his sister what she could and could not buy. Hazel's need to conform came to the fore when her mother was planning her trip to Poughkeepsie for graduation. Hazel sent several letters outlining appropriate attire. "Bring all your decent clothes," she instructed. "Even bring that upholstered green evening thing—you might need it." When Hazel got word that her mother had already purchased a suit in Billings, she wrote, "I am sorry you got a suit in Billings because I know what it will look like here both to yourself and me." Hazel insisted that her mother not "buy anything in Denver. You'll be able to do much better in N.Y."—advice she emphasized by underlining the text. The daughter simply wanted her mother to hold her "head high among all mothers here."[51] She knew her dorm mates would be watching.

Similarly, Chalmers Alexander tried to dress to the standard of his dorm mates. He wrote to his mother, "You said in the last letter that it hurt you that I did not have some fine clothes," but he assured her, "Dad can tell you from his seeing me here, I am dressed as nicely as the average run of boys." To further settle her mind, he reminded her that "next week the annual senior 'beer suits' are coming out . . . and that puts everyone in a uniform, so to speak; so I wouldn't be wearing a fine suit even if I had one."[52] Alexander also doled out fashion advice to his family, noting in one letter that he hoped his "sister got some coats like the one you bought out from Donings. That's the type that I think always looks best—dark color with heavy fur collar and cuffs."[53]

Early in Alexander's college career, his mother was primary in supplying garments and offering wardrobe advice. His first year at Princeton, he told her to send "about 10 pair of wool sox [sic] (or however many is needed by a fellow)." Not wanting to call attention to himself, he instructed her: "Do not get fancy streaked ones of loud design. They wear plenty of color here but no wild stuff." Alexander could save money on clothing sent from home. As he told his mother, "The sox here cost about $2.00 to $2.50." In Jackson, Mississippi, the socks were a dollar less.[54] By the time he was a senior, he had to call off his diligent mother. An efficient laundress reduced the need for so many items, he explained: "I get my shirts back from the janitor's wife almost the day after I send them to her. It makes no difference." Letters leading up to the request illustrated that his mother had sent several shipments of items that were not the style that he had wanted. Always in need of money, he requested, "If you have $3.00 around you might send it, for I owe that much to the woman, not having paid her anything since the week before I came home for Christmas."[55]

By the 1930s, the breach between what students wanted and what mothers wanted grew too wide to bridge. Students relied more and more on their peers for advice on what to buy. The development of the college clothing industry and the advent of college shops furthered the collegian's independence as a consumer. Student newspapers devoted entire sections to the latest trends. Cal's *Daily Californian* featured in-depth, monthly coverage of campus styles beginning in the mid-1920s and published a biannual fashion supplement for spring and fall fashions—for men and women. In 1927, the coverage of men's fashion ruffled the masculine feathers of student newspaper columnist "The Californiac." He believed the supplement was an "insidious plot" and "pitied the poor masculine gender," who "since time immoral held it below his dignity to bow to fashion's fiendish dictates." Unlike the women who could read their supplements on Wheeler Steps, he continued, Cal men "slunk away in the dank depths of Strawberry Canyon with a candle, feverishly scanning the fashion section," hoping "his associates may not discover his degeneracy."[56] Campus humor magazines offered an intimate yet exaggerated portrait of clothing on the college campus. Cal's *Pelican* and Penn State's *Froth* both ran columns on dress for men and women, and they sponsored yearly fashion shows throughout the 1930s and 1940s. Early coverage by coeds in city newspapers sometimes lacked specificity to campus fashion and referred to general styles and European collections. Names such as Schiaparelli, Lelong, and eventually Dior made regular appearances. The articles ran alongside pieces on styles from their own campus, because fitting in with one's peers was the priority. In the *Berkeley Daily Gazette*, for example, students were told to hold off on buying until they were settled into their dorms, because "to be out of step with the group is nothing short of a real tragedy."[57]

## "I'm So Sick of Tattletale Gray": Laundry and Technological Change in the Dorm

As students assumed the responsibility for clothing selection, they also assumed the responsibility for its upkeep. Laundry was an enduring annoyance of dorm life and a necessary evil. An editorial in a 1920 issue of the *Harvard Crimson* acknowledged the problem: "We in Cambridge have come to realize all too fully that, with our clothes, as with many other luxuries, the initial cost is insignificant compared to the upkeep. . . . [We wish] we were in a position to recommend the adoption of an 'Old Clothes' policy at Harvard, we would not hesitate. But unfortunately we are not."[58] Laundry had to be dealt with. Yet as "comfortable" and "practical" came to define collegians' dress, the management of their wardrobes became less of a burden. Students shunned high-maintenance fabrics and opted for easy-to-care-for items that required minimal upkeep. Coin-operated machines in dorm laundry rooms washed Orlon sweaters, rayon underpants, and elasticized socks. The rise of synthetic fibers directly coincided with the rise of casual style.

Well into the 1930s, an estimated one-third of in-residence students sent their laundry home through the mail for their mothers or sisters to clean. Cardboard or cloth laundry cases, designed to be packed and shipped with ease, were a keystone of student luggage. While the U.S. mail was the main operator, specialty companies got in on the action. Railway Express trafficked dirty clothes around New England. The company told the *Radcliffe News*, "Laundry is now second only in importance to the baggage business." Laundry shipments were a "constant throughout the year," while the delivery of baggage is "particularly heavy at Christmas and Spring vacations." The company concluded, "Students seem to like the pick-up and delivery service at both ends of the journey, [but] the popularity of the idea may also be partially based on the chance to send the bundle collect and receive it paid."[59] The delivery of the items was necessarily prompt. Dartmouth student Fredrick Baker noted in his diary in February 1937, "My laundry finally came, due last Sat. Sent it right back. 1st time in college that anything went wrong in the schedule."[60]

Over the course of her four years at Radcliffe, student Nancy Murray (Class of 1946; see figure. 1.1) used a variety of methods to ensure that she had a wardrobe of clean clothing. She sent a significant portion of her clothes home, carefully timing shipments of the packages. During her sophomore year, she made efforts to economize and decided to "send laundry every two weeks and save about $2."[61] Murray also tried using an on-campus service but grew frustrated with the quality. She complained to her mother, "I am so sick of tattletale gray!"[62] Murray also used an off-campus laundry service, which resulted in the loss of clothing. She was thrilled, however, when the situation was resolved in her favor. She told her mother, "By the way, I finally got $1.50 from the New England laundry for

Figure 3.3. Well into the 1930s, an estimated one-third of students sent their laundry home to be washed and returned. The figure was even higher in the first decades of the century. Speciality luggage makers such as KwikPak (the manufacturers of the case seen above) and parcel shipping companies such as Railway Express cashed in on collegians' need for clean clothing. The owner of this case attended Lehigh University and sent her laundry home to Pittsburgh. Other students used dorm facilities or local laundries, which picked up and dropped off the items for an additional cost. Courtesy of the Heinz History Center.

the articles lost which is a moral if not material victory. Everyone has been congratulating me on that."[63] Lost items were common. Penn Staters told freshmen, "Don't be one of those unfortunate persons who loses clothes because of lack of proper identification. Mark all your clothes with India ink or name tags."[64]

Most of the decisions to send dirty clothes home, to a campus service, to a local laundry, or to do it oneself depended on finances and on the availability of facilities in the dorm. Without any facilities in their living quarters, Princeton men used one of the many campus-based services or those of a local establishment. Both types of laundries relied heavily on student labor to sell their colleagues "tickets" for a certain number of washes or to work as delivery boys. These students, as Chalmers Alexander noted, were "working their way through."[65] At Princeton, there was a range of services for clothing maintenance that were offered by the university and staffed by working students. A shoe-shine service, tailor shop, clothing store, and barbershop were hubs of campus activity. One popular facility was the University Store, a cooperative society that was founded in 1900 and based on campus. The University Store had a laundry service that allowed students to charge fees to their store account. Rather than pay as they went, students accrued a bill and paid it at the end of the semester. Many off-campus facilities rented office space from the university and paid students to collect, tag, and transport dirty clothes to their locations in town.

The cost of off-campus versus on-campus services was sometimes negligible. Chalmers Alexander was very much interested in stretching his clothing-maintenance allowance and carefully considered his options. Upon arrival at Princeton, Alexander set up an account at the University Store, which allowed him to charge all the laundry for his first term for $25. He also bought a ticket for twenty suit pressings.[66] When his parents hit hard financial times in the early 1930s, Alexander racked up a laundry bill that became the source of much anxiety. At one point he owed an off-campus service that was giving him a better deal than the University Store more than $50.[67] Administrators at Radcliffe in 1934 estimated that laundry bills for an entire year averaged around $30 a year, "if a Cambridge laundry is used." Students looking to reduce this sum were advised to "send their laundry home, or to make use of the facilities for washing and ironing which are provided in the dormitories."[68] Students were told to budget another $10 a year for dry cleaning.

The arrival of new technologies on campus put an end to many businesses that were reliant on the shuttling of collegians' clothing.[69] A 1947 poll of universities conducted by *College and University Business* magazine, showed that 25 percent of respondents operated a campus laundry, which turned a profit at every campus. Sometimes schools denied students denied access to new technologies to protect this service or to maintain friendly relations with local laundries. At Harvard in 1949, students of the Adams and Dunster Houses petitioned the school to put coin-operated machines in the basement. The *Harvard Crimson* explained the various ways men dealt with "the weekly heap of dirty clothes": "Some carefully pack their laundry in neat cardboard cases, lug them down to the Post Office, and then spend weeks in squalor and grime waiting for the return mail. Others pile their clothes in the washbasin and alternately scrub and sneeze until a dazzling brightness is attained. But most undergraduates shoulder or dispatch their wash to Cambridge laundries which charge up to $18 to fray cuffs off of shirtsleeves." Despite the students' offers to pay for the machines, "Vice-President Reynolds poured cold water on the idea." The residents persevered and submitted the proposal repeatedly. They were concerned that without administrators' approval, "one of the best proposals of late for cutting student expenses will wind up a washout."[70]

Nothing became of the proposal, though graduate students were given their own self-serve laundry facility several years later. Undergraduates continued to send laundry home, to use local establishments, or to patronize the student-run Capital Laundry.

For women at Spelman, doing laundry was part of their weekly routine. Until 1929, the women did their own laundry in on-site facilities. Administrators mandated the task to teach life skills and to inculcate cleanliness. "The aim of the laundry," wrote administrators in 1908, "is to teach each girl how to do well the laundry work of an ordinary household." The curriculum offered "a laboratory course in laundry chemistry for those sufficiently advanced in their studies to profit by it."[71] Each dormitory was allotted access to the facilities one day a week. On their appointed day, the women got up at 4:00 A.M. and walked single file to the laundry to clean their clothes. After washing garments, the students hung them in the drying room and went to have breakfast and morning classes. After lunch, they returned to iron the garments using fire-heated irons, even when electric irons were readily available. At any point in the process, students could be made to redo their laundry if overseers considered their work shoddy. Mandatory service in the laundry room ceased in 1928, when Spelman hired on-site laundresses. Students praised the change and marked it with the publication of a humorous editorial in the *Campus Mirror*, titled "The Laundry's Soliloquy." With its demise, the "laundry" comforts itself: "If I am thought of very much nowadays, at least I am not thought of with dread." "The only time I see the girls now," it laments, "is when they hurry in with their bag of laundry and when they hurry out with a neat pile of ironed clothes."[72] The change in the use of mandatory student labor marked the final phase of vocational training at Spelman. Dressmaking and other home economics programs persisted, but the school focused on transforming itself into an institution of higher learning.

As students assumed control over the maintenance of their clothing, developments in the chemical, fiber, and textile industries provided fabrics with increased durability and fewer wrinkles.[73] Collegians became a viable market for man-made fibers because of the rigors of their daily life. Cal's fashion editors said women would "find it hard to pass up" many man-made fibers because they are "washable and non-crushable."[74] One Penn State fashion writer reported, "The college shopper eyed practicality as well as style when she selected her fall ensemble," and she recommended "Orlon—because it's easy to care for, soft as cashmere, and for the first time, at popular prices . . . was one of the most called for fabrics."[75] Sweaters made of man-made fibers or blends could be washed by machine without losing their shape. The fashion industry's *Tobé Report* noted of college shop openings in August 1948 that "nylon sweaters are selling everywhere."[76] Students wore nylon in many forms, not just as hosiery or undergarments. Spelman student Erin Goseer (Class of 1955) selected a pink nylon blouse for her class portrait (see figure 2.6). The blouse was a gift from a family friend, and, because it washed easily and was light enough to wear in the Atlanta heat, it became one of her favorite garments.

Academics and industry executives alike acknowledged the symbiotic relationship between the campus and the chemistry lab. Home economics programs at schools such as Penn State and Cal were central to consumer-end research on man-made fabrics and synthetics. In a speech to teachers of home economics, head of the Department of Clothing and Textiles at Penn State, Ruth Ayres noted how "the forties into the sixties was a period of unprecedented technological development including that of new fibers, finishes and textiles, affecting not only that industry but posing new problems and offering new opportunities to the garment industry, to the retailer, and to the consumer."[77] Women such as Ayres taught the next generation of researchers and homemakers about these new fibers and how to care for them. Penn State's Forth Annual Spring Weekend of the School of Home Economics (1953) hosted a panel, "The 'Miracle' Fibers Bring Their Own Problems." The panel featured home economics students, professors, executives from Du Pont, Celanese, and American Viscose, and retailers such as Kauffman's and Sears.[78] The home appliance and chemical industries provided home economics and textile programs with up-to-date facilities. Some even sent representatives into the classroom. In 1953 New York University's Division of General Education offered a course titled "The New Synthetics: Man-Made Fibers," taught by Ira Zane, a textile engineer for Davis Mills. A study by the Manufacturing Chemists' Association showed that thirty-four companies provided 1,036 scholarships and fellowships with an annual value of more than $1.6 million to undergraduates. Millions more went to institutions and graduate students.

### "The Bane of My Life": Making, Bartering, and Borrowing in the Dorm

The dormitory was central to the acquisition of clothing. Here, collegians made, bought, and borrowed clothing. In commandeering control of their wardrobes, students were able to get more of what they wanted. As one student editor told her colleagues: "Nothing is sadder than knowing what ought to be worn and not being able to buy it," so "why not make it?"[79] For turn-of-the-century women, sewing was central to assembling a college wardrobe because the women's ready-to-wear industry developed a few decades behind men's. By the first years of the century, college men had their pick of off-the-rack suits, shirts, and underwear.[80] College women cobbled together wardrobes from a range of sources. Home economics programs prepared students in the short term to make a campus wardrobe that was affordable and to their specifications. The women often wrote home of their latest class project. But coursework had long-term benefits as well. In the years before World War I, 63 percent of home economics majors were preparing for homemaking and 30 percent planned a career in teaching home economics. The passage of the Smith Hughes Act in 1917 fostered the growth and standardization of vocational education, and the number of programs and students in home economics grew exponentially.[81] Sewing was a popular activity for dorm dwellers. Some took to it happily. Others felt like the 1916 Penn Stater who wrote, "The bane of my life just now is sewing."[82]

Women often pooled resources to buy or rent sewing machines. In 1908, the women of Morgan Hall at Spelman raised money to buy a sewing machine for the dorm. In an effort to fill "spare hours that might otherwise have been spent in idle gossip," the women signed up for times in the evening to use the machine.[83] In 1912, Vassar student Hazel Hunkins asked her mother, "How much of that blue linen is left? Ginnie (a girl we like awfully well) has rented a sewing machine and everyone is getting on a sewing streak." Hunkins reported that "Florence has made a shirtwaist yesterday and I'm going to tackle a dress during spring vacation."[84] Sewing was an economical way for financially strapped students to stay in style. In another letter, Hunkins wrote, "This is to be a sewing letter. I have been in bed for a few days resting and I've looked over the fashion books and I have made up my spring wardrobe." Hunkins wrote of the new items displayed in local shops and of the anguish that her present financial state caused: "It is most distracting to have all these wonderful displays . . . and not have a penny with which to make yourself beautiful." She resolved to "do quite a bit of sewing for myself this vacation."[85]

Students mended garments, darned socks, and fixed buttons. They also had clothing tailored to accommodate their changing bodies.[86] Chalmers Alexander used the services of the dorm janitor's wife. He grew several inches in college, and his newfound love of exercise kept him slim.[87] For most students, however, tailoring meant letting out seams in order to accommodate weight gain. In her first two months at Cal, Agnes Edwards gained ten pounds, and she wrote to her mother, "Can you imagine how I will look after I've been here a few months more? Goodness, I hope I don't have to let my clothes out."[88] Her fears were soon realized, and she reported having to let out several of her skirts. Edwards's efforts to maintain a workable wardrobe were well documented in letters to her mother. Time was a recurring problem for Edwards. "I'm too busy to bother with clothes anyway," she wrote on one occasion. "Everyone is beginning to wear spring hats and the stores are all showing new voiles and ginghams. . . . [I] wish I had time to make some dresses."[89] Getting the right materials was also problematic. She recounted renovating her own things, as well as items given to her. During wartime, secondhand clothing was harder to come by. In 1917 Edwards wrote, "I can think of lots of things I could fix if I were home. I know I could fix a dress out of that gray silk of Milly's. Darn it, why don't people ever give me their cast offs any more? Gracie Allen gets them all the time and Mrs. Allen fixes them up so cute for her."[90]

Students with limited funds were careful to maintain their garments and rework old styles into new ones. Sewing skills varied from student to student. One told a friend that she could accomplish "menial" tasks in sewing such as attaching fasteners or binding necklines, but "the aesthetic parts, such as making little bows and rosettes, I am never allowed to do, for I have an unfortunate propensity of pulling them all out of shape with my strong athletic hand."[91] In the first decades of the century when college women still wore hats, dorm dwellers often worked collectively to trim hats, sharing feathers, bows, buckles, and pins. In 1917 a Penn Stater thanked her mother for a recent package, "The hat trimmings are just what I wanted. Little Otie Scott was here yesterday and concocted several 'creations' out of them. We were tickled to pieces."[92] Overdoing it was cautioned. Spelman women were told: "One of the most common errors is the attempt to dress up a plain garment with knickknacks and bits of finery. The result is always a failure."[93]

Renovating outdated duds was not limited to poorer students. Radcliffe's well-to-do and clothing-conscious Edith Culver worked seasonally with her mother's maid, who was sent to her Cambridge dorm to tailor clothing for the student. Despite Culver's affluent background, she commonly wrote home of how she and her dormitory pals got together to sew sequins, bows, or lace onto old evening gowns to give them a new look. On an afternoon in February 1920, she spent hours in her room sewing blue ribbons onto Dot's pink evening dress. One diary entry detailed her wardrobe maintenance: "I worked hard all A.M. pressing my dresses and sewing beads on my new taffeta. About 3:30 I went up the street, got a new pair of corsets at Skinner's and changed a pair of black silk stockings I got for Christmas for a white and got a pair of awfully good looking high brown boots at the Model shoe store."[94]

Dorm rooms also served as a marketplace where students bought and sold their clothing. Hazel Hunkins wrote to her mother in great detail of the "gorgeous" coral evening gown her wealthy dorm mate Carita wanted to sell her. "[I] would buy it in a minute," she wrote, "but I think the tight skirt is too old style to pay much for."[95] In 1919, Edith Culver reported to her parents, "After prayers, Billy had an auction of clothes in her room."[96] Radcliffe women took a unique approach to the disposal of items collected in their dorm's lost and found. They held a semiannual auction around Christmastime, where those seeking presents could buy "scores of scarcely used fountain pens and automatic pencils." Gloves were deemed the "the most elusive objects which a woman owns. Aside from the unmated ones, between 25 and 30 pairs were bid for." Other items in the 1925 auction were "wool sweaters, five felt hats, scarves of all descriptions, seven powder and rouge compacts, jade earrings and a half dozen rings." Most surprising was a wedding ring, which the *Radcliffe News* declared was "evidence of the fact that there is nothing which a college girl is not capable of losing." The auction pulled in $20; a sum given to the student government treasury.[97] Dorm dwellers created a policy that items had to be abandoned in the lost and found for three weeks to be considered for sale.[98]

Students also bought clothing from other undergraduates at other universities. In 1930, a relative of Chalmers Alexander named Thad, who attended the University of Virginia, wrote to him to ask for help selling a used raccoon coat. Thad told Chalmers that he was unable to sell the coat on his home campus, because "raccoon coats here at Virginia are about as popular as pole cats of uncured variety." Thad had bought the coat "in B.D. (before the drought)" for $525 but was willing to part with it for $150. He promised Alexander a 15 percent commission if he sold it for more. Alexander tried to sell it to several men in his dormitory but confided to his mother that any efforts were in vain because the craze for fur coats had long passed. "I might as well try to sell a white elephant," he wrote. When Alexander reported that he could not find a buyer, Thad suggested that Alexander mail the coat back, insure the package, put moth nests in the pockets, and collect the insurance money.[99] Figure 1.4 provides an example of the kind of raccoon coat Chalmers was trying to sell.

When the situation allowed, students gave away clothes and accessories to dorm mates. Agnes Edwards benefited greatly from a pair of shoes given to her by her roommate. She told her mother not to worry about her often-dire clothing situation: "I have a new pair of shoes too. Mary had a pair, tan with white tops that she hadn't worn so very much and her feet grew or something . . . [The shoes] fit perfect and are very nice for summer."[100] Some students passed on clothing to family members at home. Chalmers Alexander found a Dobbs derby of the "latest cut" that was left outside his dormitory "by some drunken dunce." He sent it to his younger brother Albert and instructed his mother that, if it didn't fit, "maybe Marion Tobias might like it or if it won't fit him, give it to Leland, if it won't fit him give it to Bilbo." Chalmers noted that if the owner came looking for the hat, his mother would have to send it back.[101]

One of the most popular and pervasive ways for dorm students to obtain clothing was to borrow it. A defining feature of dorm life was the open sharing of personal items, such as packages of food sent from home and school supplies. The *Radcliffe News* explained, "Communism has been tried at various times, but never has it reached such actual success as in a college dormitory." Clothing was particularly transient, as the article confirmed, "No new evening gown? Betty or Mary or Fran has one that would fit beautifully and she wouldn't in the least mind lending it."[102] From the 1900s through the 1960s, women's fur coats were a highly coveted item and were commonly borrowed from dorm mates. In 1918, Radcliffe's Edith Culver reported having spent an afternoon "in town for the sole purpose of shopping." After window shopping and buying a few Christmas cards, she and her friend ate "a college ice at Baileys" and then walked down "Tremont and Boylston streets commenting on every fur coat we saw." She concluded, "After dinner Tinkie borrowed my evening coat to wear to symphony with Ruth Blackman."[103] Despite having one of her own, Culver routinely borrowed furs from her neighbors.

The prevalence of borrowing and lending clothes in dormitories prompted concern among parents and etiquette writers alike. A 1936 advice book scoffed, "Campus humor magazines would go out of print if the students neglected to borrow, for all their pages proclaim that at college a co-ed is known by her roommate's wardrobe." The author told undergraduates, "Although you do want to be collegiate in this manner of lending," there were basic rules of the "borrowing game." These included: "Never borrow anything that you cannot afford to replace. Expect to lend unhesitatingly to any girl from whom you borrow. Return underwear, handkerchiefs and hose carefully laundered and dresses pressed. Return everything you borrow promptly with a word of appreciation for its use." The book recommended that one wear her own clothes, as "they were bought to express your individuality," but added that "there are times when even a lady must borrow. But no one objects if she borrows like a lady!"[104] Men borrowed, too. Stanford men were told: "One very great [thing] in ruining perfectly good friendships is the college habit of borrowing," which "depends entirely on the degree of friendship and of ability to loan."[105]

Despite good intentions, many borrowers and lenders were brokenhearted when items were lost or damaged. Agnes Edwards wrote to her mother in despair after a roommate lost her purple garnet ring. She explained, "I myself didn't lose it but it was what I might have expected for letting anyone else wear it. It made me sick."[106] Pomona College student Marjorie Cherry asked her mother, "Where is there a hole to hide in?" when she borrowed and lost Eleanor Herrington's "beautiful new black coat with gorgeous fur around the collar and cuffs." She wrote, "Please bear witness to a solemn swear. I shall never borrow anything again! I know you've always warned me about borrowing but I would do it."[107] On occasion, dorm mates borrowed without permission. When Hazel Hunkins's wealthy dorm mate, Carita, went to visit her brother John for the Yale-Harvard football game, her roommates had "a very wonderful time . . . at her expense." Hunkins told her mother, "Last night Florence wore C's daisy chain dress of embroidered crepe, Louise wore a lovely tan satin with golden brown marquisette over it and I wore a gorgeous coral cha[r]meuse satin beaded and real lace under the marquisette." The borrowing lasted all weekend, noted Hunkins: "Today Florence is wearing C's dark green crepe and I'm wearing an embroidered white one. Tonite [sic] a pink one." The women eased their guilty consciences by agreeing, "C's clothes are really much better looking on us than they are on her because she is unfortunately short and thick set."[108]

■ Life in the dorm required comfortable, practical clothing that could be worn to any spontaneous happening on campus. At Radcliffe, women favored easy-to-wear clothing because "informal get-togethers" could "take place in the individual dorms on slight provocation."[109] Or, as was the case at Dartmouth April 1924, a group of drunken frat boys could enlist the help of dorms dwellers to come to the quad and vote in a mock election for the next mayor of Hanover. The leaders, one student recounted, "were thoroly [sic] and delightfully plastered, stood upon barrels and gave the funniest speeches imaginable—and all of this at midnight so it was quite a typical college prank."[110] Cold hallways, late-night cramming sessions, and dorm room dance parties all demanded functional garments. Few frills were needed. Lounging called for loose-fitting clothes that allowed the student to put her feet up on the desk or crawl under her bed to fetch a runaway ping-pong ball.

In the dorm, students experienced firsthand the cultural tension that is produced when new technologies collide with established methods of how to do things. Students' insistence in assembling and maintaining their own wardrobes broke the hearts of mothers and local laundry owners alike. Coin-operated laundries in dorm basements coincided with the rise of synthetic fabrics. Radcliffe women told freshmen that "first and foremost" they should "pack [their] wardrobe trunk with essentials." When it came to lingerie, hosiery, and socks, they declared, "Nylon is a fabric just made for the busy college girl."[111] Collegians proved a receptive audience to man-made fibers, which were more affordable and easier to clean than natural fibers. Garments in synthetics or synthetic blends met with solid reviews from students who willingly embraced DuPont's slogan, "Better Things for Better Living . . . Through Chemistry."

At the most intimate level, the study of dorm clothing adds nuance to the personal meanings of dress: trying not to look too "high brow" for a "freshie," being comfortable enough to sit on the steps while waiting for the other women to come home from their dates, avoiding several hours behind an ironing board. These meanings were primary in students' daily decisions to embrace casual style.

### CHAPTER FOUR

# On a Date

Nearly every student had at least one—a date. Even Chalmers Alexander went to dinner with "that Russell girl," a soon-to-be Smith freshman, "plump in tendency but so far not plump, rather pretty with irregular teeth," who "dresses in the New York manner."[1] Student letters to parents, notes scribbled in diaries, and odes to the subject in campus newspapers all confirm that dating defined most students' social lives. "Dates are quite important on a campus," Spelman women agreed, and "may be anything from a few minutes spent in an evening to the most formal college proms."[2] For many collegians, the prom was the culmination of the collegiate year. For decades, the prom demanded a tuxedo or the more formal tailcoat, which was worn with a top hat, a waistcoat, and gloves.[3] Female prom-trotters had a wardrobe of evening gowns, a host of accessories such as gloves, opera capes, dancing slippers, and the all-important dance card, used to keep track of her parade of partners.

With the rise of alternative, less-supervised forms of dating, the popularity of formal dances slowly waned—and the most formal elements of the American wardrobe disappeared. Fraternities and sororities had their own events that began to eclipse the prom and required less elaborate attire. Informal dances, house parties, and movies gave collegians other options. Not all collegians had such liberties. Into the 1950s, Spelman administrators still monitored women's socializing through "calling hours," an hour on several afternoons a week when Morehouse "Willies" came to dorm reception areas or walked on campus with students. White, middle-class students at Penn State had far more freedom from supervision. A 1950 survey of students showed that 83 percent of women named movies as their first choice for a date, with sporting events coming in second, and formal dances a distant third.[4] Figure 4.1 shows the kinds of clothing Penn Staters

Figure 4.1. A fraternity party at Penn State's Alpha Epsilon Pi in 1954 shows the many incarnations of casual style. Students wore flannel shirts, T-shirts, sports socks, penny loafers, V-neck sweaters, pedal pushers, and jeans in an array of combinations, bringing comfort and versatility to the American wardrobe. Proms and formal dances waned in popularity because alternative forms of dating offered less supervision and more privacy. A survey at Penn State in 1950 named movies as a most popular choice for a date and sporting events as the second. Formal dances were a distant third. Courtesy of the Penn State University Archives, Pennsylvania State University Libraries.

wore on such dates. These "new systems of courtship," says historian Beth Bailey, "were inextricably tied to new understandings of youth and to the development of a youth culture."[5] Students no longer wanted to dress up in their parents' clothes to be watched by a hawk-eyed hostess. Booze and backseat make-out sessions were far more enticing. As a national collegiate culture solidified in the late 1920s, the old guard openly "deplored" the "sex stimuli" of "motion pictures, magazine illustrations, stage costumes, and the fashion for every day attire." Yet the more avant-garde students believed youth should "divorce ourselves from the old parental attitude which held that a non-marital sexual relationship is immoral."[6] Dating practices changed, and the prom became passé.

As a result of this transformation in courtship, the clothing worn to formal events lost its position of prominence in the collegian's wardrobe and its specificity. Students looked for versatile clothing that served a variety of occasions. Dark suits replaced tuxedos; cocktail dresses replaced evening gowns. The word "formal," which once held concrete connotations, became a catchall term. One Penn State coed explained that when it came to dress, the word "formal" meant "anything from a cocktail dress to a full-length gown."[7] Women bared their shoulders, backs, and legs. As a student fashion editor put it, her turn-of-the-century counterpart "would probably faint from shock to see the new evening gowns coeds will wear."[8] As the 1960s arrived, the opportunities to wear any kind of formal wear became increasingly rare. In 1962, the chairmen of the junior prom committee at Penn State admitted that the "probability of another Junior Prom is very unlikely." To break even, 500 tickets needed to be sold. Only 230 were purchased.[9]

### "The Highest Exemplification of Social Activity": Dancing and the Evolution of the Junior Prom

For decades, the junior prom was the pinnacle of an undergraduate's social calendar. Most schools had senior proms, but by the end of their final year, seniors were too focused on commencement activities to plan and promote a gala event. Formal parties for freshmen and sophomores were popular but rarely called "prom"—a term reserved for use by upperclassmen. According to Radcliffe's student newspaper, the junior prom was "a great event in a college career, which makes every Freshman and Sophomore sigh for the faraway day when she will be a Junior."[10] Penn State's humor magazine, *Froth*, scoffed at the idea that "the term is simply a shortening of the word Promenade." Editors hypothesized other possible origins for the term: Could it be the "prominent citizens among the patronesses"? Or was the term "from the numerous letters to tailors from the various male participants—epistles embodying a promissory note for the rental of . . . dress suits"? Most likely, they surmised, the term came from the fact that "the Prom invariable leads to serious thoughts and promotes promiscuous promises to love, honor, and obey."[11] Established social etiquette defined behavior and dress.

In the early twentieth century, Ivy League proms were elaborate and expensive. Men wore tailcoats, white gloves, canes, and silk hats. At Yale, the junior prom involved a week-long litany of activities and was considered "the social event of the year."[12] The events were so intense that some students, such as President Taft's son Robert Alphonso, "became one of the many post promenade infirmary patients."[13] Without women on campus, men had to invite them in—a process that required an official invitation, a chaperone, and paid accommodations for a weekend of events. The associated costs of an Ivy League prom made it exclusive—even to many of the students. In 1910, the cost of the Yale prom for a couple was rumored to be upwards of $500, a figure debunked by the *Yale News,* whose unofficial survey put the "general average" around $125. This included "flowers, carriages or automobiles, hotel bill, amusements, such as theaters, dinners, or concerts, and miscellaneous items."[14] Twenty years later at Princeton, the cost of tickets (and the lack of a date) kept the penny-pinching Chalmers Alexander from attending. He wrote to his mother, "All the lads are now getting ready for the Junior Prom. Tickets for couples are $8.00—a new winter hat."[15]

Prom-goers could cut costs by inviting a local date—if a man could get one. Princetonian John Peale Bishop (Class of 1917) noted that indeed there were a few local women, "but they are hedged about or wear flat-heeled shoes."[16] An invitation to an Ivy League prom was a hot ticket, and "society girls" from cities on the East Coast train line "consider it worth their while to run down . . . and be amused by these fresh-faced young fellows."[17] Part of the host's responsibility was to secure individual dances for his date. Edith Culver bragged to her mother that her MIT prom date, a friend named Dexter, got her "lots of nice men to dance with. . . . [There was] Vanderburg who dances like a streak [and] rushed me . . . and Johnny Walker also cut in on me twice."[18]

The women of the Seven Sisters were easy pickings for Ivy Leaguers. Harvard men had their opinions about the women at each school. Smith women believed in "Study, Sport, and Sex—all in their proper place," but their strict administrators aimed to ensure that their "fun is untarnished by limiting the girls' nights away from college (*always* chaperoned) to seven per term." This rule required planning if a man wanted a prom date.[19] The "trouble with Vassar," Harvard men felt, "is that it's so far away."[20] Wellesley proms were "more ornate than those at Radcliffe," but both schools "display, as is the case at most women's residential colleges, a strait-laced, blue stocking attitude that makes one look for a corner to hide in."[21] The rivalry between Wellesley and Radcliffe for Harvard men's attention endured, but most Harvardians believed, "Wellesley girls are prettier, but Radcliffe is more convenient."[22]

The women of the Seven Sisters had their opinions as well. Radcliffe women believed the ideal prom date was one "who knows how to dance, is taller than you and does not suggest that 'we sit this one out.'" For their part, women should strive to be "the kind of girl who does not plant her spike heel on your instep [or] drape her arm around your neck, and uses a subtle perfume that goes to your head but does not hit you in the eye."[23] In a 1928 article in the *Radcliffe News* titled "How to Ask a Man to the Prom," the editors acknowledged that Yale men were impulsive, and suggested a prom-goer should "shoot him an urgent special delivery two days beforehand. He might accept the invitation." For Dartmouth men, they advised, "give him a month's notice so that he can get his Tux out of hock and start saving up for flowers." For their nemeses at Harvard, a gal could just "ring him up Prom Night and suggest he come over for a few dances." Princeton men were eager and easy to entice: "A sweet little note to that friend of your brother's will do the trick."[24] Princeton men were acknowledged throughout the Seven Sisters as "rather smooth numbers," mainly because "a man from foreign territory is always a little more sensational than the fellow from next door." Wellesley women thought Princetonians were the "best dressed and the savoir-fairest," but Cliffies considered them "a trifle on the collegiate side."[25]

Getting a prom date did not guarantee a good time, however. Radcliffe's Eleanor Gilbert (Class of 1918) began her college career as a shy wallflower who was told by her well-meaning mother that she must attend dances as often as possible. Her mother wrote, "Don't be afraid [to] talk and enter into things." To be a social success, Eleanor must "be unconscious of yourself—dance and have a good time." Most of all, warned her mother, "if you stay away from things, the girls will either think you are a crank, or haven't any clothes."[26] Gilbert took the advice to heart and three years later, she wrote to her mother about her junior prom: "Well, the prom is over, and it was a great success." Unfortunately, her date "was also the same as ever. We counted up about a half a dozen social errors for him during the evening." Thankfully, another student's date "knew the leader of the orchestra, so he winked at him when he wanted the music repeated." She reported that she ate "two or three helpings of everything" on the menu, including chicken salad sandwiches, olives, ice cream, cake, coffee, and punch.[27]

The junior prom at the Seven Sisters was the culmination of a "carefully planned weekend, which swoops upon the males (not always Yalies) fortunate in an invitation."[28] In 1926, Wellesley's prom was a weekend affair. On Friday night, they had a 6:15 dinner, but the official prom lasted until 2:30. Saturday featured "various kinds of entertainment such as tennis, golf, canoeing, motor parties and picnics," not to mention "an afternoon tea dance," and "an evening with Tony Sarg's marionettes which acted out Treasure Island."[29] Boston papers printed the highlights of the event. Proms at the Seven Sisters and the Ivy League attracted national press coverage. This subjected Princeton to the kind of public scrutiny that administrators feared. In 1921, the editors of the *Daily Princetonian* warned their readers that the junior prom was an "affair that is more than local in importance and will draw both guests and attention from all parts of the country. It is one of the standards by which the University is judged." Editors told students that the "general impression" of Princeton was "not improved by even such small evils" as "smoking on the Gym floor and appearing on Nassau Street in the small hours of the morning with girls in evening dress." Students should remember: "The Prom is not a Prom Committee's dance, nor the Junior Class dance, but a dance at which every Princetonian should consider himself the host."[30] In the early 1920s, Princeton boasted nearly 1,600 attendees to their junior prom.

By the mid-1910s, the junior prom had gone mainstream, as colleges and universities instated the tradition to celebrate the time of year when "the mind of man naturally wanders from his labors to recreation." The more middle-class students of Penn State considered the event as "the highest exemplification of social activity in this college," and it attracted hundreds of couples.[31] At the Penn State prom, one could see "youth in all of its glory" and partake in the "carefree madness quite symbolic of the wine of youth."[32] As more and more middle-class Pennsylvanians came to college, the jump in Penn State's enrollment helped to fill class coffers. For men, more students also meant more women from which to choose. Men inviting out-of-towners irked Penn State women. One told her parents: "I wish you could see the 'stunners' that have infested this 'burg." But with her dress and fur wrap, she promised, "I 'be ain't' so far behind the rest."[33] By the end of the 1920s, Penn State's prom had become "a most lavish affair that has thrilled the heart of many a maiden—and these stories of marvelous times have spread far and wide."[34] On the dance floor, bodies were bared, as "shapely legs, made even more enticing by shimmering silken stockings, put to shame the artificial decorations that drape the ceiling. Passion runs high. So do the prices at the door. It is the night of the Junior Prom!"[35]

The student culture of each campus shaped the school's proms and formal dances. At Spelman, many dances did not require dates, and women extended a blanket invitation to the men of Morehouse. The men who came to Spelman events and calling hours on a regular basis were called "Spelman Willies." There were often more women than men, and the less social members of the group were left to their own devices. After one formal dance, the editors of the *Maroon Tiger*, the Morehouse newspaper, chastised their classmates about "the line of girls who didn't get an op-portunity to dance." These women "had spent as much time on make-up, and had sung all day as gaily as the popular girls, and after this thorough routine they could but sit and look on, because there were too many men and too few gentlemen invited."[36] Given the religious inclinations of Spel-man and Morehouse and the socioeconomic status of many of its students, elaborate events that required students to rent or buy expensive clothing were generally discouraged by the administration. However, the students themselves insisted upon a prom through the 1950s. To many, the prom celebrated the end of one's college career. Fifty years later, Erin Goseer (Class of 1955) remembered the red and pink floral-print silk she used to create a strapless dress for her long-awaited prom. More than the dress, she remembered the shoes: "My cousin Eryn and I wore the same size shoes so she loaned two pairs of her pretty high-heeled shoes that matched. . . . I felt a little sad when I had to return these beautiful shoes."[37] Indeed, the fact that Spelman women planned and partook in the most formal of cam-pus traditions demonstrated that they found comfort and confidence in a right of passage (and the associated forms of femininity) that many of their white classmates considered to be outdated.

The middle-class students at Cal preferred low-key settings for social-izing, and formal affairs were limited to one or two per year. Informal dances were the most popular events. To a large degree, this preference reflected a student culture built by undergraduates who lacked both the knowledge of proper etiquette and the appropriate attire. Some students were amazed at just how casual dances at Cal actually were. Agnes Ed-wards wrote of one event where she wore her "white net dress, as it was informal and even then felt rather dressed up." She noted her classmates' preference for casual clothing: "there were lots of sports costumes."[38] In-formal dances also fit the bill for students who were not part of main-stream social networks. The International House, home to foreigners and first-generation Chinese and Japanese students, hosted five dances a year, "including a fall informal, a Halloween dance, a Big Game Formal dance, a dance given by the Russian groups, a barn dance and weekly informal dances."[39] These activities allowed a diverse cross-section of Cal students to participate.

A recurring issue for students at Cal was that many students did not know how to dance—a problem that the university's athletic department and extracurricular groups tried to remedy by offering dance lessons. In 1914, men at Cal learned traditional Irish dance as part of their physi-cal education requirements. After class, administrators began to offer men instruction "in the tango, maxixe, fox trot, and one-step, which were just beginning to gain public favor." The response of the men was remarkable: "Instead of rushing to the dressing rooms as they had done in the past when dismissed, the men lingered in large numbers and Harmon Gymnasium was turned into a ballroom crowded with male dancers, swaying back and forth."[40] Similarly, in the 1940s, the university's Assembly Dance Committee raised money for its events by offering men and women dance lessons for a small fee.[41] Cal students stood in contrast to those of the elite schools, who picked up the latest dances on weekend trips to New York or Boston. One Radcliffe student reported home in 1928 that all of her classmates were great dancers who "can tango or do some fancy steps" and that "nearly everyone plays an awfully good game of tennis."[42] Each campus had its own prom traditions but the event's formality and significance was universal into the early 1930s. As Stanford's Burnham Beckwith wrote to his mother in 1923, the junior prom "is a big thing at any college."[43]

## "At the Top of the Social Scramble": Frat Parties, "Getting Tight," and Sex

Fraternities profoundly influenced campus culture. Early in the century, fraternities were key players in the popularization of the prom. Their members served on committees, decorated venues, and sold tickets. Fraternities organized private booths where brothers and their dates lounged during the event. By the 1950s, however, fraternities were a key reason for the prom's demise. As one Penn State student explained, fraternities used their own events, termed "semi-formal," to "get around the social necessity" of attending class proms.[44] The fraternity man's shift from prom propagator to deserter marked the changing role of his organization on campus. Fraternity members no longer retained sole custody of the social scene. As the "barbarians" (the term used for nonfraternity men) grew in number, collegians abandoned the prom en masse for more affordable, casual events. Drinking and sexual experimentation marked the collegiate experience and became increasingly favored for Friday night fun.

For the first half of the twentieth century, fraternity members reigned on campus.[45] The author of *Why Go to College?* noted that they were the ones who "choose athletic managers" and "exert the 'pull' which controls editorship upon the college papers." They also "determine largely the presidents of classes, and in some cases the elections to senior societies."[46] Fraternities provided members and their dates with a range of informal and formal events to attend. As one social critic noted, "The Greek-letter society is found at the heart of undergraduate social activities." At Morehouse, men considered fraternities "quite constructive organizations and . . . the nuclei of collegiate social entertainment."[47] Fraternity members were generally considered the best-dressed men on campus, mostly because many (though certainly not all) were more financially well off than their barbarian counterparts.[48] Sociologist Willard Waller's study, "The Rating and Dating Complex," claimed that for a man to be successful, he must be in "one of the better fraternities, be prominent in activities, have a copious supply of spending money, be well-dressed, 'smooth' in manners and appearance, have a 'good line,' dance well, and have access to an automobile." Fraternity men dominated collegiate dating, but their desirable dates, according to Waller, were not necessarily sorority women but those who were asked out by the most men. When it came to dating, "nothing succeeds like success."[49]

Parents, administrators, and students alike scrutinized the social lives of fraternities.[50] Excessive drinking topped the list of complaints. In 1923, a woman named Mrs. E. H. Raymond wrote to Cal's dean of men to ask his advice on selecting a fraternity for her son. The dean told the mother and the student that he should not "be puritanical or narrow" but should avoid a fraternity that "showed any tendency to bringing intoxicating liquor into their entertainment, or to indulge in loose, careless conversation."[51] Such warnings reassured parents but were often dismissed by students. In another letter to Cal's dean of students, a mother reported her daughter's recent experiences at a fraternity formal where "members were intoxicated and lying on the floor." Several brothers "made vulgar remarks to her and squirted soda water at her." The woman "would not divulge the name of the fraternity involved" because she felt "loyalty to it since her husband belonged to it at Yale."[52]

Socializing was central to life in a fraternity house. Dartmouth's Richard Eberhart (Class of 1925) wrote his father a letter about living with his Alpha Delta Phi brothers: "It is great living at the house; about all we do is sleep, eat and be merry." Eberhart mentioned boxing lessons that he received from a fellow fraternity member, his quest to perfect his marbles game, and afternoons spent shooting at targets in the back yard. "Reading, pool, and cards also occupy the stage . . . but [I] can't get down to real studying yet," he added.[53] Dartmouth's fraternities were under constant scrutiny from administrators, who were left to deal with complaints from parents, visitors, and police. During much of the administration of Ernest Martin Hopkins (1916–45), fraternities were not allowed to house more than a third of its membership, and dining facilities were prohibited altogether. Such control was necessary, Hopkins believed, because "the conditions of fraternity life at Dartmouth are so different from those in most colleges."[54] The college's rural location and all-male student body encouraged a brand of masculinity that prioritized drinking, sports, and pranks.

Membership in a sorority guaranteed a social life. One sorority member told her mother: "By belonging we get in on lots of dances and affairs and meet so many more people."[55] Clothing was of primary importance for a woman to be accepted into the sorority and to fit in once she became a member. In a humorous article titled "How to Get into A Sorority," Penn State's *Froth* magazine told women who were rushing: "Make sure your clothes look expensive. Wear heavy tweeds, or cashmeres [and] be careful that your skirts are the length that is being worn. More girls have been cut for unfashionable hemlines than for any other reason." Above all, "never wear the same thing to the same sorority twice."[56] At sororities, women learned about the latest styles. Pomona student Marjorie Cherry told her mother, "Had Phi Kappa meeting last night—sometimes I wish I hadn't joined that organization. There is so much artificiality and sorority-ishness in it now, especially with regard to bidding girls. So many of the old girls are in favor of cute peppy frosh with looks, personality and money." "Did enjoy the fashion show that followed," she added. "College girls modeled the beautiful clothes. Teppy wore the most heartbreakingly sweet green formal—made of all over lace."[57]

Formal dances were a defining aspect of sorority life, and these events, whether girls-only or mixed-sex, demanded appropriate clothing. As one advice book offered, "Except for rushing, girls wear their old evening dresses at stag parties when only girls are there; a new formal is always saved for men."[58] At coed institutions, students secured dates for friends or dorm mates. Cal student Agnes Edwards needed any help she could get. She described to her mother the receiving line at a formal dance held by her sorority: "I pretty nearly had a nervous prostration when the first one came down the line. As I told you, one of the girls had gotten a man for me, he didn't prove to be very good-looking but he certainly can dance, and of course that's most important at a dance."[59] Edwards shied away from social situations that required dates. In 1919, she told her mother, "What I don't like about college dances, you have to have a specific man and stick with him all evening and when you don't know him it isn't any fun at all."[60]

For students such as Edwards who struggled to pay tuition bills, the demands of the sorority's social calendar were a constant concern. In 1918,

Edwards's mother "asked about an evening dress for next year." Given the shortage of men during the war, Edwards believed, "I don't suppose there will be so very many opportunities to wear one."[61] Indeed she did have such opportunities. Her sorority entertained soldiers stationed on campus, and Edwards kept her mother up to date on the many dances that she attended in the name of patriotism. In the spring of 1918, she hosted a dance for aviators and later wrote home, "Some of the fellows were regular flirts but, of course, that didn't worry us any." They were a welcomed change from "those college fellows who mostly get bored to death." She told her mother after one dance that she had "a peach of a time—the best time I've had for ages because they were all so wide awake and are *real men.*"[62]

Sororities hosted many events, including on-campus entertainment for servicemen. During World War II, groups such as Cal's Panhellenic War Council organized competitions for the Sorority of the Month. Women were given points for rolling bandages, selling war stamps, harvesting and canning, and donating blood. During and after the war, sororities recast themselves to be more focused on service than socializing. Even those rushing were told to keep it casual. Cal's Panhellenic told freshmen, "Simplicity of taste always has been the keynote of any well dressed person, and this is especially true of your wardrobe at Cal. We are trying to make this rush season as informal as possible."[63] Within a few years, the group decreed, "Campus clothes will be worn to all rush parties."[64] Despite attempts to reform their image, sororities retained their reputation as exclusionary. In 1949, scholar Janet Kelley argued that participation in Greek life ensured "the members of a sorority all have status on the campus by virtue of their membership in that sorority."[65] In 1945, a critic of Greek life wrote in *Life* magazine: "The adolescent tragedies inflicted on some of the girls who are excluded has made the whole college sorority system a foremost issue in U.S. academic life today."[66]

The arrival of World War II veterans altered the social hierarchy of the campus. The vets had little tolerance for frat-boy regulations. In 1946, solider-turned-student Bob Thorn (Cal, Class of 1946, and member of Sigma Phi Epsilon) wrote in an article titled "Veterans and Fraternities" that in order to attract veterans to the Greek system, outdated rites of passage must be abolished, because "it is too much to assume that the veteran of 23 or more relishes being at the mercy of the whims of some 'fresh-out-of-high-school' paddle wielder." Thorn argued that regimentation and hazing "have been passé since the passing of the raccoon coat and beaver hat."[67] At Princeton, veterans who were freshman were excused from wearing dinks (beanies) and black ties, but civilian freshmen were forced to comply, since they were "not to be yet considered men, despite the fact that they are part of the university." The double-standard dealt a crippling blow to the "dink" tradition that had been foundering for nearly a decade.[68]

As the barbarians increasingly influenced student culture, fraternities lost much of their allure. Historian Helen Lefkowitz Horowitz writes that hedonism had once been the "exclusive prerogative" of fraternity men but in the wake of the war was "now shared by any college student who chooses it." Popular sites for "indulgence and fun lie off campus in bars, rather than in the fraternity house."[69] In 1937, "Dating and Rating" author Walter Waller argued that at large, state-run universities, "dating is almost exclusively the privilege of fraternity men, the use of the fraternity parlor and the prestige of fraternity members being very important." They were, he claimed, "at the top of the social scramble." A researcher at Penn State replicated Waller's study in 1950. He found that dating was no longer dependent on membership in fraternities and that more activities were available to students than those offered by the Greek system. Rather than formal dances, daters favored movies, house parties, and sporting events.

The shift in how and where students socialized reflected a remarkable increase in their autonomy—a change that came to fruition in the years after World War II but had been brewing since the mid-1920s. As the century progressed, collegians commandeered more control over their social space, and chaperones were the first to go. Etiquette writers urged collegians to view chaperones not "as a watch-dog or wet blanket[s] but as an asset to a good time." Few students considered them as such.[70] In the mid-1920s, students sidestepped or outright ignored many of the regulations. As Paula Fass explains, "Chaperones were invited by, conveniently seated in the parlor, superficially engaged in conversation (often the chore of the freshmen), and kept out of sight and hearing of the real activity on the dance floors, entertainment areas, and unlit grounds outside."[71] Female students pushed for later curfews and were granted them. Rather than being supervised by chaperones, women's off-campus activities were tracked by sign-in/sign-out policies at dorms.

With the emergence of a national youth culture in the late 1920s, female undergraduates no longer had to pretend that they were "non-sexual beings." Rather, "as they cut their hair, shortened their skirts and lit cigarettes, coeds and their sisters in women's colleges announced that they were ready for fun."[72] Changing attitudes toward sex redefined collegiate culture. The Charleston embodied this transformation, "generating a discourse that intertwined apprehension about gender, class, race and aesthetic value."[73] Critics feared that the rhythmical music and movements would "excite sexual urges that, without adequate social or internal controls, will pose dangers to young people."[74] Students mocked social critics. In 1925, Penn State editors joked that the dance was "the invention of a maniac" who "should be stopped," because "once-modest maidens, instead of tripping the light fantastic are ripping the tight elastic." The biggest problem with the dance, they declared, was that most Penn Staters did not know the steps, and admitted, "We wish we could do it."[75] Another student feigned fear of the dance's influence: "The Charleston menace is now stalking the American colleges. . . . If these stories are credible the present rage will leave in its path a swath of ruined buildings unequalled in extent in this country since Sherman's memorable march." The article confirmed that the Charleston caused the dance floor to collapse at the State College for Women in Atlanta and that the board of trustees at the University of Indiana prohibited the Charleston from being performed in the student union. At William & Mary, administrators banned it, because, they asserted, "dance should emphasize grace and beauty, and as the latest fad preserves neither of those qualities, it should hold no place on the program of college dancing." Tulane administrators were subtle in their approach. They simply handed attendees at the freshman/sophomore dance a note that read, "You are requested not to dance the Charleston tonight." The higher-ups at Smith created a rule that women who were living on the third floor of the dorm were not allowed to practice the dance in their rooms. True to form, Oberlin College bucked the trend and taught the Charleston in gym class. Despite administrators' efforts to eradicate the dance, students kept doing it.[76]

Automobiles, says Beth Bailey, were "the best and most private option for sexual privacy" and were easily parked behind dormitories so students could make out or have sex.[77] Penn State's student-issued "Co-Ed Commandments" told women, "Thou shalt say 'no thank you' when offered a drink" and "Thou shall not sit out dances in cars," but not everyone listened. Radcliffe student Bailey Patterson (Class of 1932) wrote about riding around with "Bee," the brother of a friend. They "drove out to Cambridge and parked (to my amazement) behind the Stadium. Bee leaned over and kissed me twice . . . and I nearly passed out!" After a while, she continued, "a police car came around and made us move on." Patterson confided, "It's funny how being kissed will almost entirely blot out another person." A previous suitor named Arthur, she wrote, "is very dim in my mind right now."[78] Patterson also wrote of a date to a movie with a man named Richard Bennett, who "held my hand all during the movie so I suppose I wasn't surprised when he put his arm around my shoulders." Bennett moved in for a kiss, but "wouldn't stop when I told him to. I didn't let him kiss me but I had to hold my hand over my mouth all the time. He was terribly strong and I had all I could do to hold him off." During the incident, she "was darned mad and scared too."[79]

Drinking and sexual experimentation often went hand in hand, sometimes with disastrous results.[80] Patterson wrote of a bridge-playing session at a friend's house that led a man named Tom to get "drunk as a lord." He "kept turning out all the lights and trying to make me lie down on the couch beside him." She refused, but "because he was such a big lummox, and so much stronger than I, he succeeded in soul-kissing me several times." When she rebuffed further advances, "he was perfectly vile, and said the most awful things to me. He said my lips maddened him and made him want to tear off all my clothes! He said 'I'll bet you aren't any more a virgin than a cat.' I simply couldn't believe my ears." Patterson added, "[I] didn't dare slap him because I was afraid I'd never get away from him." The next day, her neck was bruised and her jaw and chin were "actually painful to the touch." Her arms were "sore as though I'd been doing some unaccustomed exercise, and it was all just from trying to hold that brute off."[81] Despite Prohibition, Patterson drank regularly and even attended a speakeasy with her mother. She recorded an applejack drinking session with college pals: "Marion was pretty tight and partly unconscious. . . . She began to race and heave around and Emily had to get in bed with her to hold her down."[82]

Major campus events, such as the prom, brought out boozing in full effect. Chalmers Alexander, a vehement Prohibitionist, wrote to his mother in 1929, "Junior Prom is tomorrow nite [sic] so I suppose after it there'll be a great liquor shortage over all the U.S."[83] At Dartmouth's formal dance held during the annual Green Key Weekend, a student named Frank Bridges became so intoxicated that he made a "public and disgusting spectacle" of himself, which was "seen by dozens, if not hundreds of people." The president of the college, Ernest Martin Hopkins, the student, and the student's father, who was the leader of the Chicago Ethical Society, exchanged several letters heatedly debating the circumstances that led to Bridges' dismissal from Dartmouth. The young man claimed he had not been drunk but had vomited and passed out due to a stomach virus and believed he was "owed an apology by someone." The school's insistence on his dismissal caused his relationship with

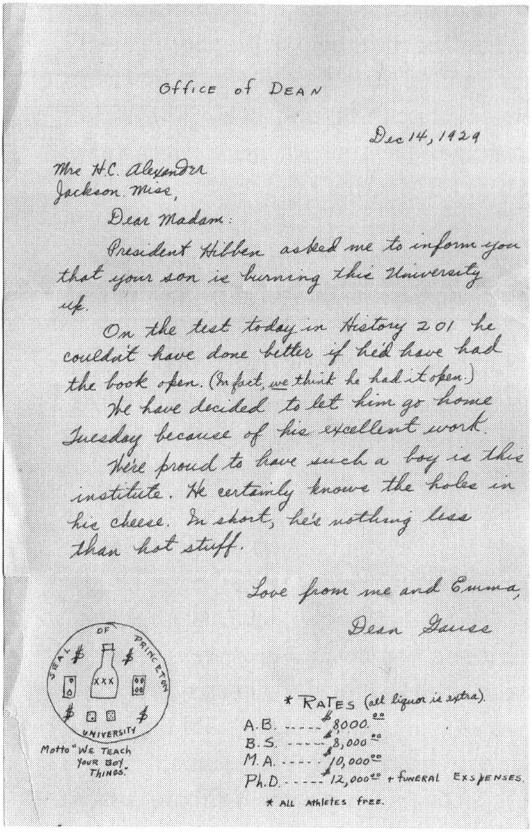

Figure 4.2. Chalmers Alexander (Princeton, Class of 1932) wrote to his mother in Jackson, Mississippi, nearly every day. His letters home detail daily life at Princeton—dorm pranks, difficult exams, and campus events. Chalmers wrote often of the tailored suits of his well-to-do classmates and his own clothing needs. Chalmers's insight into life at Princeton is particuarly telling as he was a religious man living among "the type who will never see heaven unless a miracle happens"(letter dated 16 September 1928). This mock letter from Dean Christian Gauss attests to Chalmers's more playful side. An avid Prohibitionist, Chalmers reinvented the Princeton seal, complete with cards, dice, and a bottle of liquor. Courtesy of Princeton University Library.

his father to be "strained to the point where a complete breakoff would not be an impossibility." The president was enraged by Bridges' general "smart-aleckism." He exclaimed, "There have been few men of whom I have known who have done the College more injury than you did." Despite Bridges' claim, his dismissal for getting drunk at the college formal was not repealed.[84]

## "A Button-Down Oxford with a Tux": Formal Attire Becomes Not So Formal

As the popularity of formal dances began to wane, students who did attended them wanted multipurpose garments that could be used for a range of "dressy" occasions. Men opted for dark suits instead of tuxedos, and women choose body-revealing cocktail dresses. Black was preferred because the women considered it sophisticated and believed that "if you only have a few dresses, you won't tire of it so easily."[85] The delineation between "formal" and "informal" got fuzzier, as the dean of women at Purdue noted in 1955: "Formal dress for a member of the younger crowd encompasses a greater variety of styles today than it did even a few years ago."[86] Students opted for versatile dress clothes, and bought fewer of them. Radcliffe women were told in 1920 that they needed five formal dresses. By the late-1940s, they were advised that "one or two should see you through."[87] For men, the transformation in formalwear came in two phases. First, the tuxedo replaced dinner dress (that is, tailcoats)—a change that had been coming since the turn of the century. Then, in the early 1950s, the dark suit replaced the tuxedo. An ensemble that served for formal dances did double duty for a job interview or an evening at the theater. By the mid-1950s, a tuxedo was no longer a prerequisite to participate in on-campus formal events. One student handbook told new students that "if you have a tux, bring it along, although you won't be out of line without one."[88] Events such as Penn State's 1957 prom were billed as "semi-formal," so men wore suits instead of renting tuxedos.

In the first decades of the century, male prom-goers wore either tailcoats—complete with waistcoat, white gloves, and a silk top hat—or a tuxedo. Tuxedos had minimal accessories and gave a more informal air. To a large degree, the choice was a matter of personal preference and finances. In 1907, Robb Carson opted for the tuxedo, writing to his parents, "It certainly was mighty good of you to offer me such a fine Christmas present as a dress suit coat, but I think I can get along all right without one. My tuxedo is a peach."[89] Men at Penn State and California often rented tuxedos for formal events. Early in the century, advertisements from local merchants with tuxedos to rent were common in school newspapers. Fraternity men were more likely to buy tuxedos because they had more occasions to wear them. The men of the Ivy League maintained a preference for tailcoats into the 1930s. A writer for a retail trade magazine skulked around Yale's formal events to see what the students favored. In 1931, he confirmed, "During the past year at Yale University, fully 60 percent of the men who attended the 'proms' and other formal evening functions wore the full dress suit or 'tails' as they are popularly known." The other 40 percent wore tuxedos. The reporter reminded merchants that Yale students were "always conservative and always correct" and that these were the students who "influence the styles of the men's clothing in the majority of colleges in the country."[90] Formal dress trends at Princeton in the early 1930s reflected a similar preference. In 1931, Chalmers Alexander confirmed the peaceful coexistence between full dress and tuxedos.

Figure 4.3. Hundreds of couples attended Penn State's junior prom in the 1920s. In this picture from 1923, men wear either tuxedos or tailcoats and women wear the low-waisted, sleeveless dresses associated with the "flapper" look of the late 1910s and early 1920s. Penn State's humor magazine wrote of the event: "Legs, made even more enticing by shimmering silken stockings, put to shame the artificial decorations that drape the ceiling. Passion runs high. So do the prices at the door. It is the night of the Junior Prom!" Courtesy of the Penn State University Archives, Pennsylvania State University Libraries.

Alexander wrote to his mother on the night of his class's junior prom: "On the way back from library last nite [*sic*], I passed by the Gym where Prom was being held. The girls I saw entering had perfectly beautiful evening gowns—silver, red, gold, blue, green and slippers and trappings to match. Must have cost oodles of money. A big number of boys in full evening dress (the rest had tuxedos) and tall opera hats (same as silk topper or stove pipe hats, except that they are on black dull heavy silk cloth and folded up flat). Nobody ever has a very good time. The floor is crowded and packed."[91]

The college man's biggest complaint about dressing formally was how to properly accessorize—a problem that was far more pronounced at state colleges than at Ivy League schools. One Penn State student dreaded the prom and the agony of "the two-hundred-watt lights" when he would be wearing "the new tux; the stiff shirt; to say nothing of that damn collar." These kinds of formal ensembles are seen in figure 4.3. Such fancy events, he believed, "seem to cast a spell of liberality over the poor, inexperienced,

worldly unwise Johns and Adams."[92] Editors of California's humor magazine, the *Pelican,* offered advice in "answer to a number of inquiries as to
when it is proper to wear a Tuxedo." They explained:

1. When you own a Tuxedo
2. When the tailor is pressing your only suit, and your roommate's
does not fit you.
3. When your roommate's Tuxedo fits you.
4. When you expect a rough party and you want to prevent people
from throwing things.
5. When you want to get the family's permission to use the car.
And any other time you may want to hide among the waiters.[93]

Formal dress tips offered by fashion editors at state schools stressed the
basics—knowledge that was second nature to most Ivy Leaguers. Shoes
were a major source of confusion, as demonstrated in a 1933 *Froth* article
titled "Why I Am Not the Best Dressed Man." Poking fun at Penn State's
chapter of Sigma Alpha Epsilon, the writer joked, "I am an S.A.E. and some
people think black and white sport shoes aren't to be worn with a set of
tails." Penn State's student handbook told men that for a formal dance they
should "be sure the shoes are shined and [wear] black socks; no others."[94]
Penn Staters had to be told that wearing a tuxedo with the accessories of
formal dress was considered bad form. A fashion editor for the *Daily Collegian* explained, "At the IFC Ball chic dressers will tear their hair at the
sight of broken combinations of top hats, white ties, and tails. These accessories should all be worn together. A Chesterfield is the proper topcoat."[95]
In general, the students of California shunned formality. In 1933, the Eastern college women's trend for prom dresses with long trains prompted a
California fashion writer to explain: "Here in our Western environment,"
such trains were as out of place and "as amusing as a top hat would be on
her escort."[96] Even at their most formal, middle-class collegians were less
formal than their counterparts at many elite schools, who held onto formal
social events well into the 1960s.

Cal students led the charge to replace tuxedos with dark suits. In 1953,
the women's executive board convened to plan the school's junior prom,
which was to be held at the St. Francis Hotel in San Francisco. The women
decided that "the dress will be formals (for women) and dark suits (for
men)."[97] Such was also the case at Penn State, where one observer of the 1951
junior prom observed the "shifting kaleidoscope of color," where the "men
with their dark suits" intermingled with the women decked out in "various
hues."[98] Beginning in the early 1950s, the junior prom was promoted in the

Figure 4.4. The popularity of formal events waned in favor of events such as Penn State's Dungaree Drag in 1948, which brought out students in their most casual clothing. Men rolled up their sleeves, and women their pants' cuffs to make already informal ensembles even more comfortable. Slouchy hats, hair bands, charm bracelets, and painted fingernails demonstrate the personal touches students used to personalize casual style. Events with themes such as square dancing, the Wild West, and sailors and pirates allowed students to attend university-sponsored functions in casual clothing. Hosted by the women's group the Cwens, this dance had a "girl-ask-boy" theme and was held at Rec Hall. Courtesy of the Penn State University Archives, Pennsylvania State University Libraries.

student newspaper as a semiformal, a distinction that would have allowed men to choose either regular suits or tuxedos.

The elite schools began to follow the trend. In the 1950s, dark suits replaced tuxedos at many—though certainly not all—of their formal events. In 1954, Princeton's eating clubs voted to forgo formalwear at any of their events. By then, most of the school's previously formal dances "now demand [a] jacket and tie instead of tuxedos. . . . [Students] expect that either or both will be shed before the end of the evening."[99] Local haberdashers documented the five-decades-long march toward informality. In 1957, several gathered to be interviewed by a local fashion reporter. A lifelong clothier named Mr. Lahey recalled that most men wore tails only "until 1920 or so, but . . . the tux came in and now they can even wear plaid cummerbunds. Today many will wear anything. Even a button-down oxford with a tux." Mr. Wendroff of retailer Harry Ballot's recalled a time "when no student ever went home for Christmas without tails, silk hat, a Chesterfield and white gloves. Now who wears tails? The Glee Club."[100]

For women, two trends led to the decline in the formality of prom attire. First, women bought fewer formal dresses because they had fewer occasions to wear them. Instead of several evening gowns, they purchased a "catchall" dress that could be accessorized to fit a variety of occasions. The 1946 Spelman handbook advised women, "A good idea is to choose a design that is 'in-between' enough to be worn to both formal and semi-formal occasions and not decorative as to become tiresome after being worn two or three times."[101] Simplicity and versatility became rallying calls of prom-dress shoppers in the late 1940s. Second, the dresses women wore to the prom became more diverse in design and showed far more skin than those from the turn of the century. Short cocktail dresses were worn alongside backless, floor-length numbers, and women selected these styles to fit their personal tastes and body types.

In the first three decades of the twentieth century, the popularity of formal dances made having a suitable dress a necessity. Letters home, diary entries, and student newspaper reports document the emotional and physical energy women invested in selecting and maintaining their formalwear. A Spelman student confided in her diary, "[I] spent practically most of the afternoon pressing the ruffles on the new green mousseline I was to wear to the junior-senior prom. . . . [It is] the sweetest garment I think I've owned to date, and chic." She wanted to keep it in good condition, so she "put it away in lavender and mothballs."[102] Serious prom-trotters cultivated a wardrobe of gowns. Hazel Hunkins's wealthy friend, Florence, was invited to the junior prom at Union College. Hunkins told her mother, "Florence is having 3 new dresses made, a beautiful brown shamuses and a lavender crepe de chine and a pink accordion plaited."[103] Clotheshorse Edith Culver and her mother shopped the Boston and Providence department stores for a new dress for her to wear to the high school prom of Arson, a family friend. The women spent two days tracking down the perfect frock. Culver bought other outfits, including an orange dress with blue feathers that she intended to wear to a fraternity dance and a brown lace number with a matching hat for a Harvard tea dance. Such indulgence was a luxury beyond the means of many collegians, who often sewed their own formalwear or swapped with dorm mates. A report of Spelman's prom commented on the women "in their dainty dresses, many of them dormitory-made, flitting here and there like gay butterflies."[104]

As the popularity of proms waned, women opted for multipurpose dresses, and the discourses of student fashion editors reflected the newfound appreciation of versatility. Rather than encouraging a range of wardrobe options, editors told women to buy one or two dresses and make them work for every occasion. The old guard understood the women's need to be "more practical" in their dress selection and their need to avoid an "extreme style and vivid color that will stamp your dress indelibly on everyone's mind." Yet the young women's insistence on black showed that they were not tied to the fashion dictates of their mother's generation who considered wearing the color bad form for young women. Much to the chagrin of one etiquette writer, a collegian's "first choice for an evening dress will be black; for a freshman's dream of sophistication is very low-cut and slinky, and she wears it with sinister, dangling earrings and elongated eyebrows." She told college women, "At twenty-five, you will look more kindly on the more youthful chiffons you should be buying now." But if women did choose black, she added, "Just remember that other girls will be buying black, too, and be certain that yours fits your type."[105]

One key to achieving versatility, said student fashion editors, was to be creative. Penn Staters were advised not to purchase a new gown but rather to use "formals left from your pre-college days." Of course, they added, "if you are buying something new, a dinner dress and jacket is by far the most practical and useful choice," because the ensemble was easily re-fashioned: "With the jacket, it can go to a dinner dance, and without it, to the formal dances."[106] Renovating a simple dress with sequins or beads was the advice of Spelman fashion editors, who told their colleagues, "If you are really creative and industrious, there is no limit to the ways in which you may use them."[107] The popularization of the simple, multipurpose frock by prom-goers blurred the distinction between "dressy" and "formal" to abstraction. A single garment was now suitable for nearly any and every occasion.

Not only were collegians buying fewer, more versatile dresses, but the dresses they wore to proms and formal dances became more diverse in design, so much so that by the end of 1960s fashion writers and mothers alike complained that nearly anything qualified as "formal enough." Most noticeable was the amount of skin the dresses revealed. Turn-of-the-century prom dresses were ankle-length and often featured long sleeves or high-necklines—or both. Yet, beginning in the mid-1910s and in keeping with general style trends, prom frocks with shorter hemlines and no sleeves or low necklines were in vogue. The shift to showing more skin nettled more conservative college students. After a 1917 sorority formal, Agnes Edwards wrote to her mother of her classmate's clothing: "Mother dear, if you think that my little dress is low in the neck, you ought to see some of them. As Mary says, they're held up by the grace of God. But they're certainly pretty and if I ever have an honest to goodness evening dress, as I hope to, it's going to be not as low as some are, but low enough to deserve the name."[108]

During her first years at college, Agnes Edwards struggled to reconcile the new styles of eveningwear with her personal sensibilities. After another formal, she confided, "Some of the girls have very wonderful dresses but I imagine I'd feel very queer in them because there isn't very much to them."[109] By her senior year, Edwards became comfortable donning revealing formalwear. In her last year at California, she wrote home of the hubbub her homemade gown caused at a recent formal dance: "You should have seen the girls—and heard them. It's the first time they've ever said anything much about anything of mine. I told one girl that you and I made it and she said it certainly looked like one from the shops." Even with the rave reviews, Edwards admitted, "I felt a little funny in it at first. It's a little more evening-fied than any I've had before."[110]

The prom dresses of the 1930s brought to bear another part of the female form—the back. The new silhouette scored big points with the opposite sex. One fashion writer reported, "The fellows remain partial to the off-the-shoulder or strapless back number."[111] Yet etiquette writers warned women that the look was not for everyone: "For formal evening wear, a backless evening dress is more or less enchanting," but should only be worn "if you have the 'skin you love to touch.'"[112] Within a decade, legs took center stage. In 1947, a Penn State fashion columnist told women attending the Interfraternity Council formal that "a short evening gown will really put you in the IFC spotlight."[113] The postwar trend for shorter formal dresses arrived during the years of Christian Dior's much publicized "New Look"—a silhouette that featured fitted bodices, cinched waists, and calf- to ankle-length hemlines. The silhouette was not in sync with collegiate tastes or needs, and the New Look got a lukewarm reception among American youth.[114] Penn State's *Froth* ran an entire issue devoted to lambasting the look.[115] Penn State men despised the style, calling it "nothing but the brain child of clever dress manufacturers—always searching for the extra dollar." Radcliffe women described it as "hideous" and "unflattering." When the *Harvard Crimson* asked one Cliffie for her opinion of the style, she just screamed.[116] A faculty member in the home economics department at Penn State summed up the reason why the New Look would not fly with her students: "The clinched-in waist is just not comfortable. College girls have too much good sense to want to sit in classrooms with their waists pinched-in by a rigid girdle." To woo Penn

State women, said the professor, "designers will have to keep their clothes practical."[117]

■ Collegians began the century tied to the mores and morals of their parents' generation. Dating was a supervised activity, and proms were the pinnacle of the collegian's year. Over the first half of the twentieth century, the prom "was replaced by dining and dancing, Coke dates, movies, 'parking.'" Amid these changes in American culture, the act of courtship "became more and more a private act conducted in a public world."[118] A student joke from Penn State in 1947 featured two women students talking to each other:

> Student One: All this stuff you read in college magazines is a bunch of hooey. I'm a college girl and I haven't smoked, necked, or drunk beer yet.
> Student Two: How long have yuh been in college?
> Student One: I just registered.[119]

The clothing that collegians wore on dates and to public events such as the junior prom was an essential means of expressing not only who they were but also who they were not.

In this respect, two important standards governed the clothing choices of collegians. In the 1960s, these standards came to profoundly shape not only collegiate wardrobes but the American wardrobe as a whole. Students' insistence on practicality played heavily into their rejection of formality in dress. Tailcoats and tuxedos were worn once or twice a year, while a dark suit fit a variety of social settings. The accessories of formal dress became far too complicated for collegians' developing tastes. White gloves, silk hats, and waistcoats were discarded in the early 1930s, and even more basic items vanished after World War II. One etiquette writer in the 1950s complained, "Few college women now have a coat that they use only for evening or formal wear."[120] Collegians' disassociation with established codes of formality gave them the opportunity to express their individuality—an opportunity they certainly took advantage of. A Princeton student from the late 1950s boasted, "I wore boots to Junior Prom [and] refused to wear a tie, no matter how formal the occasion."[121] In the 1960s, a report in *Women's Wear Daily* confirmed: "Radcliffe girls buy saris for $40 instead of a long dress for formal occasions."[122] Such independence was a far cry from the attitude of Edith Culver, who spent two days scouring the boutiques of Boston with her mother on a quest for the perfect frock to wear to Radcliffe's 1919 Freshman Jubilee.

Interestingly, elite schools and historical black colleges held on to the prom years past Penn State, but even they relented due to lack of student interest. The end of formal events at college ensured that entire generations of middle-class Americans grew up and did not know how to tie a bowtie or dance in heels. The collegians who rejected the prom at Penn State in 1962 rejected similar formal events as they graduated and moved into their middle-class lives. As all vestiges of formality waned, sartorial standards increasingly emphasized individuality and versatility.

### CHAPTER FIVE

# In the Gym

In May 1930, the editors of the *Dartmouth* challenged their readers to "bring forth your treasured possession—be it tailored to fit or old flannels delegged" so that the men could "lounge forth to the supreme pleasure of complete leg freedom."[1] The students rose to the challenge. The Shorts Protest of 1930 brought out more than 600 students in old basketball uniforms, tweed walking shorts, and newly minted cutoffs (see figure 5.1). The demonstration caused a rush on local merchants such as Campion's and Dudley's, who sold upwards of 300 pairs of shorts; the college's co-op sold 250 pairs. The editors believed that they had managed to break down, if only for a day, the formalities that forbade shorts in public. They proclaimed, "Emancipation is complete" but admitted that "the style is young" and hoped that "time will prove it valid."[2] Once the provenance of Boy Scouts and British day hikers, shorts became fashionable in the 1930s, and college students made that happen.

Shorts began as gym garb but became a staple of casual style. So did oxford shoes, sports coats, and button-down-collar shirts. The fashion industry dubbed these garments "sportswear" and by wearing them, collegians lived out their allegiance to the campus's all-important sports culture. By the late 1910s, clothing worn for sports defined campus dress. A trade publication for the menswear industry explained the pervasiveness of sportswear: "Even those men who do not play golf or tennis prefer this style for regular campus wear."[3] In 1922, Bessie Rudd, an instructor at Radcliffe, told a journalist that the "common sense styles of the modern girls are directly attributable . . . to the introduction of sports here at college." She continued, "The more women go in for healthy exercising, such as tennis, golf and walking, the more they become addicted to wide, short skirts, and sensible shoes."[4] The integration of sportswear into the American

Figure 5.1. The Dartmouth Shorts Protest of 1930 called for men to come out and "lounge forth to the supreme pleasure of complete leg freedom." The event, organized by the editors of the student newspaper, challenged their readers to "bring forth your treasured possession—be it tailored to fit or old flannels delegged." As the above picture illustrates, that's exactly what they did. The man in patterned hose appears to have purchased shorts, as demonstrated by the clean hem, but others wore cut off pants. The man in the middle wears lederhosen with ragged socks and a mended shoe. The protest was covered in regional newspapers and helped to introduce shorts to the wardrobes of American men. Within several years, college men across the country were wearing shorts when the weather permitted. Courtesy of the Rauner Library, Dartmouth College.

wardrobe was closely tied to an emerging cultural emphasis on youth and health. Mass acceptance of these clothes attests to a new appreciation for the athletic body—a form freed from layers of fabric and body-distorting undergarments. As much as the demise of the tuxedo and the evening gown documents the death of the most formal aspects of the American wardrobe, sportswear as street wear documents the rise of the informal.

Sweaters and shorts proved sportswear's most popular offerings. Their path to mainstream acceptance reveals when and where standards of formality changed in the first half of the twentieth century. Beloved by collegians for their relaxed fit and durability, the popularity of sweaters and shorts demonstrate how specific garments morphed from athleticwear, to campus favorites, to fundamental aspects of casual style off campus. In an article called "Big College Market," the sweater industry reminded retailers that collegians' preference for knitwear "will be aped by high school girls, office girls, factory workers, and just home girls in the country over."[5] Housewives and businessmen soon followed. A 1938 marketing report confirmed, "Sweaters are a fashion of great magnitude"; they had grown from being the provenance of "school and college girls, [of] the career girl as well, and [of] the smart matron in city and suburb alike."[6] Sportswear trends cultivated on the campus seeped into everyone else's wardrobes. The popularization of sweaters and shorts coincided with the emergence of new technologies such as knitting machines and synthetic fibers, the consolidation of the American fashion industry, and the development of California as a cultural tastemaker.

Shorts and sweaters provide tangible examples of how and why our understanding of masculinity and femininity changed. Men were the first to don sweaters and shorts, and the adoption of these sports-inspired garments raised only a few eyebrows. Early in the century, the male undergraduate's predilection for the sweater prompted the *Harvard Lampoon* to offer a humorous definition in 1908: "Sweater: Something to be worn on every occasion and in all places. Always decorated with enormous letters and fashionable at teas, dances, weddings, etc."[7] As the century progressed and older men chose to copy these collegiate trends, the conservatives among them lambasted those "who have no sense whatsoever of what a grown man ought to look like, which is an adult." "Short pants," said a naysaying journalist, "are for small boys." "Garment-wise, adult America has gone back to college," he complained. Missing the irony of how casual his parents considered his own generation's clothing, the author noted that he was from the "era of Harold Teen and John Held Jr.," when men wore "Harris tweed coats" and "gray flannel pants." He said that the Bermuda shorts (such as the ones in figure 5.2) made "the American man look about as silly as the American woman looks sloppy."[8]

On women, sweaters and, even more so, shorts provoked enduring and caustic commentary from college administrators, townspeople, and social critics, who called the garments "unflattering" and "unfeminine." In 1955, at a luncheon for industry executives, Margaret De Mille, the fashion director at Bloomingdale's, asked, "How often have we all be horrified by the indiscriminate use of shorts?"[9] Women's male classmates minced no words. Boston College student Ed Galotti told a panel of college women and department store buyers: "Anything is better than a sweater."[10] A writer for Penn State's *Froth* was far more ruthless when he asked his brethren,

Figure 5.2. Jeans, khakis, sweaters, Bermuda shorts, and button-down-collar shirts defined campus dress at Berkeley through the 1950s. Here, students in the late 1950s celebrate the capture of the Stanford axe, a campus tradition since 1899. In the first decades of the century, Cal was rife with traditions associated with clothing. Seniors wore sombreros and juniors wore plugs—hats they decorated themselves to proclaim their academic status. The much-loved "Pajamarino" was held in mid-October and brought out men in their pajamas to compete against one another in games and stunts. Until the mid-1950s, women were not allowed to wear their pajamas to the event. Courtesy of the University of California Archives.

"Have you ever seen a Bermuda Burger? Of course you have. If you think you haven't, take notice [of] the only piece of flabby flesh protruding from a coed's lower Bermudas and knee socks."[11] As figure 5.3 attests, "Bermuda burgers" were certainly not the norm. As a fashion reporter summarized in 1936, however, college women believed that shorts and sweaters were "typical of the brisk, active young girl of today."[12] In the interest of comfort and practicality, women insisted on borrowing "men's clothing," and by the late 1950s, they made few excuses for their preferences.

Sportswear—in its many and varied forms—supplied the foundation for casual style. As the twentieth century progressed, clothing meant to be worn only to the gym morphed into multipurpose garments that were

Figure 5.3. In the 1950s, college women wanted to wear "Bermudas on practically all occasions," but school administrators at coed schools such as Penn State limited when and where the shorts could be worn. The fight to wear Bermudas demonstrated a new kind of Penn State woman. In a letter to the editor in *Daily Collegian*, a student asked, "Must we sit back and accept this rule made by the dean even though almost 100 percent of women students oppose it?" Women's Bermuda shorts came in a range of fabrics, including cotton, flannel, tweed, and suede. Courtesy of the Penn State University Archives, Pennsylvania State University Libraries.

worn not only in the gym but also to class, to town, to church, and on dates. As Penn State's *Froth* wrote of the sweater in 1932, "In the old days it was only worn on the football field or when the gang went out to a jolly corn roast. Now it is worn in the classroom as well as for sport."[13] These clothes were worn loose, washed when needed, and discarded when they wore out. The American fashion industry made sure there was always more to buy. A defeated style reporter admitted in 1942, "We all know how our American youth goes in for baggy, shapeless clothes that are far from figure revealing."[14] The popularization of sportswear demonstrates the dynamic nature of collective taste. Shorts and sweaters were deemed "unfeminine" in the 1920s, but opinions changed by the 1950s. With time—and youthful defiance—sportswear became, in the words of one student, "very much accepted now by a great many people—on and off University campuses."[15] Many of the new proponents of casual style needed a little direction. For middle-class men hoping to hop on the bandwagon, *Esquire* outlined the proper accessories to wear with the shorts, "which extend to a point just above the knee": knee socks, a business shirt, tie, and jacket. The editors asked those men who still had reservations, "What more reassurance do you want that it's O.K. to be comfortable?"[16]

## "Looking Like Something Salvaged from the Bundles of the Poor House": Sweaters, Sizing, and Sloppy Joes

Knitting had been around for nearly 2,000 years when sweaters became fashionable in the late nineteenth century.[17] Long considered more "costume" than "fashion," sweaters, as their name implies, were about sweating. Practical and comfortable for rowing, football, golf, and rugby, the sweater took on symbolic meaning when male collegians emblazoned them with letters to denote accomplishments in sports. Yet college women became the more ardent supporters of the sweater. In 1940, a Harvard student explained, "At one time, sweaters were considered mostly for men. That's out today. One instinctively thinks of a woman in a sweater." After all, he wondered, "Where would a girl be without a sweater? Out in the cold."[18] College women and the many others who followed their fashion cues found the sweater to be a remarkably versatile garment. Men, too, expanded their wardrobes exponentially by mixing and matching sweaters with sports coats, khakis, corduroys, and jeans.

Itself an upstart on the American fashion scene, the knitwear industry knew why sweaters became such prized possessions for collegians. The garment was in keeping with the "practical character of clothing demanded

by this market," and it was college youth "toward [whom] knitwear designers and stylists point when they create new things."[19] Despite being the
creators and consumers of knitwear trends, collegians butted heads with
magazine editors, manufacturers, and retail executives who struggled to
understand their preference for what they deemed oversized, misshapen
garments. College women engaged in a four decades-long battle to wear
sweaters that made them "feel so free and comfortable."[20] In the end, nay-
sayers became proponents, demonstrating the allure of the garment as
practical and easy to wear. By the late 1940s, an African American newspaper told its middle-class readers that American women wore "sweaters for
every occasion and almost every age and walk of feminine life."[21]

The collegiate craze for sweaters began with the letterman's sweater,
which costume historians believe "denoted initiation and acceptance as
well as individual accomplishment in a sport."[22] The sweaters first appeared in the last years of the nineteenth century at Ivy League campuses.
At Princeton, the letterman's sweater took various forms, ranging from
the turtleneck to a boat-necked, ribbed cable-knit. Most were black with
a large orange P on the center of the chest. Other universities took to the
practice and made the sweater uniquely their own. Figure 1.2 shows the
kind of hip-length, fitted letterman's sweater that athletes wore at Penn
State in 1908; in this case, the letter B is on the arm, indicating that the
wearer was a member of the baseball team. At Cal, each varsity team had a
letter that incorporated imagery related to their sport. The baseball team's
sweater, for example, featured a glove and bat resting against the side of
the large C. At Morehouse, team coffers did not allow unnecessary spending, so students raised funds to buy letterman's sweaters, as did student
body president Marshall Cabiness on one occasion. On all campuses, the
letterman's sweater was revered. In 1907, Harvard student James Rosenthal
wrote to his father of the hubbub caused when an actor appeared on a
Boston stage in a Harvard letterman's sweater. Rosenthal explained, "Such
insignia is one of the most private and exclusive characters, and it is not
supposed to be worn by anyone who has not been granted it." Even though
the actor was indeed a Harvard graduate, he should have known better
than to wear the unearned emblem.[23]

For college women, varsity sports were few and far between. The students developed their own criteria for getting a sweater and considered
it a prize well won. Interclass competitions offered an opportunity. Vassar student Hazel Hunkins wrote to her mother: "Just to let you know that
yesterday I played left wing in the Freshman Soph hockey game and I won
my numerals. So now the next time you see my sweater you will see a nice

big 13 on it." The number represented her class, the Class of 1913.[24] Radcliffe began awarding letterman's sweaters around 1912, and each year the student manual, the *Red Book*, outlined the requirements for earning one. In 1914, it explained that if a woman played "three games against other colleges, the Athletic Association [would] award a white sweater with a red R for hockey, and a grey sweater with a red R for basketball."[25] University administrators used the sweaters to encourage participation in gym events. At Penn State, where women's athletics played second fiddle to men's, administrators implemented a point system. Ten points were given for "being a first class team member of major sports," which included hockey, basketball, and track. "Second-class" members of those teams were given five points. Team managers got six points, and any woman who walked seventy miles in a season was awarded ten points. Once the student accumulated fifty points, she received "a sweater and an Old English's [cologne]"— presumably to complement her masculine tendencies or to mask the smell of exercise.[26]

Men and women adopted the sweater as an emblem of school pride and athletic ability, but the garment became a staple of casual style because it was practical. Agnes Edwards found the sweater to be well suited for Berkeley's unpredictable weather. In September 1918, she wrote to her mother: "I initiated my sweater today. I like it so much. It's just warm enough for these spring days and it is such a pretty shade of blue."[27] Fearful of standing out, Edwards was often the last to jump on the bandwagon of a new trend. A year earlier, Edwards reported that nearly "every girl has a knitted sweater and you see every color under the sun." She admitted, "I don't know whether I want one. I'm afraid the craze might die out suddenly."[28] It did not. The "craze" for sweaters grew exponentially in the years surrounding World War I. College women knitted for servicemen and to supplement their own dwindling wardrobes. "Everyone here knits," Edwards told her mother. "The girls carry those big cretonne bags around with them and knit during lectures and meetings and on the street cars."[29]

College students from across the country spearheaded the sweater's transition from functional to fashionable in the 1920s. What the *Radcliffe News* called "an epidemic of sweaters" came amid a broader trend led by French designers such as Gabrielle "Coco" Chanel and Jean Patou for jersey knits, used in women's two-piece suits, and for long cardigan sweaters.[30] American knitting companies such as Jantzen and Bradley pumped sweaters, swimsuits, and athletic gear into department stores.[31] Jantzen's annual output of swimsuits, for example, grew from 600 bathing suits in 1917, to 4,100 in 1919, to 1,500,000 in 1930.[32] Knitted sportswear had a national market but the industry was becoming increasingly associated with the West Coast. In 1937, a trade publication for the industry acknowledged, "To an increasing extent the California manufacturers of knitted sportswear and beachwear have been penetrating the eastern market." The writer attributed the growth of the knitwear industry to Hollywood and California's "energy and creative ability." Manufacturers teamed up with retailers to use the "California ballyhoo as an aid to their merchandising."[33] California's burgeoning knitwear industry provided the actual garments, and the state's reputation as the "'new frontier' in leisure, pleasure and good living" created eager consumers.[34] Collegians were the first in line.

Women's sweaters of the late 1920s and 1930s were more demure and detailed than those of Agnes Edwards's day. The gauge of the knit was smaller, collars and cuffs added a polished appearance, and accessories such as pins, scarves, and dickies allowed for unlimited experimentation. Sweaters offered collegians variety at a bargain price, and women bought three or four for the cost of a suit. Sweaters were no longer practical add-ons for a windy day; they became the foundation for a complete outfit. Sweater-based ensembles inspired creativity. A survey of women's colleges conducted by *Harper's Bazaar* in 1934 reported that at "Vassar the only thing to wear is a short tweed skirt, sweater buttoned on backwards, and flat heeled shoes." Women at Smith favored "a string of pearls with a sweater and a ribbon or bandeau around the hair."[35] Pearls with sweaters was so prevalent at Radcliffe that the editor of the 1938 yearbook told seniors to try a new accessory for class pictures because "too many sweaters worn with pearls would look monotonous."[36]

Accessories were paramount for achieving versatility. Radcliffe women recommended dickies to "perk up . . . sweaters after the first newness wears off," but the accessory was also useful in "freshening [outfits] when sweater necks are hopelessly stretched."[37] Spelman fashion editors told readers, "Class-time is skirt and sweater time" and called it "good 'clothes sense' to get serviceable ones in colors that go well with many blouses and sweaters, as well as your own complexion."[38] Female students used sweater accessories to accent their individuality. At a 1938 roundtable held by a Boston department store to better understand what college women wanted in sweaters, the respondents endorsed "gadgets"—a catchall term for pins, Liberty of London silk scarves and kerchiefs, sweater clips, and embroidered monograms.[39] By the eve of World War II, the college woman's preference for sweaters came to "amaze" the editors of *Vogue,* who in 1939 reported that 80 percent of female collegians owned between five and fifteen sweaters.[40] Upperclassmen at Boston colleges told incoming freshmen: "You should have at least four pull-overs and four cardigans when you enter the college gates and you should increase that to eight of each kind come the finals in June."[41]

Much like their sisters, college men first adopted sweaters because the garment was comfortable and practical. In the early 1910s, college men supplemented their letterman's sweaters with patterned pullovers that were worn with knickers, textured hosiery, Norfolk jackets, and heavy-soled oxford shoes. By the mid-1920s, such golf-inspired sportswear had gone mainstream, and sweaters were worn "more generally than ever before by men of all classes."[42] In the late 1920s, the sweater was a welcomed addition to or replacement for the standard shirt and tie combination. The men of Cal were well known for their sweaters paired with dirty corduroy trousers. They wore the ensemble to class, to campus events, and on dates. Much to the annoyance of their female classmates, Cal men wore sweaters without button-down-collar shirts and ties underneath. The school newspaper reported that women "nominated to oblivion . . . sweaters worn without shirts" because "semblance of neatness should be sought on campus."[43] The versatility of the sweater endeared it to college men. At the height of the Depression, Penn State men praised the garment as multipurpose. *Froth* noted that "the depression has cast its pall on sartorial effulgence" and "estimated that this article of dress has taken the place of at least four shirts on the average per week." The humor magazine prophesied, "The formal turtleneck shirt will probably be seen at the outstanding social functions this fall."[44] Indeed, the Depression had a marked impact on clothing production, but even more so on retailing. According to the Census of American Business, nationally, retailers of women's apparel and footwear suffered a 48 percent and 47 percent decrease in net sales, respectively, between 1929 and 1933. Men's ready-to-wear retailers' and family clothing stores' net sales decreased by 59 percent and 66 percent, respectively.[45]

As did women, men wore sweaters on their own terms and for their own purposes. A missive on campus dress at Princeton in the 1940s reported, "Sweaters continue to be worn in that cute backwards, inside out style."[46] As Princeton student R. M. Lichenstein demonstrated in the late 1940s, sweater use was an individual choice made on a daily basis. As part of his undergraduate thesis in psychology, Lichenstein surveyed 420 of his colleagues and concluded that all "men like to attend classes in casual dress." However, he also reported that the "incoming Frosh who wants to orientate himself to the Princeton style will probably pick a sweater for class attendance," but an upperclassman was more likely to wear a coat and tie because he had other campus responsibilities, such as club meetings and dinners. Lichenstein had asked students to identify clothing that they believed "constituted the Princeton pattern of dress." Sixty percent of the students chose the sweater.[47]

Sweaters were central to collegians' casual style. For women, however, the garment came with mixed reviews from administrators, fashion editors, and male colleagues. Critics lauded well-fitted, fine-gauge sweaters with delicate details such as bows or beading but condemned oversized, chunky-knit sweaters with too-long sleeves and misshapen necks. A journalist for a Massachusetts newspaper noted that women "might wear the baby sweaters, those little fluffy things that fit tightly and come only to the waist" for evening events, but such sweaters "'cut no ice' for daytime wear." Women preferred "their sweaters to be hip length and baggy. Two sizes too large is just about right."[48] Critics deemed baggy sweaters unfeminine and even unsanitary. In 1939, an etiquette writer acknowledged that "gals have to be comfortable," but argued that a sweater that was too big and worn too often "falls in with underthings as an item which collects odors and aromas" and reminded women, "Sweaters need to be washed often."[49] A *Harvard Crimson* reporter wrote adamantly of "the untidy, form-concealing pullovers" that his Radcliffe neighbors wore when "pretending to be men."[50] One Harvardian, who wrote an intermittent fashion column for the *Radcliffe News,* published a diatribe about the "evils" of oversized sweaters, as well as those "scrupulously ornamented with pompoms and angora lace!" He wanted to see women in tailored, simple sweaters that "soar to lofty summits of aristocratic casualness" and "suggest a British title vacation in the Lake Country."[51] Penn State men agreed that bulky sweaters were not attractive. One noted, "It would be hell to date a babe who was wearing one of these damn things."[52]

Fashion writers, manufacturers, and retailers understood that college women "love and insist on comfortable clothes," but the late-1930s craze for "sloppy joe" sweaters really struck a cord.[53] The sloppy joe was an extra-large cardigan or pullover that came to midthigh and had sleeves that were so long they had to be pushed up. Some fashion industry executives saw the sloppy joe as an opportunity to cash in on the college market. One manufacturer thought the name was "undignified" and suggested it market the sweaters under the name "Slop-Ons" because it was "catchy," had "promotional value," and "characterized in a synthetic word the casual effect that the garments seem to create."[54] Many retailers and industry observers believed that the popularity of the sweaters was fueled by college women's insistence on dressing alike. Syndicated advice columnist Dorothy Dix wrote of the trend: "If all other girls are wearing sloppy Joe sweaters and dirty shoes, Maud goes about looking like something that has just been salvaged from the bundles of the poor house."[55]

Some critics enlisted the help of college men to bring reason to the women's irrational preference for oversized sweaters. In 1940, Slattery's had a fashion show with an all-male jury that "represented average male opinion of Betty Co-Ed's Clothes." When asked their opinion, "the boys vetoed sloppy sweaters, pushed-up sleeves, and sweaters buttoned up the back."[56] In a survey of northwestern campus trends, the fashion editor of the *Chicago Tribune* observed that the average male student "appears to have the idea that the average female student ought to be more ornamental" and that women were "handicapping their natural attractiveness by freakish or careless styles of dress." Along with sloppy joes, bare legs, and flat shoes, men disliked it when women showed up on campus looking "like new arrived peasants from central Europe, female wrestlers in training, Hollywood stars, tavern man-grabbers, night club hostesses, and councillors of high school students' summer camps." The men "positively steamed" about "calculated sloppiness," but they also complained of "'silly' dresses (meaning ruffles, too big prints)," "noisy jewelry, especially charm bracelets," and "too much makeup." The men's opinions of clothing that looked like menswear were resolute: "Keep out of slacks, pants or shorts and any other strictly masculine makeup if you want to keep your desirable femininity, girls."[57]

With little regard for the opinions of department store buyers and male colleagues, college women put away the sloppy joes when they tired of the trend. By the mid-1940s, women began to prefer more tailored sweaters. A 1944 report from Wellesley noted that "tucked-in sweaters and colorful belts are nudging out the 'box' sweater and the baggy cardigan."[58] In 1946, Spelman fashion editors told readers, "Sloppy Joe sweaters and sagging skirts are out" and "you'll want to tuck those small knit sweaters."[59] The fashion industry chalked up the return of the fitted sweater to the return of men to campus after the war. A publication for the knitwear industry explained, "These men, who for the most part have just returned from service, many from a rough and tumble existence in the jungles or wasteland areas, are wanting to see the girls looking neat and feminine."[60] Penn State men thanked the influence of Hollywood, declaring, "With the advent of Lana Turner and Jane Russell the sweater has soared from its doldrums and projected its personality unto the public."[61] Despite a brief reprieve for oversized sweaters in the second half of the 1940s, college women took up the sloppy joe again in the 1950s. In 1956, "shaggy" sweaters "that used to be called 'sloppy Joe' length and shape" were once again "enthusiastically approved" by the college-bound.[62] In the early 1960s, college women quickly adopted the roomy and ribbed "poor boy" sweater. A Barnard College fashion writer described this incarnation of the sloppy joe as a "big, floppy sweater" worn with "wild, ribbed, diamonded stockings."[63] In 1960, Barnard student Mary Jo Kline wrote to her parents of her new favorite sweater: "It's such a good color. . . . It should go with almost everything I own. Since it's cotton, it's comfortably light, while fashionably 'bulky.'"[64]

Indeed, women's preference for sloppy joes, oversized sweaters, and baggy sweatshirts demonstrated a fundamental shift in the relationship between women's clothing and their bodies. Fashion executives called the 1960s "the Age of the Body," agreeing that "today's body feels free, unconfined, uninhibited, and natural." But they acknowledged that cultural standards are not challenged and recast over night. Rather, the "increased interest" in "the liberated body . . . has been years in the making."[65]

### "Becoming Normal Casual Wear": Men, Women, and the Double Standard of Wearing Shorts

When the men of Dartmouth first sauntered forth in their homemade short pants in the spring of 1930, they did so for practicality's sake. The school newspaper advocated shorts not only for "tennis, for golf, for basking in the sun" but also "for attendance at the most aristocratic of classes, for study in the library and dinner at the D.O.C. house." The men knew they were pushing fashion's boundaries and encouraged their colleagues to join the campaign, because "all the reputation of college men in general for sartorial guts hangs in the balance."[66] Their fashion statement met with national press coverage and concern from Boston clothiers, but not from school officials, who ignored the trend. On college men, most observers heralded shorts as progressive. In 1955, *Esquire* reassured readers, "You can now wear shorts for sports and informal business anywhere the weather's hot, and no one is going to bat an eye."[67]

When women took to shorts, they did so under school-imposed regulations that limited when, where, and how the garment could be worn. In 1960, the women of Barnard College hit the streets to protest an administrator-penned ban of shorts and slacks. Observers felt the edict was for the women's own good. As a fine arts instructor noted, "Most of the girls in shorts look like third-rate Rubens." The well-publicized battle, which women ultimately won, ignited national controversy as to the place of shorts in the American woman's wardrobe. An etiquette writer in Ohio snipped that "the real battle" should not be with shapely students, but with the "grownup women in shorts," such as "mother and grandma who don't seem to realize shorts publicize their bad points and classify them as auditioning for horror films."[68] Casual style for men and for women was based on many of the same garments, but double standards hampered women's widespread adoption of "unisex" items, such as shorts, that took time to shake the reputation of being "distinctly male clothing."[69]

Bicycling did for shorts in the 1920s what it had done for sweaters in the late 1890s. A renewed public interest in both bicycling and tennis, the growth of a demand-responsive sportswear industry, and the development of beach tourism brought shorts to the interest of leisure-minded Americans.[70] Shorts first showed up on the college campus as part of gym and basketball uniforms. At Penn State in the late 1920s, men donned shorts paired with T-shirts and sweatshirts, and their peers at Cal purchased similar uniforms. The women at Penn State and Cal wore bloomer-inspired numbers that hit mid-thigh. Spelman students wore their bloomers with knitted stockings for added propriety. Women's gym togs were the focus of public interest from early in the century. In 1909, the *Boston Sunday Post* featured an article on Radcliffe's annual "Gymnastics Jubilee," despite the fact that the event was closed to the public. "Attired in blue bloomers with crimson ruffles," the paper reported, "the girls danced about the gymnasium floor in happy glee." Of the events on the parallel bars, it reported, "Some caught their bloomers on the bars and then there was trouble."[71]

Nearly three decades later, the women's gym uniforms still provoked interest. In the second half of the 1930s, Radcliffe updated its antiquated gym uniforms, a move praised by the students and covered in regional papers. *The Boston Post* devoted an entire page to the change, proclaiming, "Yes, it's finally happened. That conservative sister school of the venerable and distinguished Harvard university has at last torn herself away from the floppy jersey bloomers, the standard gymnasium uniform for years—and she has blossomed out, a new woman, in shorts!" The shorts themselves were pleated and featured a new addition to sportswear—the zipper. They were worn with a custom-made shirt with pearl buttons and came with both sweatpants and a short, pleated skirt to be worn when the students were not engaged in active play.[72] According to Frances Badger, the director of Radcliffe's physical education department, the 1938 change was a long time in coming. She was "very much surprised to find the girls in jersey bloomers" when she took the position five years earlier. After all, she noted, "shorts are so very much the present day mode, so much more comfortable and practical." Some of Radcliffe's old guard grumbled, but Badger stood by her decision. "There is no moral question involved," she asserted, and she could not understand "why anyone should question shorts when those terribly abbreviated bathing suits, halter tops, and play suits . . . without so much as a lifting of an eyebrow."[73] The students themselves rejoiced at the sanctioned addition of shorts to their wardrobes. Mildred Madden, the fashion writer for the *Radcliffe News,* admitted, "It may look strange to us for a while to see our athletes attired in something closely resembling underwear," but the new ensembles ensured that "Radcliffe athletes should present a smooth appearance on any field."[74]

Indeed Radcliffe was late in the game in adopting the garment as its gym uniform, but other schools were just as cautious in allowing female students to be seen in public in shorts—whether for fashion or exercise. According to a 1935 *Boston Globe* article titled "Colleges for Women Taboo Shorts for Women Except for Sports Wear," "Shorts are okay for college girls on the tennis court or for sun-bathing in some secluded spot but at most all girls' colleges in Massachusetts the wearing of shorts on any other occasion is taboo. That is the situation in a nutshell." Wellesley's dean, the article reported, said, "Let the girls wear shorts" but quickly added, "All shorts must be covered with a skirt or coat except on the tennis courts." The requirement for covering up actually extended to "all sports costumes" and demonstrated the widely held opinion that shorts were for active playing, not for everyday wear. Administrators, according to the paper, created and enforced many of the rules regarding shorts in order to "keep enough clothes on their students to avoid shocking New England townsfolk."[75] Communities across the country shared the concern about shorts being too revealing. The mayor of Grafton, West Virginia, made front-page news when he summoned a group of shorts-sporting women to his office and told them that "'shorts' may be the thing at Marshall College, or at the summer resorts but here in Grafton—no, siree!"[76] The public's opinion about women in shorts was a deciding factor in when and where the students could wear the garments.

College men were not subjected to the same level of scrutiny or control, but their interest in shorts also made headlines. On 14 May 1930, the men of Dartmouth followed the rallying call of their student newspaper the *Dartmouth* by donning short pants on campus to attend all of their day's activities. In the weeks leading up to and following the demonstration, it made news in university publications and garnered attention in the local and national press. The editors of the *Dartmouth* initially launched the campaign as a protest against the public dislike of short pants. The sweltering heat of early May prompted the editors to ask themselves why men went about "swathed in clothes to the toes." They wondered, "Where was liberty, where was the undying spirit of people that poems are written about, where were people's knees?" Above all, they asked, "why doesn't Hanover wear shorts during the spring?" The paper called up "Eagle Scouts and liberal-minded men" to buck convention and wear shorts because "shorts are inexpensive, shorts are debonair if you have a debonair swashbuckling mind, shorts are saving on flannels, shorts are rarely carried to the pressing bandit."[77] The editors aimed to dethrone "the would be dictators of fashion" and to give students "a chance to be different with a vengeance, not for the sake of being different but in the name of good sense."[78]

While the practicality of shorts was part of the initial allure, the comfort of the garments endeared them to Dartmouth men, who showed up en masse to support the cause. More than 600 students wore outfits that ranged from high school basketball uniforms, to Boy Scout shorts, to old trousers with the legs cut off. In the following day's editorial, the organizers congratulated the men who withstood the chilly weather of an afternoon that turned out to be unseasonably cold and told them to put away their shorts until the next time "you may want to sit on the Senior Fence and drowse in the sun."[79] Though the demonstration may have seemed like just another example of collegiate frivolity, the organizers and their followers saw importance in their actions. They considered it "no idle matter of a day: It is possibly the most logically radical movement since males stepped out of armored vests and trousers late in the Middle Ages."[80] To them, the public acceptance of shorts was about their own ability to defy and define fashion trends to suit their own needs. Even more so, the men understood that in order to make shorts "like airplanes, common enough to escape all notice," it was essential that they end the "stigma of the man who appears with pants slashed to the knees": being regarded as effeminate.[81] As the paper had explained in its call for demonstrators, "We don't want men who are near the danger line of being called sissies. They couldn't carry the thing off." Invoking a Dartmouth-defined masculinity, the editors called forth "every able-bodied man in Hanover, . . . the rugged element (for whom) the wearing of shorts would be the emblem of a mind hard enough so that no one could stand in the same block and accuse them of being beautiful around the knees or chocolate éclair in disposition."[82]

The editors' emphasis on a body-baring masculinity attracted the endorsement of unlikely supporters. One student's mother wrote to the school's paper to say she was "glad to know at least one place inside

Christendom, where men may go about their business in clothes that are comfortable and neat." She noted with excitement, "You've started something that will be far-reaching."[83] The most interest came from the New York and Boston press. The story was picked up by Associated Press and taken national. Student newspapers at Harvard and Princeton covered the story, and Fox Movietone News showed up to record the day's events. The college's administrators paid little attention, even when the men staged an afternoon fashion show on the steps of Robinson Hall. The show demonstrated the versatility of shorts by highlighting the range of available styles, including those for sports, lounging, and morning and afternoon wear, as well for formal and informal evening wear. Those in the fashion establishment did not share the enthusiasm for the public acceptance of shorts. The *Dartmouth* reported, "Curses have been coming through the clenched teeth of Rosenthal and Maretz, Rosenberg, Burns, Brooks Brothers, and half the national clothing houses and textile industries in America."[84] A "Prominent Boston Clothier" wrote of the demonstrators, "Having no brains to make them famous, of course they must use their legs, even if they are knock-kneed," and he called the "average American student . . . the most brainless of any student in the world."[85] While fashion executives fumed, the general public followed the story carefully. The *New York Times* reported, "An overpanted humanity (male mostly, married and helpless) will watch with fervid eagerness the progress of this audacious defiance of scared customs."[86] Within a few years, shorts gained ground with men on other campuses, including the sartorially staid Chalmers Alexander, who reported to his mother in the spring of 1932 that the pair she had sent in the mail arrived on time.[87]

*Dartmouth* editors believed that the day was near when "the short was a permanent item of dress," and by the end of the 1930s, their prophecy came true.[88] Not until the early 1950s and the mass adoption of the knee-length Bermuda did shorts become a legitimate fashion trend that bridged the gap of age and socioeconomic status. Even as sales of the shorts skyrocketed, however, many university administrators continued to deem Bermudas inappropriate for general wear and relegated the garments to private areas of campus. At Penn State the dean periodically forbid men to wear shorts to the cafeteria, but their vehement reactions usually sent administrators into submission. Penn State's women, on the other hand, did not wield such collective strength and struggled for more than two decades to overturn administration-imposed regulations.

The vogue for roomy, knee-length shorts called "Bermudas" first came to the fore in the late 1930s. Fashion writers attributed the trend to the growth of the island as a vacation spot for collegians. Students considered the shorts "perfect for bicycling across rambling campuses," and "[they] were swept up by Smith and Vassar girls as all-around campus wear."[89] In August 1939, *Mademoiselle* magazine featured the garment in its back-to-school issue. In the wake of the Second World War, the shorts hit their stride. A Barnard graduate of the era believed that women took to the fashion because they were tired of the blue jeans and men's shirts of the early 1940s. "Why," she recalled, "we never knew anything so elegant as Bermuda shorts."[90] By the early 1950s, Bermuda shorts were a fundamental part of the male and female collegian's wardrobe. In 1955 a fashion reporter told women that Bermuda shorts, knee socks, and sweaters were "the Uniform at schools across the country."[91] Indeed reports from campuses in every region reported the pervasiveness of the craze for Bermudas. While both college men and women wore the shorts, most of the national coverage and public concern again focused on women.

What distinguished women's Bermudas of the late 1940s and 1950s from the athletics-inspired shorts of the 1930s was both the cut and the material. Most shorts from 1930s were made of cotton because it was lightweight for summer wear and easily washed. They commonly had an A-line cut and featured pleating at the waist. At first glance, they resembled a skirt. The Bermuda shorts that college women popularized in the late 1940s had a waist that was similar to that on men's pants, were obviously shorts, not skirts, and often had patch pockets as accents. Moreover, because they were worn in year-round, the shorts came in a variety of fabrics. Grey flannel emerged early as the most popular fabric, but following the war, women began to wear wool versions in various brightly hued plaids. In *Vogue*'s 1946 back-to-school issue, a pictorial of campus togs featured a student in Bermudas paired with a dark, form-fitting, wool-knit shirt and a thick black belt. The caption read: "A habit: long shorts. Forming habit: unexpected materials. Suede, in this case, wonderful yellow suede."[92]

Given the variations available, women purchased more than one pair. One report in 1955 confirmed, "Whether permitted in classes or not, Bermuda shorts go everywhere else on campus, and even to parties. Minimum owned per girl is six."[93] At Skidmore in 1958, women claimed that "eight pairs of Bermudas form the basis of the wardrobe."[94] By the mid-1950s, the shorts came in varying lengths, each with its own moniker. A fashion reporter explained, for example, that "Jamaicas [are] shorter than Bermudas and Nassaus."[95] The allure of the shorts to college women and men was the same: comfort. However, men openly mocked their sisters in shorts. A British visitor to Penn State in 1955 was shocked at the site of women in Bermudas, which were worn "regardless of the suitability of their figures—and I do mean suitability—they are clad in form-fitting shorts of the most outlandish type."[96] Princeton men complained that Bermudas contributed to unoriginality in dress. Their humor magazine, the *Tiger*, noted in 1959, "Nine college girls out of ten don't know how to dress. They live in a world of Bermuda shorts, anonymous sweaters, nondescript blouses, and knee socks."[97]

At Penn State in the 1950s, the rules for men and women were issued by the students' respective deans and demonstrate the gendered nature of administrators' dress codes. Men were told where they *could not* wear shorts; women were told where they *could* wear shorts. For women, as one student put it, "circumstances under which they (shorts) can be worn have been so closely defined that the whole situation has become slightly ridiculous."[98] When Bermudas first hit the Penn State campus in the late 1940s, women were allowed to wear them only in certain parts of the dorm that were inaccessible to the public, such as bedrooms and study lounges,. The ground floor of the dorm, the golf course, and campus lawns were off-limits. As with men, the dining hall was the primary area of contention. A draft of the dean of women's 1947–48 rules for on-campus housing specified, "Bermuda shorts and kilts may not be worn in the dining halls except during finals when they may be worn for all meals except Sunday noon." Handwritten notes on the draft documented some parents' reactions to the rule. One note read: "Many adverse criticisms this year [when] parents and new students were here for counseling. One parent thought she wouldn't let her daughter come if that were acceptable dress!"[99] In the late 1940s, many parents felt that such attire had no place on campus. Ironically, less than a decade later, they, too, would be wearing the garments to community events, private parties, and shopping excursions.

Penn State administrators considered Bermudas to be acceptable dress on very specific occasions, and the shorts remained a highly contested garment for both men and women. Over the course of the 1950s, students were unrelenting in their efforts to gain official permission to wear shorts on their own terms. Even when that permission was repeatedly denied, many students wore Bermudas anyway. On 30 April 1954 Penn State student Daniel Grove, who hosted the radio show "Groovology," organized Bermuda Shorts Day. Men attended classes and their other daily activities in Bermudas and knee socks. In spite of the dean of women stepping in to reiterate that female Penn Staters "may not wear Bermuda shorts for any purpose other than a recreational activity," some women wore the shorts in defiance. Grove's purpose was simple, "it is hoped that not only today but everyday will be Bermuda Shorts Day on the Penn State Campus."[100]

Students called the deans' rules "unfair," "illogical," and "unjustified." Referring to the "archaic attitude" of administrators, one woman declared, "Bermuda shorts are quite acceptable—morally and in appearance. They are becoming normal casual wear."[101] Dean of Women Pearl O. Weston, was steadfast in her belief that "dormitories and the campus are not appropriate places for recreational attire such as shorts."[102] Despite ongoing petitions from the women's student government, Weston would not allow shorts to be worn in public areas. A student summarized the dean's opinion: "Bermudas are just fine for sports but not for anything else, because here at Penn State, we want to turn out fine well-bred young ladies, and ladies wear shorts only for sports." "Don't Vassar, Smith and Bryn Mawr turn out 'well-bred' ladies?" the student asked. "They wear Bermudas on practically all occasions except to formal dances, special dinners and church services. . . . Must we sit back and accept this rule made by the dean even though almost 100 percent of women students oppose it?"[103]

Dean Weston had no official power over male students, who were free to wear shorts anywhere but the dining hall. However, in the spring of 1954, she outlawed Bermuda-clad men from entering women's dorm lobbies and lounges, because the garments "could not be considered appropriate daytime garb for men any more than could coattails and formal dress suits." Men who needed to pick up their dates at the dormitory were asked to phone from another location. Women who insisted on wearing shorts on campus or on dates were required to wear a skirt or a long coat when leaving or returning to their dorm rooms. The Women's Students Government Association Judicial Board of Review gave "blackmarks" to those who did not comply with the rules.[104]

Despite the relative freedom of male Penn Staters to wear shorts on campus, they pushed for even more leeway, arguing that the late-1950s dining hall restrictions were outdated. "I was under the impression that student affairs are run by student government," Penn State undergraduate Donald Chalmers told readers of the *Daily Collegian* in September 1955. He felt the dining hall restriction was "unfair because the students had no say in formulating such a policy."[105] In the second half of the 1950s, student governments began writing their own rules regarding curfews, dress codes, and the like and then submitting them to the deans for approval. Time and again, the deans denied both men's and women's requests to wear Bermuda shorts to evening meals.

A 1962 request by the Men's Residence Hall Council asking for carte blanche "was called 'unacceptable' by the dean of men's office." Assistant Dean of Men Raymond O. Murphy argued that the rules helped to "develop

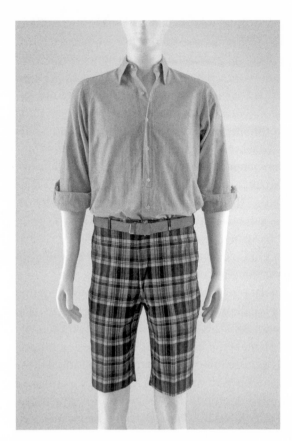

Figure 5.4. Bermuda shorts for men were most commonly made of cotton and came in a range of colors. Madras Bermuda shorts became popular for both sexes in the mid-1950s, and students paired them with oxford shirts, crew-neck sweaters, and the occasional T-shirt. The 1950s pair pictured here demonstrates the roots of what is now known as "preppy" style. Madras Bermuda shorts, colorful, adjustable belts, and rolled-up sleeves have endeared the preppy look to a range of Americans both on and off the college campus. Courtesy of The Museum at FIT.

a respect for proper dress" in residents who would relocate to downtown apartments as upperclassmen. The editor of the *Daily Collegian* wrote, "Any person who has not learned respect for proper dress by the time he has reached college age cannot be taught this respect by an administration-produced and enforced dress code."[106] Most significantly, the editor recognized the dean's "double talk" and acknowledged that the deans played male and female students off of each other to ensure neither group was successful in its requests—one sex being allowed while the other was denied would be unfair. "If AWS [Association of Women Students] and MRC [Men's Residence Hall Council] want to become more than pawns of the dean's offices," he suggested, "they will have to coordinate their efforts in all-community matters such as this and then fight with all their resources for their beliefs." Collaborative efforts ensued, and in the fall of 1966, both the men and women of Penn State sported their Bermudas when and where they pleased.

■ As with so many elements of casual style, sweaters and shorts came from the gym. Their origins were unmistakable. As an 1896 columnist reporting on the "passing of the sweater into the feminine realms" noted, "the adoption of the sweater seems to indicate that athletics had become a serious pursuit among women." Yet, he continued, even "women who never walk when they have the requisite sum for a street car ride buy sweaters with airy indifference as to the original purpose of the garments." Much like their daughters and granddaughters would come to realize, the author believed, the "sweater is so really useful."[107] Collegians of both sexes used sweaters to diversify their wardrobes. Mixing and matching sweaters with blazers, pants, shorts, and the college woman's perennial favorite, pleated, plaid skirts, collegians increased their clothing options exponentially and made versatility a defining aspect of casual style.

Shorts, sweaters, and other borrowed sportswear put collegians at the center of a cultural standoff. One critic declared in 1957, "There has never been a sloppier-looking generation than this current crowd."[108] Despite such assertions, Americans across the board took to sweaters and shorts for occasions that ranged from active sports to Saturday barbeques to informal business meetings in the 1950s and 1960s. Americans had all but forgotten the origins of the garments. Categories that once defined how we bought and sold clothing lost their meaning. As the Fashion Group International told its members in 1972, "Indeed most of our old familiar labels are outmoded today: misses, juniors, budget, 'better,' loungewear, leisurewear, half-sizing, sportswear." They asked, "When was the last time you lounged? Or wore something from Sportswear for your favorite sport? . . . [American consumers] aren't the same customers so easily labeled by age, by income, by size."[109] By the second half of the 1960s, what Americans wanted was clothing that was not only easy to wear but also constitutive of their own individual identities and lifestyle.

# Conclusion

I have always thought of fashion as what people really wear for the
prevailing lifestyle, and the prevailing lifestyle today, at least in the Western world,
is American. McDonald's and motorcycles, camping and car life,
casual and do it yourself.
—Priscilla Tucker, contributing editor to *New York Magazine*, to the
Fashion Group International, 7 October 1975

This book is about more than clothing. It is about how, when, where, and why cultural standards are tested and then recast. At its most overt, casual style broke with thousands of years of tradition when we used clothing as a steadfast delineator of race, class, gender, and age. Things got a whole lot trickier in the twentieth century. Male (and female) CEOs sported ponytails to the office, and suburban seventh-graders turned their hat brim one tweak too far. At its most personal, casual style redefined our relationship to our clothes: how we want them to fit, what parts of our bodies we want them to cover, and when we want to replace them.

*Dress Casual* only cracks the surface of the 1960s, an era most of us associate with dressing down. In reality, the change was a long time coming. As historian Thomas Frank points out, the 1960s witnessed revolutions in business practices, manners, music, art, and taste that all shared "a common hostility for hierarchy, for inherited wisdom, and for technocratic ideas of efficiency." Armed with demographic studies and new ideas about market segmentation, manufacturers of many things, including clothing, came to "the now commonplace insight that targeting slightly different products to specific groups of consumers is significantly more effective than manufacturing one uniform product for everyone."[1] Retailers broke down departments and floors into sections and boutiques, a process that required "quite a bit of logic," according to the president of Bonwit Teller, Mildred Custin, in 1967. She acknowledged that the buying "market is so vast today that we are still constantly trying to distill the needs of the consumer."[2] Custin and her colleagues abandoned the educational mission of the last generation of retailers. Instead, these suburban executives aimed to meet, rather than shape, consumers' choices. More and more, these consumers shopped in the suburbs. By the end of the 1960s, over 50 percent of all sales in the United States occurred in the suburbs. The phenomenal rise in suburban living made "the shopping center indeed the new life style of retailing." In 1962, there were 6,500 shopping centers across the country; by 1972, there were 14,800. Sales went from $59 billion in 1964 to $140 billion in 1972.[3]

Not everyone was buying in the 'burbs. Department stores lifted the idea of the boutique from urban centers, but even after the shift to shopping malls, many downtown boutiques thrived. Some called it the "Off, Off, Off Seventh Avenue" trend or the boutique movement, and it offered buyers what a reporter described as "a little of this and a little of that, a little business and a little off the cuff, a little theatre and a little chaos."[4] In the midst of a rapidly splintering consumer market, retailers understood that some shoppers just couldn't be won over by parking lots and layaway. Executives actively discussed the potential for the boutique shopper (and all associated "nontraditional" shoppers) to influence American youth at large. In 1966, teenagers spent $15 billion on stuff—clothes, records, sporting equipment, beauty products. Retailers admitted, "We're no longer keep up with the Joneses, we keep up with the young."[5] Failure to keep up meant losing the market. An advertising executive believed the young American was a "customer in rebellion." "How about that sign of protest worn at Berkeley?" she asked. "It might be rephrased to read, 'I am a consumer. Don't fold, bend, or mutilate.'"[6]

Ripped jeans, roomy tunics, oversized army jackets, and long hair became more common on college campuses as the decade progressed and were adopted by students regardless of their ideological leanings. In 1968, one student noted, "On the Princeton campus, it is no longer possible to predict a man's politics by the length of his hair."[7] Long hair on men both intrigued and confused the old guard. In 1966, James Laver, a renowned historian of dress, recounted a recent experience to a group of fashion industry executives. He had walked "behind a young couple [who] were the same height, both with long hair, both with jeans, both with pull overs." He said, "I couldn't tell them apart, until I looked at them from the side." A step behind the times, Laver declared, "Clothes of the sexes are beginning to overlap and coincide."[8] Soon, centuries-old rules about how to restrain women's bodies also became breachable. "I find bras uncomfortable," a college woman told *Women's Wear Daily* in 1969. "Half the girls I know don't need them anyway. Besides, I think that clothes look better without them."[9]

The dilapidated dress of 1960s student culture played up an aspect of dressing down that had bothered critics for decades—and still does. Casual clothing was worn too big and too broken in, and college students were the long-standing, top offenders. Since the 1930s, many students interpreted casual style to be a "grubby button-down shirt or the over-sized sweater."[10] In 1945, a veteran attending Penn State described the "typical Joe College" man as "dressed in baggy brown trousers and plaid wool shirt topped by a beige corduroy jacket."[11] College women became known for their "frayed and faded blue jeans rolled to the knee, men's shirts with flapping tails, and moccasins, run down at the heel, broken and gaping, with toes protruding."[12] Shoes were worn until they fell apart. In 1959, another Penn Stater wrote of his sister's footwear, "The crazy cobblers of today may as well give up on their Trotters, Ki Yaks, trios, Leprechaun Boots, [and] Cantas Boots" because "they will still never be able to produce the hole-in-the-toe sneaker that graces the foot of every IN coed." When it came to beat-up sneakers, he added, "It makes no difference that they look like hell. Our girls want 'em and our girls'll have 'em. Even Dean McCoy can't change that."[13] Certainly not all collegians or proponents of casual style wore clothes until they were rags. Those who did further entangled "casual" with "sloppy" and helped to erode formal dress standards to allow for "worn in" to become a sought-after state. "New" and "clean" lost their universal appeal.

The versatility that endeared casual style to collegians in the 1930s and 1940s and then to their parents in the 1950s became the calling card of the American wardrobe in the 1960s. Our need for versatility killed off the remaining vestiges of formal dress because there just weren't enough occasions to warrant more than one suit or evening dress. In the oh-so-long history of people putting clothing on their bodies, the active pairing of sweaters, T-shirts, and sweatshirts with shorts, jeans, leggings, and the occasional skirt was a completely new way of thinking about and interacting with our dress. Versatile clothing was a practical way to maximize one's wardrobe, but it was also part of a broader shift in how we use clothing. With casual as the sartorial baseline, 1960s clothing increasingly became about "living out" one's individuality and lifestyle. An editor of *Money* magazine believed that the "ready availability" of a comfort-focused life, "even to people of quite modest incomes, is one of the features of modern life that would probably astonish our forefathers the most."[14]

Figure C1. In the 1970s and 1980s, fashion designers offered their own interpretations of casual style. This boomer-inspired sweatsuit by Norma Kamali from 1981 is her creative take on the kind of jersey knit fabric that had been used for gym garb since the mid-1920s. An editor of *Money* magazine believed that the "ready availability" of comfort, "even to people of quite modest incomes, is one of the features of modern life that would probably astonish our forefathers the most." Courtesy of The Museum at FIT.

The emphasis on individuality in dress that echoed through the 1960s became the rallying call of the 1970s. This was particularly pronounced for women, whose casual clothing became the darling of mass manufacturers and haute couturiers alike (see figure C.1). Whether their improved social status was real or perceived, American women in the 1970s bought and wore clothing to fit her needs. These clothes were easy to wash, easy to wear, and easy to replace. Referencing Christian Dior's body-constraining New Look, American designer Jeanne Eddy clarified, "Make no mistake about it. This is not 1947." Rather, her casually dressed client "believes in her individuality." Eddy declared, "Welcome to the 1970s . . . and the liberated woman. . . . How can you be a slave to fashion, if you're going to be a liberated woman?"[15] Many women found an open playing field intimidating. "Today is the age of options for American women," said trend-forecasting guru Laurel Cutler. "There is so much freedom that it is almost frightening. So frightening that many women, mostly older, mostly out of the big cities, are clinging to the old bonds, as though they were still there."[16] As the 1970s progressed, casual clothing increasingly dominated all aspects of women's dress. This meant fewer hats, pantyhose, and dress coats, and more of the stuff women wanted—pants, maxi dresses, and men's blazers. "The prevailing look is casual," said an industry observer. "It's the way we live today. Let's not spoil it by judging with antiquated standards." By the end of the 1970s, "antiquated standards" withered and died. The clothes were "loose, easy, and relaxed."[17]

Man-made fibers became primary to the manufacturing of casual clothing in the 1960s and 1970s. For decades, Americans struggled to accept these fibers as alternatives to natural ones. Advancements in the fibers themselves and the sustained efforts of chemical companies to work with designers to offer fashionable options turned the tide. In addition to their improved durability, washability, and fashionability, these fibers could be blended in innumerable combinations. Lycra scored big with consumers. Historian Regina Lee Blaszczyk writes in her history of DuPont's engagement with the fashion industry, "Riding on the cultural fetish for comfort, Lycra proved the flexible goose that laid the elastic golden egg."[18] The fiber's worldwide earnings grew from $6.3 million in 1964 to $30 million in 1969. Lycra was part of a wider turn toward man-made fibers. In 1969, textiles mills wove more man-made fibers than wool or cotton. Of the 11.9 billion pounds of fibers used in textile production in 1980, 73 percent were man-made, 26 percent were cotton, and 1 percent were wool.[19]

Not only were the fabrics made of man-made fibers easy to wear, but they fit the body in ways that were becoming increasingly desirable as the 1970s progressed. Fabrics made of Lycra hugged curves and snapped back into shape time and again. Polyester jersey draped the body to reveal more than flaunt, but unlike its cotton counterpart, its disco-bright colors never faded. In the 1980s, a cultural interest in the toned body turned workout wear—perhaps the most functional of casual clothes—into street fashion. Women wore sweatbands and cut-up sweatshirts, leggings, and bodysuits paired with colorful high-top sneakers and were completely unaware of the kinds of rules that hemmed in the choices of sporty collegians in the 1920s. "Fashion for fitness, body clothes for exercising, dance, or just for 'whatever' has exploded into a multi-billion dollar business," said a marketing man.[20] In the 1980s, tennis shoes accounted for more than 25 percent of the shoes sold in the United States.[21] By the end of the 1990s, casual style was in the office with few excuses. Some called it "business casual" and attributed it to the work culture of Silicon Valley, where twenty-something millionaires just didn't want to wear ties. Today, business casual is so pervasive that in many parts of the country, we turn to look twice at a man in a suit.

The wildfire that is business casual started amid a bigger and badder shift in the American clothing industry: the outsourcing of apparel production to overseas. Outsourcing reconfigured manufacturing from a national system of textile production in the middle South and garment production in New York and California to a highly mobile global network. Economist Shah rukh Rafi Khan writes, "Following the 'flying geese' model, the textile and clothing industry has been relocating to the cheapest sites of production."[22] The move offshore began in the late 1950s to places like Japan and Mexico, then went to Hong Kong and Taiwan in the 1960s, South Korea in the 1970s, and then onto Central America and South East Asia (Bangladesh, India, Sri Lanka, and Pakistan) in the 1980s, 1990s, and 2000s.[23] Cotton is still grown in the American South, but it's woven and made into T-shirts in China—the motherland of offshore clothing production.[24] In 1961, 3 percent of our clothing was imported; in 1985, 33 percent; in 2000, 90 percent.[25] In 2011, 97 percent of our clothing was imported.[26] It's not all sweatshirts, jean shorts, and tennis shoes, but, given our predilections, the vast majority of imports is casual clothing. Paradoxically, even though so few of our clothes are made on American soil, we still consider our casual clothing an indicator of a flourishing democracy. "Our clothing and our lifestyle have reflected each other—reinforcing our independence and individuality," as beauty-queen-turned-politician Bess Myerson put it in 1975. In twentieth-century America, she added, what we wear is not "a uniform of rank or class—as they were in many of the lands from which our people fled."[27]

Both economically and culturally, casual came at a cost. Ask the hosiery, millinery, or foundation garment industries—if you can find them. Who doesn't watch a well-costumed historical drama and get a bit nostalgic for such studied elegance? Social critics and grandmothers are still complaining that we have become a nation of slobs, more concerned with comfort than respectability. Americans in the nineteenth century prized respectability, diligence, and thrift. They also wore top hats and tailcoats to demonstrate just how respectable they were. Through our clothing, we live out social and cultural change in real time. A return of top-hatted "respectability" is unlikely. As a Radcliffe professor noted in 1920, once we have "known the joys and comfort of unrestricted movement, we will be very loath to go back."[28] Dressing to capture a bygone era is best left to historical reenactors and the patient connoisseurs who scour vintage stores for the kind of craftsmanship not found in our "Made in China" wardrobes.

The more heady and less observant among us complain that mass-produced, Gap-sold casual clothing has made achieving true individuality way too difficult and caused the masses to be "indistinguishable by their clothing."[29] There is no denying the lemming-like tendencies of some of us to dress in nearly identical outfits with slight variations of accessories, fabric, or color. Group participation and individual expression are not mutually exclusive. In fact, fashion theorist Georg Simmel argued in 1900 that our competing urges to "fit in" and "stand out" are what power the ever-churning wheels of the fashion industry. Mass production enables not only casual style but also personal style, and, as Yves St. Laurent put it, "style allows one to go beyond fashion."[30] Style is a crafted personal identity. That isn't done by Madison Avenue, or Seventh Avenue, or the culture industry, or one's social betters. No matter how bland or extravagant, an individual's style is his or her own. Jeans, cardigan sweaters, T-shirts, sandals, khaki shorts, and button-down-collar shirts are the foundation of the modern wardrobe, but the options to experiment are endless. Context is everything. Hence, the difference between the white T-shirt my uncle Bob wore and the one Marlon Brando wore. A peewee soccer coach in Poughkeepsie may wear the exact same pair of cargo pants as a mural painter in Seattle or a street musician in New Orleans. Each person picks and pairs these garments to suit their own needs and identities.

The rise of casual style demonstrates how, where, and why cultural standards change. Clothing is but one measuring tape; sexual mores, etiquette, and language could serve a similar purpose. Clothing is such a useful tool because it is profoundly visual and utterly inescapable. To put too much stock in the visual, however, allows changes in dress to be easily dismissed as going from "this" to "that." In the case of collegians, to merely compare the tweed knickers and slicked hair of *This Side of Paradise*'s Amory Blaine with the dirty, "COLLEGE" sweatshirt and uncombed mane of *Animal House*'s Bluto is just too easy. When visual change is studied in conjunction with the written historical record, seemingly arbitrary trends are emboldened by their contexts. Material culture analysis adds another layer to the study. All one has to do is hold a Harris tweed blazer to see how well-suited it is for rainy October mornings on the Princeton campus. Tracking seismic shifts in how we behave—whether those shifts are in what we wear, how we talk, or where we eat—is best done with a wide lens. John Held drawings, a graduate's coat in a museum in Pittsburgh, and a report from

Nassau Hall confirm that "coon-skin coats [were] almost as thick as flies" on the Princeton campus in 1924.[31] An integrated study that incorporates visual, written, and material sources allows for a nuanced understanding of how the processes that challenge cultural standards are lived out on the day-to-day level.

The mass adoption of casual style does not reflect cultural change. It is cultural change.

# Notes

## ABBREVIATIONS

FGIR  Fashion Group International Records, Manuscripts and Archives Division, Humanities and Social Sciences Library, New York Public Library

ODSAR Office of the Dean of Student Affairs Records, University Archives, Cecil H. Green Library, Stanford University, Stanford, Calif.

PSU  University Archives, Special Collections Library, Pennsylvania State University, State College, Pa.

PUA  Princeton University Archives, Seeley G. Mudd Library, Princeton University, Princeton, N.J.

RSCL  Rauner Special Collections Library, Dartmouth College, Hanover, N.H.

SLH  Radcliffe College Archives, Schlesinger Library, Radcliffe Institute, Harvard University, Cambridge, Mass.

UAUCB University Archives, Bancroft Library, University of California, Berkeley, Calif.

UAUM  University Archives, Elmer L. Andersen Library, University of Minnesota, Twin Cities, Minneapolis, Minn.

## INTRODUCTION

1. "Clothes Requirements for Radcliffe Are Simple," *Radcliffe News*, September 1938, 2.

2. I use the word "style" to describe a manner of dress that a person assembles from available garments "to define, to present, to communicate, to deceive, to play with," his or her identity (Maynard, *Dress and Globalisation*, 5). In my use, "style" is more enduring, personal, and expressive than "fashion," which I interpret to be the ever-changing assortment of garments produced by a multivectored interaction between consumers, the media, and manufacturing and retailing industries. This book suggests "style" is constitutive of one's larger lifestyle. This book has the goal of "penetrating the skin of style and drawing out its hidden meanings" (Hebdige, *Subculture*, 78).

3. The Fashion Groups, letter to Vice President and Mrs. Nelson A. Rockefeller, 10 March 1975, FGIR, box 99, folder 2.

4. Bledstein, *Culture of Professionalism*, 288.

5. "Enter: A New Candidate for Casual Honors," *Boot and Shoe Recorder*, 15 July 1945, 15.

6. Riesman, Glazer, and Denney, *Lonely Crowd*, 157.

7. "College Men Grow Fashion Conscious," *Daily Collegian*, 10 September 1952, 8.

8. Since the 1930s, the majority of Americans have self identified as middle class (see Brander, *Middle Class in America*). Efforts to quantify the middle class have take a backseat to questions of why and how all of these middle-class people "lived out" their own interpretations of middle-class culture. As cultural historians have shown, this has included what they've looked at (Savran, *Highbrow/Lowdown*; Seguin, *Around Quitting Time*), what they've listened to (Hayes, "White Noise"; Newman, *Radio Active*), and what they've eaten

(Diner, *Hungering for America*; Bentley, *Eating for Victory*; Belasco and Scranton, *Food Nations*). I argue that buying and wearing casual clothing was constitutive of the middle-class experience in the late 1940s and 1950s. In the 1960s, casual clothing served as the basis for an American wardrobe that was increasingly an expression of one's personal identity and one's lifestyle—both of which could be beyond the confines of class. My analysis is in keeping with that of Bill Osgerby, who argues in *Playboys in Paradise*, "Like Bourdieu's 'new petite bourgeoisie' of 1960s France, the ascending middle class of 1950s America established their status as a social formation through the consumption of distinctive cultural goods and signifiers" (81). As Marina Moskowitz writes in *Standard of Living*, "While material culture certainly did not create the middle class, it did identify the growing group, both to themselves and to others, on a national scale" (2). Casual clothing was a visual marker of one's middle-class status and a way that Americans lived out their social and cultural identities.

9. Alexis, "Changing Consumer Market."

10. Tobé Coller Davis, "The Business of Fashion," speech to Harvard Business School, ca.1957, Tobé Coburn School For Fashion Careers, Records, box 2, folder Advanced Retail Management folder, Manuscripts and Archives Division, Humanities and Social Sciences Library, New York Public Library; Stuart, *American Fashion Industry*, 19.

11. "Special Report to the Apparel Merchandise Manager," *Tobé Report*, 15 July 1965, 2.

12. For a discussion of the historiography of fashion and the body, see Corrigan, *Dressed Society*, chap. 4.

13. Veblen and Chase, *Theory of the Leisure Class*, 108. Though Veblen's bustled and bowler-hatted subjects seem nearly comical today, there's no underestimating the influence of trickle down theory when it comes to how we study style, fashion, and culture more generally. As historian of consumption Jackson Lears admitted, "Veblen cast(s) a long shadow" ("Beyond Veblen: Remapping Consumer Culture in Twentieth Century America" in Hollander, *Marketing*, 28). Those who came after Veblen, built upon, modified, and updated his downward dissemination of dress trends. German social philosopher Georg Simmel clarified that the individuals who participate in fashion are caught between "adaptation to society and individual departure from its demands" (*On Individuality and Social Forms*, 295). Yet, Simmel assures us that "Fashions are always class fashion, by the fact that the fashions of the higher strata of society distinguish themselves from those of the lower strata" ("Philosophy of Fashion," 187). French sociologist, Pierre Bourdieu's *Distinction* offers up what one economist generously called a "'trickle round' of tastes" (Trigg, "Veblen, Bourdieu, and Conspicuous Consumption," 106). Despite many theoretical trap doors, Bourdieu's omnipotent *habitus* ensures that the men of Princeton have an outrageously unfair advantage to define taste.

14. The social meaning of dress is too imprecise to be a language, as suggested by Alison Lurie in *The Language of Clothes*, and too mercurial to be affixed to a complex system of signs and signifiers, as proposed by Jean Baudrillard and Roland Barthes. Sociologist Susan Comstock documents the rise of jeans as a working-class phenomenon during the Depression in "The Making of an American Icon." See also the Global Denim Project at University College London for scholarship and art devoted to all things denim.

15. Blumer, "Fashion."

16. Horowitz, *Campus Life*, 6. For statistics on women attending college, see Solomon, *In the Company of Educated Women*, and Newcomer, *A Century of Higher Education for American Women*. While the number of women students grew significantly,

their percentage vis-à-vis men remained the same, averaging 40 percent for the period studied.

17. Pennsylvania State University, *Introducing Penn State*, 1955, 2. Founded in 1855, Penn State serviced only a few hundred students in early years of the century, but enrollment grew to nearly 5,000 in 1936 and 17,500 in 1961. Cal's growth was even more impressive. In 1900, enrollment topped 2,000, with nearly 40 percent of it women. In 1930, the total grew to more than 9,000 and then 23,000 in 1948. Cal was one of the largest schools in the United States. The role of the G.I. Bill in shaping the demographics of college attendance is beyond the scope of this book. For more information on the historical significance of the G.I. Bill, see Suzanne Mettler's *Soldiers to Citizens*.

18. "What the Young Man Will Wear," *Daily Princetonian*, 21 January 1924, 2.

19. University of California, Berkeley, Student Handbook, 1941, 4.

20. *Your Way Around Campus*, 1948, Women's Student Government Association and Association of Women Students Records, box 1, folder 16, PSU. This document is an orientation pamphlet.

21. "Cliffies Defend Female Sloppiness," *Harvard Crimson*, 29 November 1948, 3.

22. In terms of my research, Morehouse is the most underdeveloped of the schools studied here due to the general lack of sources at the Morehouse archives. Most of the material about Morehouse is taken from Spelman sources and an incomplete run of the student newspaper, *Maroon Tiger*. For a more detailed and fuller discussion of black male students during the first decades of the twentieth century, see chapter 6 of Martin Summers's excellent *Manliness and Its Discontents*.

23. Langston Hughes, "Cowards from the Colleges," *Crisis* 41, no. 4 (1934): 226. In 1929, Spelman, Morehouse, and Atlanta University entered into an agreement that allowed for students to share facilities, including classrooms and libraries, as well as some extracurricular activities. Around this time, Spelman discontinued its high school and many of its vocational programs to focus on transforming itself into a full-fledged liberal arts college for women.

24. Spelman College, *Fortieth Annual Circular of Spelman Seminary for Women and Girls*, 2.

25. Lowe, *Looking Good*, 3.

26. "Miss Vogue," *Spelman Spotlight*, 11 November 1960, 3. In "Black Women in the Academy," Alicia C. Collins writes that despite consistently outnumbering their male counterparts, female black students have remained "almost totally absent from the research literature." For an overview of the literature on black women in black colleges, see Marybeth Gasman's "Swept Under the Rug?"

27. The general lack of sources related to African American students at colleges such as Penn State, Cal, and Radcliffe make a comparison with historically black universities and colleges (HBUCs) nearly impossible. Indeed, I found little mention of black students at predominantly white schools. However, enduring dress codes at HBUCs allow us to assume that there was a more stringent regulation of casual clothing at these schools than at mixed-race schools. At Penn State, for example, black students might have been inhibited to dress down by unspoken social rules rather than specific regulation from administrators.

28. Sherry Suttles, letter to her mother, 3 October 1965, Sherry Suttles Papers, Barnard College Archives, Lehman Hall, Barnard College, New York.

29. For more on the Afro, see Walker, *Style and Status*, chap. 6. For more on black student unrest at Columbia, see Bradley, *Harlem vs. Columbia University*.

30. The history of Princeton in the twentieth century is meticulously documented in James Axtell's *The Making of Princeton University*.

31. "Style Contagion," *Saturday Evening Post*, 9 May 1931, 6.

32. "Undergraduate Dress at Princeton," *Princeton Alumni Weekly*, 1 January 1931, 720. For more on Princeton, see my work, including "The Evolution of Collegiate Clothing," and "Student Culture and Clothing."

33. "The Toggerie Worn at Princeton," *Harvard Lampoon*, 3 November 1926, 117. Harvard was not a primary case study, but serves as an important foil to both Princeton and Radcliffe. The writer of the *Post* article cited in note 31, confirmed the widely held impression that "Harvard holds to a tradition of careless dress—well-made clothes seldom dry-cleaned and never pressed."

34. "Types of Pretty Girls in the Freshman Class at Radcliffe," *Boston Journal*, 19 October 1905, 4.

35. "The Student Vagabond," *Harvard Crimson*, 14 October 1931, 4.

36. "Questionnaires Reveal Oddities of Fashions at Girls' Schools," *Daily Collegian*, 9 October 1934, 4. Many period sources use the term "girls" to refer to college women. I avoid using the term, except in its original context.

37. Hebdige, *Subculture*, 130.

38. Chapter 1 demonstrates the active negotiation between consumers and clothing producers, department store buyers, and fashion editors and presents the multivectored exchange that serves as the middle ground between production and consumption, which, as historian Susan Strasser points out, "are and always have been intertwined aspects of human cultures" (*Satisfaction Guaranteed*, 291).

39. Debby Applegate, "Henry War Beecher and the 'Great Middle Class': Mass-Marketed Intimacy and Middle-Class Identity," in Bledstein and Johnston, *Middling Sorts*, 111.

40. Important works on the cultural rituals of the middle class in the twentieth century include Aron, *Working at Play*; Hornstein, *Nation of Realtors*; Clarke, *Tupperware*; and Farrell, *One Nation Under Good*. For a recent and comprehensive history of the middle class, see Samuel, *American Middle Class*.

41. Veblen and Chase, *Theory of the Leisure Class*, 102. Cultural historians who have considered clothing as a primary lens for analysis include Kathy Peiss, Nan Enstad, Reggie Blaszczyk, Michael Zakim, and Thomas Frank.

42. Lipovetsky, *Empire of Fashion*, 4 .

43. Mrs. Perry Meyers, "A Million Small Dreams" (speech, New York City, May 1954), FGIR, box 76, folder 11.

44. Riesman, Glazer, and Denney, *Lonely Crowd*, 157.

45. "Men's Shoe Business Goes to College," *Boot and Shoe Recorder*, 19 August 1939, 40.

46. Chalmers Alexander to his parents, 4 May 1930, Chalmers Alexander Letters, PUA.

47. Ibid., 21 September 1928.

48. Marjorie Cherry to her parents, 30 April 1930, Marjorie Cherry Rohfleisch Papers, SLH.

CHAPTER ONE

1. Jaffe, Bronx, and Konter, *Collegiate*.

2. "Back-To-School Merchandising to Feature Knits," *Knitted Outerwear Times*, 16 July 1937, 45.

3. "On the Campus," *Princeton Alumni Weekly*, 3 April 1936, 567.

4. Fass, *The Damned and the Beautiful*, 126.

5. Flugel, *Psychology of Clothes*, 159.

6. National Center for Education Statistics, *120 Years of American Education*, 75.

7. Horowitz, *Campus Life*, 27, 33.

8. Frank, *Conquest of Cool*, 25.

9. Betsy Talbot Blackwell, "Remarks" (speech, 19 September 1969, New York City), FGIR, box 79, folder 1.

10. Nancy Murray to her parents, 25 September 1942, Anne Nancy Murray Morgan Papers, SLH.

11. Chalmers Alexander to his parents, 13 February 1931, Chalmers Alexander Letters, PUA.

12. D. H. Gardner survey results showed that in 1932, 50 percent of college men and 25 percent of college women in land-grant colleges were earning part of their way through school. See "Student in the Land-Grant College Survey." Throughout the period studied, industry groups and colleges tried to determine how much the average student spent on clothes. At Cal in 1940, $250 bought clothing for two years (see "Average Budget for Two-Year Period Computed," *Daily Californian*, 20 September 1940, 4). At Drexel, what a student studied influenced her expenditures. In 1940, average yearly clothing expenditures for Drexel women was $182.55. The women in the School of Business Administration spent on average of $282. The most frugal students were those in the Home Economics program who commuted from home and spent on average $164 (see Reba Irwell Edelman, "Trends in the College Wardrobe," *Journal of Home Economics*, May 1940, 315). Women who commuted to campus adhered to a more formal standard of dress, as they spent more time in the public eye than campus-bound students.

13. U.S. Department of Education, *Historical Summary of Faculty, Students, Degrees, and Finances.*

14. Osgerby, *Playboys in Paradise*, 31.

15. Rotundo, *American Manhood*, 1.

16. "Physical Care and Development of Students," *Princeton Alumni Weekly*, 17 February 1915, 450. For more on youth and sport, see Lewis, "Sport, Youth Culture and Conventionality," 132.

17. "Former Student Tells of Gymnasium at Yale," *Daily Californian*, 30 January 1912, 2. For more on gymnasium architecture at Yale, see Ryan "Architecture of James Gamble Rogers."

18. "The Sweater Fund," *Maroon Tiger*, April 1939, 1. In 1926, Morehouse students raised more than $3,000 to contribute to a gymnasium.

19. Morehouse College, *Annual Catalogue for Morehouse College for 1917-1918*," 4.

20. Summers, *Manliness and Its Discontents*, 244.

21. For more information on J. C. Leyendecker, see Turbin, "Fashioning the American Man," and Martin, "Great War." Also see Eric J. Segal, "Normal Rockwell." Segal analyzes the use of clothing and body type in Rockwell's work to argue that the illustrator heavily influenced the representation of white, middle-class masculinity.

22. Osgerby, *Playboys in Paradise*, 33. Osgerby ties the icon to the emergence of a leisure-based consumption for men. Two important works on masculinity, consumption, and magazines are Pendergast, *Creating the Modern Man*, and Clark, *Creating the College Man.*

23. Cooper, *Why Go To College?*, 3.

24. "Column from Vanity Fair," *Pelican*, January 1925, 50. *Vanity Fair* remained a key part of the American publishing world through the 1920s, but it hit economic troubles during the Depression, and its readership was folded into *Vogue*'s in 1936. *Vanity Fair* was revived in 1983 and remains a popular magazine today. For more information on *Vanity Fair*, see Ward, "Vanity Fair Magazine and the Modern Style." Both *Froth* and *Pelican* were more dependent on advertising dollars than student newspapers. Student editors used fashion columns to attract both readers and advertisers.

25. "The College Girl's Wardrobe—What Should Go in the Freshman Trunk," *New York Times*, 9 September 1906, 26.

26. Lowe, *Looking Good*, 60.

27. Gordon, "Gibson Girl Goes to College," 211.

28. Mary Bunker diary, 6 February 1890, Mary Hawthorne White Bunker Papers, SLH.

29. Gilman, Hill, and Deegan, *Dress of Women*, 39.

30. "A Fresh-Air Cure," *Radcliffe News*, 18 January 1934, 2.

31. Ellen Gerber traces the slow development of intercollegiate women's sports in "Controlled Development of Collegiate Sport."

32. Warner, *When the Girls Came Out To Play*, 220.

33. Gordon, *Make it Yourself*, 115.

34. Patricia Campbell Warner details the entire history of the gym suit in her excellent essay, "The Gym Suit," in Cunningham and Lab, *Dress in American Culture*, 140–79.

35. "What the Young Man Will Wear," *Daily Princetonian*, 21 January 1924, 2.

36. "To the Frosh," *Froth*, September 1923, 13. For an overview of how the collegian has been portrayed in American literature, see Boys, "American College in Fiction."

37. "College Shops Braced Again for Fall Rush," *New York Times*, 15 August 1960, 26.

38. U.S. Department of Education, *Historical Summary of Faculty, Students, Degrees, and Finances.*

39. "The Flapper," *Froth*, May 1922, 14. Also see Yellis, "Prosperity's Child."

40. Horowitz, *Campus Life*, 123.

41. Fass, *Damned and the Beautiful*, 22, 231.

42. "Instruction Says Modern Styles Are More Sensible," *Daily Californian*, 7 July 1925, 4.

43. The 1920s saw a boom in clothing manufacturers, mostly small operations working either for themselves or a bigger maker. These "jobbers" lived a tumultuous existence as increasingly powerful retailers balked at advanced orders and other manufacturers undercut bids. For more on the development of fashion production in the first decades of the century, see the chapter "Manufacture of the Fashion System," in Fine and Leopold, *World of Consumption*. For an explanation of the significance of clothing to business history and a review of literature, see Robinson, "Importance of Fashions in Taste." Historian of clothing Elizabeth Wilson points to mass production as essential to the existence of modern fashion. She writes, "Originally fashion was largely for the rich, but since the industrial period the mass-production of fashionably styled clothes has made possible the use of fashion as a means of self-enhancement and self-expression for the majority" (*Adorned in Dreams*, 12).

44. "The Princetonian's Dictionary," *Harvard Lampoon*, 3 November 1926, 114.

45. C. Ford, "Ready-Made College Types," *Vanity Fair*, September 1926, 72.

46. "Balanced Attire for Radcliffe: Fashion Linked to Comfort Reigns at College," *Boston Post*, 21 January 1931, 19.

47. "Symposium on Hats," *Radcliffe News*, 21 November 1924, 3.

48. "Fifty Year Review," *Radcliffe News*, 7 January 1938, 3.

49. Spelman College, *Promotional Pamphlet*, 1931.

50. "The Old-Fashioned Girl," *Campus Mirror*, 15 December 1927, 2.

51. "Our Dress," *Spelman Messenger*, March 1912, 3.

52. "Shoes and Ships and Sealing Wax," *Campus Mirror*, 15 November 1928, 4.

53. "Gone Are the Days When," *Campus Mirror*, 21 June 1935, 2.

54. "How to Sell to College Boys," *National Retail Clothier*, 11 September 1924, 60.

55. This advertisement ran in *Vanity Fair* in October 1926 on page 35.

56. "Princeton Grad Flayed," *Daily Princetonian*, 1 October 1926, 2.

57. "Clothes Make the Man," *Froth*, October 1928, 11. In *Letters to His Son on the Art of Becoming a Man of the World and a Gentleman* (1774), Philip Stanhope, Lord Chesterfield (1694–1773), offers a range of advice, including on the topics of dress and fashion.

58. Cooke, *Brooks Brothers*, 64. The term "Oxford" was used to describe the button-down-collar shirt, but it takes its name from the weave of the fabric. The weave was named for the University of Oxford. Other important clothiers include Kuppenheimer (1876) and Hart, Schaffner & Marx (1872). Both firms were headquartered in Chicago and manufactured for their own retail stores around the country. For more information see Kuppenheimer promotional pamphlet, *Tempered Clothing*, 1921.

59. Fitzgerald, *This Side of Paradise*, 73, 77. Shoemakers Franks Brothers, founded in 1865 and also based in New York, advertised in the *Daily Princetonian* as early as 1903. For more on the modern influence of Brooks Brothers on menswear, see Mears, *Ivy Style*, and Banks and de La Chapelle, *Preppy*.

60. Hazel Hunkins to her mother, 1 December 1910, Hazel Hunkins-Hallinan Papers, SLH.

61. "Compulsory for Campus," *Vogue*, 15 August 1937, 38.

62. Herman's Smart Shop advertisement, *Daily Californian*, 15 September 1927, 5.

63. "Mrs. Goodall Predicts Styles," *Radcliffe News*, October 24, 1929, 3.

64. "College Shops Braced Again for Fall Rush," *New York Times*, 15 August 1960, 26. This article identifies the origins of the college shop as trunk shows to college campuses.

65. Edith Culver diary, 16 January 1919, Edith Culver Hagar Papers, SLH.

66. Ibid., 8 February 1919.

67. Entry for 5 September 1929, Bailey Patterson Sweeney Diary, SLH.

68. Ibid., 31 December 1930.

69. Ibid., 2 July 1931.

70. Ibid., 11 January 1930.

71. "Those Wheaton Girls," *Radcliffe News*, 10 November 1939.

72. "Silverwoods Uses Windows to Attract College Trade," *National Retail Clothier*, 19 July 1938, 86.

73. Rhea Seeger, "Want Their Co-eds Neat and Natural," *Chicago Daily Tribune*, 26 December 1937, G3.

74. "Fall Styles for College Show War's Impact," *New York Times*, 5 August 1942, 15.

75. Nystrom, *Fashion Merchandising*, 211.

76. "College Shops Launch Campus Fashions in New York," *Tobé Report*, 17 August 1939, 11.

77. "College Shops: The Undergraduate as Salesgirl and Customer," *Life*, 8 September 1941, 63.

78. "Clothes? Here Is Advice on Some Musts," *Daily Collegian*, 7 September 1939, 4. For more information on the rise of the academic study of marketing, see Leach, *Land of Desire*, 157–64.

79. "Chicago Company Announces College Fashion Contest," *Radcliffe News*, 12 January 1934, 1.

80. "Student Wins Honors," *Emporia Gazette*, 19 April 1934, 16.

81. "Student Designers Given Opportunity to Sell Work," *Adelphi College Fortnightly*, 11 October 1940, 2. Similar articles appeared in the *Radcliffe News* and the *Daily Collegian*. Women were more commonly polled or asked to participate, but manufacturers and retailers enticed men with contests and giveaways. In 1924, the well-established clothier Hart, Schaffner & Marx sponsored an essay-writing contest on the "theory of wages" with a prize of $5,000. See "Hart, Schaffner & Marx," *New Student*, 29 November 1924, 4.

82. This advertisement ran in the *New York Times* on 16 August 1931 on page 10. In this context, the word "smart" is synonymous with "fashionable."

83. "College Shops Open with New Smart Styles," *Chicago Daily Tribune*, 4 August 1941, 16.

84. "Shopping Suggestions," *New York Times*, 25 August 1935, X5.

85. "College Shops Braced Again for Fall Rush," *New York Times*, August 15, 1960, 26.

86. "Silverwoods Uses Windows to Attract College Trade," *National Retail Clothier*, 19 July 1938, 86.

87. *Tobé Report*, 25 September 1938, 3.

88. "College Shops: The Undergraduate as Salesgirl and Customer," *Life*, September 8, 1941, 63.

89. Joan Projansky to Mary Beth Little, Office of Publicity Papers, box 9, folder 63, SLH.

90. "Radcliffe Version of Campus Fashions Decrees Snuggly Woolens for Winter Boston Breezes," *Radcliffe News*, 2 September 1941, 3.

91. "Guide to Recreational Reading," *Campus Mirror*, December 1939, 4.

92. "History of the Class of '37," *Campus Mirror*, May/June 1937, 3.

93. "Voted Most Popular," *Vogue*, 15 August 1937, 38.

94. "35% Now Wear Slacks on Campus," *Vogue*, 15 August 1939, 153.

95. Osgerby, *Playboys in Paradise*, 49. *Esquire* sidestepped accusations of effeminacy and dandyism because so much of its content focused on heterosexual sex and featured illustrated pinup girls. For more on *Esquire*, consumption, sex, and masculinity, see Osgerby, "Bachelor Pad as Cultural Icon." For a study of turn-of-the-century bachelordom, see Chudacoff, *Age of the Bachelor*. The partnership between the Princeton student publication and *Esquire* was in March 1947.

96. "Gentleman's Home Journal Finds Favor at Harvard," *Radcliffe News*, 20 October 1933, 3.

97. "Living on Campus in '48," *Esquire*, September 1948, 38.

98. "Best Idea of the Week," *Boot and Shoe Recorder*, 23 August 1941, 29.

99. "Radcliffe Girls Model Fashions during Summer," *Radcliffe News*, 14 October 1938, 3. The hoopskirt is just one example of students rejecting styles pushed by fashion editors and store buyers. The Edwardian-era-inspired fashions of the late 1930s were of little interest to college women, who preferred streamlined, comfortable clothing for day and body-revealing cuts in eveningwear.

100. "Record Sales," *Tobé Report*, 31 August 1939, 1.

101. "Casualness Becomes Keynote of Fall Fashions as Sloppy Sweaters Drop from Parade," *Daily Californian*, 20 September 1940, 2.

102. On the history of undergarments in the twentieth century, see Farrell-Beck and Gau, *Uplift*.

103. "Woolknits Gets Opinions on Knit Goods from *Mademoiselle*'s College Board," *Knitted Outerwear Times*, 2 August 1941, 1.

104. "Shopping Suggestions," *New York Times*, 25 August 1935, X5.

105. Office of Publicity at Radcliffe College, memo, 10 September 1947, Office of Publicity Papers, box 6, folder 61, SLH.

106. "We Cover the New York College Shops," *Tobé Report*, 12 August 1943, 9.

107. *Tobé Report*, 17 July 1952, 5.

108. "New Clothes for the College Set," *Berkeley Daily Gazette*, 18 September 1948, 21.

109. Jeane Eddy, "Fall Fashion Group Commentary," (speech, 6 June, 1970, New York City), FGIR, box 79, folder 4.

110. "Clothes? Here is Advice on Some Musts," *Daily Collegian*, 7 September 1939, 8.

111. *Tobé Report*, 24 August 1938, 2.

112. The giant cart motif was used by McCreery's in New York in 1943, and a knitting area was a suggestion by *Tobé* to retailers in 1940.

113. "New York College Shops in Full Regalia," *Tobé Report*, 14 August 1952, 7.

114. "Cry Is for Better Grade, Even on a Smaller Budget," *Women's Wear Daily*, 3 June 1942, 14.

115. "Coed Requires Ten Outfits," *Daily Collegian*, 9 July 1941, 4.

116. *Daily Californian*, 27 February 1942, 11.

117. *Tobé Report*, 14 August 1942, 2. Radcliffe women took to wearing shorts because "such grace and line should not be hidden under slacks which also waste material vitally needed for the army and navy." Radcliffe women calculated that if they bought shorts instead of pants, they would save enough yardage to make 125 to 250 uniforms. The administrators of the college voted unanimously to allow the women to wear shorts as part of their war effort. See "Army Clad in Garb Donated by College," *Radcliffe News*, 6 February 1942, 1.

118. "College Promotions Receiving Big Play," *Boot and Shoe Recorder*, 15 August 1942, 14.

119. *Tobé Report*, 16 July 1942, 7.

120. Nancy Murray to her parents, 27 February 1943, Anne Nancy Murray Morgan Papers, SLH.

121. "Victory Models Can Be a Waste, Too," *Campus Mirror*, November 1942, 2.

122. "A.I. Clothes are Wartime Necessity," *Berkeley Daily Gazette*, 7 August 1944, 27.

123. Pennsylvania State University, *Home Economics Handbook*, 1942, 6. For more on the impact of war regulations on the dress of Radcliffe students, see "War Has Caused Refashioning of Nearly All College Clothes," *Radcliffe News*, 16 October 1942, 2. Many married students were on coed campuses such as Penn State and Cal during the war. Wardrobes of young wives were a bit more dressy and versatile than those of their unmarried colleagues.

124. Nancy Murray to her parents, 17 September 1943, Anne Nancy Murray Morgan Papers, SLH.

125. Ibid., November 1944. The correspondence to her parents about her permanent occurred over a several-week period in early November 1944.

126. "We Nominate for Oblivion," *Daily Californian*, 16 February 1940, 5.

127. "Men Preen Feathers as Females Snicker," *Harvard Crimson*, 11 May 1950, 4.

128. "More on Blue Jeans," *Carnegie Tartan*, 26 February 1946, 2. Carnegie Tech became Carnegie Mellon in 1967.

129. "Male Fashion Board Bans Bustles," *Radcliffe News*, 12 November 1948, 1.

130. "Damsels Defy Dior," *Harvard Crimson*, 13 November 1953, 1.

131. "Seven New Looks for the Smart Girl In and Out of College," *Vogue*, 15 August 1946, 32.

132. "New York College Shops in Full Regalia," *Tobé Report*, 14 August 1952, 7.

133. "Work and College Linked by Styles," *New York Times*, 6 August 1943, 12.

134. "Office and School Get Same Styles," *New York Times*, 12 August 1954, 14.

135. "Silhouettes and Profiles," *Berkeley Daily Gazette*, August 16, 1940, 17.

136. *Tobé Report*, 8 August 1957, 6.

137. "Shop Will Cater to Junior Sizes," *New York Times*, 24 August 1960, 35.

138. "Scattered Goods Bane of Shoppers," *New York Times*, 25 September 1955, 1.

139. References to Bergdorf Goodman's new shop are found throughout the fashion press at the time. *Tobé Report* covered it and the store's research on the market on 19 April 1956. For more information on the usage of the word "junior," see Harder and Thompson, "Who or What Is a Junior?"

140. McCardell, Leser, and Cashin facilitated the popularization of sportswear. These women began their careers in the 1930s and became prominent names in the 1940s and 1950s. For more on their influence, see Iverson, " 'Early' Bonnie Cashin"; Robinson, "American Sportswear"; and Yohannan, *Claire McCardell*. For information on the role of retailers in the promotion of these designers, see Webber-Hanchett, "Dorothy Shaver," and Leipzig et al., "It's a Profession That Is New."

141. *Tobé Report*, 30 August 1952, 4.

142. "New York College Shops in Full Regalia," *Tobé Report*, 14 August 1952, 8.

143. "Casual Wear for Men Is Gaining Favor," *Gettysburg Times*, 5 April 1955, 8.

144. "College Shops Braced Again for Fall Rush," *New York Times*, 15 August 1960, 26.

145. "High Schoolers Heed Call of College Shop," *New York Times*, 2 September 1967, 25.

146. "The College Shop Scoreboard," *Tobé Report*, 19 August 1948, 7a.

147. Kay Cornith, "Listen to Young America," speech to Fashion Group International, 14 February 1962, FGIR, box 77, folder 10. Work on teenage girls and the history of American girlhood include Schrum's excellent *Some Wore Bobbysox* and Douglas's *Where the Girls Are*.

148. National Center for Education Statistics, *120 Years of American Education*, 75.

149. "Campus Togs Extend Past Campus," *New York Times*, 6 August 1959, 87.

150. George Sokolsky, "The Vassar Problem," *St. Joseph News-Press*, 16 May 1962, 8. Sokolsky was a nationally syndicated Associated Press writer.

CHAPTER TWO

1. "Fashion News From Our Vassar College Reporter," *Tobé Report*, 25 July 1940, 4.

2. Agnes Edwards to her parents, 15 August 1917, Agnes Edwards Partin Papers, UAUCB.

3. "Do Not Let Your Daughters Wear Them," *Spelman Messenger*, May 1917, 6.

4. "Little Paternalism at Michigan," *Daily Princetonian*, 10 March 1928, 2.

5. "On the Campus," *Princeton Alumni Weekly*, 14 April 1950, 10.

6. "Dean Discusses Changes in Undergraduate Dress," *Daily Princetonian*, 13 December 1963, 1.

7. Social Policies Suggestions for the Use of Women at University of California, poster, November 1952, Records of the Office of Student Activities, box 16, folder 15, UAUCB.

8. "Sport Coat More Valuable to Man's Wardrobe," *Daily Californian*, 24 September 1937, 7.

9. "Most Male Students Prefer Informal Sports Clothes," *Centre Daily Times*, 26 April 1948, 3.

10. Osgerby, *Playboys in Paradise*, 14.

11. "Myself and My College," *Spelman Messenger*, March 1926, 2.

12. "Too Many Restrictions at Spelman," *Spelman Spotlight*, 15 December 1961, 2.

13. "Girls Take to Boys Clothes for College Wear This Fall," *Boston Traveler*, 25 July 1940, 23.

14. The most useful sources for understanding administrators' policies on student dress are found in the papers of deans of men, of women, and of students. Records of student conduct boards, dorm councils, and freshmen orientation materials also offer documentation of rules for dress and more general guidelines for what was worn on campus and when. For more information on the history of deans of men and women, see Schwartz, "Reconceptualizing the Leadership Roles of Women" and "Rise and Demise of Deans of Men."

15. For more on the early origins of the suit, see Kuchta, *Three-Piece Suit*.

16. "The Well Dressed Man Crossing the Ocean," *Harvard Crimson*, 7 April 1923, 2. According to fashion historian Anne Hollander, the suit is the incarnation of modernity and has remained remarkably unchanged by time. Variations in pant length, coat cuts, fabric preference, and accessories are "constant internal changes," subject to the whims of fashion. Its basic form, however, has endured. In "shifting their social and sexual meaning," argues Hollander, "tailored suits have proved themselves infinitely dynamic, possessed of their own fashionable energy." The presence of the suit in male wardrobes, she posits, has stabilized men's dress in a way that women's clothing has not enjoyed. See *Sex and Suits*, 4.

17. "From the Raw Material," *Men's Wear*, 11 May 1910, 80.

18. "In Matters of Campus Clothes," *Princeton Alumni Weekly*, 23 February 1901, 509. An important source on changes in menswear during this period is Diane Maglio's master's thesis, "From the Gilded Age to the Jazz Age." Many fashion historians believe that the Norfolk was one of the first jackets styled to be worn with nonmatching pants. The term "tweed" comes from the Scottish word "tweel," a handwoven cloth, though many historians mistakenly attribute the word's origins to the Tweed River. The most popular variety is Harris tweed, made in the Scottish islands of Lewis, Harris, Uist, and Barra in the Outer Hebrides.

19. "Fashion Front," *Froth*, February 1934, 32.

20. Anderson, "This Sporting Cloth," 171.

21. Osgerby, *Playboys in Paradise*, 35.

22. Cromwell and Wilson, *Arms of Industry II*, 615. This source documents how the government secured the materials to make uniforms and details the evolution of various military uniforms.

23. "The General's Uniform," *New York Times*, 29 February 1920, E2.

24. For more information on the post–World War I clothing market, see Sonneborn, "Price Factors in Men's Ready-to-Wear Clothing"; Agnew, *United States in the World Economy*; and Glover, *Development of American Industries*.

25. "No Radical Change in Styles," *National Retail Clothier*, 19 July 1923, 56.

26. Fitzgerald, *This Side of Paradise*, 43. With the first sale of a short story, Fitzgerald bought a pair of white flannel pants and kept them until 1934.

27. "Princeton Boys Dress in a Uniform," *Life*, 6 June 1938, 31.

28. Advertisement, *National Retail Clothier*, 19 May 1932, 117.

29. "Fashion Front," *Froth*, February 1934, 32.

30. "A Guy Has to Be Cagey," *Daily Californian*, 16 February 1940, 4.

31. Edwards Voorhies to President Sproul, 3 March 1942, CU Collection 14, box 7, folder 6, UAUCB.

32. *Red and Black*, 26 February 1925, 1.

33. Stanford University, *Stanford Handbook*, 1940, 40.

34. Morehouse College, *Annual Catalogue for Morehouse College*, 5. Historian Joe Martin Richardson argues that "discipline in black school[s] was usually more strict that in the average American college" as a means of fostering success. He writes, "A college education was looked upon by blacks as a difficult and sacred attainment." See *History of Fisk University*, 84.

35. Dumas and Hunter, *Benjamin Elijah Mays*, 32.

36. Carter, *Walking Integrity*, 367.

37. Miller, "Past, Present and Future."

38. "Be Men Not Dinosaurs," *Atlanta University Bulletin*, July 1922, 2.

39. "Commencement Address," *Spelman Messenger*, July 1931, 3.

40. "Appropriate Clothing for Different Occasions," *Spelman Messenger*, December 1924, 3.

41. "How to Be the Best-Dressed Man," *Froth*, May 1931, 28.

42. "Round the Town," *Froth*, October 1947, 28.

43. "We Bite. Why Do They?," *Daily Californian*, 30 August 1925, 2.

44. "More Class Headgear," *Daily Californian*, 20 August 1925, 2.

45. "In Defense of Old and Dirty Cords," *Daily Californian*, 30 August 1925, 2. As with many campus fashion trends, dissenters also voiced their opinions. Harry V. Hopkins (Class of 1926) responded to this letter to the editor, "For a man who is supposed to be educated at the place of a college man to be going about in filthy trousers for the sake of tradition or any other excuse looks to me like an incompatibility" (*Daily Californian*, 17 September 1925).

46. Pennsylvania State University, *College Customs and Co-Ediquette*, 1942, 4. This pamphlet was reproduced on a yearly basis at Penn State through the 1940s. Information in the pamphlet varied slightly by year.

47. "Most Male Students Prefer Informal, Sport Clothes," *Centre Daily Times*, 26 April 1948, 12.

48. "Safety Valve . . . Protest Wearing Ties in Dining Hall," *Daily Collegian*, 23 September 1953, 5.

49. "Dorm Dress Rule: Passing the Buck," *Daily Collegian*, 13 March 1954, 4.

50. "More Students Write on Nittany T-Shirt Issue," *Daily Collegian*, 18 November 1958, 4.

51. Stanford University, *Stanford Handbook*, 1957, 34.

52. "Sloppy Dress Alarms the Princeton Tiger," *Daily Princetonian*, 29 October 1959, 2.

53. "To the Editor," *Daily Collegian*, 18 November 1958, 4.

54. "Informality Pervades Campus Dress," *Daily Princetonian*, 22 February 1954, 1.

55. Hollander, *Sex and Suits*, 40.

56. Nancy Murray to her parents, 18 January 1943, Anne Nancy Murray Morgan Papers, SLH.

57. "Pulling in the Slack," *Radcliffe News*, 15 October 1943, 2.

58. Radcliffe College, *Red Book*, 1957, 34.

59. Spelman College, *Freshman Handbook*, 1955, 17.

60. Spelman College, *Student Handbook*, 1959, 6.

61. *List of Rules*, memo, Dean of Women Papers (General Vertical File), folder "Women in General," PSU.

62. Students of Davidson Hall to Dean of Students, 11 July 1967, CU Collection 14, box 16, folder 15, UAUCB.

63. "Why College Girls Dress That Way," *New York Times*, 10 December 1944, SM28.

64. My discussion of the Seven Sisters is largely limited to the comparison of Vassar, Smith, Wellesley, Radcliffe, and Barnard. Mount Holyoke and Bryn Mawr were largely off the radar in terms of mainstream press coverage and the Ivy League social scene. Mount Holyoke was highly religious, and its students had the general reputation of being morally conservative. Bryn Mawr women had the reputation of being unfashionable nerds.

65. R. Le Clerc Phillips, "The Problem of the Educated Woman," *Harper's Monthly*, December 1926, 61.

66. "Why College Girls Dress That Way," *New York Times*, 10 December 1944, SM28.

67. "Why College Girls Dress That Way," *New York Times*, 7 April 1946, 104. Note that the title was used for two different articles in the paper, one in 1944 and a second published in 1946.

68. "Girls Take to Boys Clothes for College Wear This Fall," *Boston Traveler*, 25 July 1940, 23.

69. "Why College Girls Dress That Way," *New York Times*, 10 December 1944, SM28.

70. "Cry Is for Better Grade Even on a Smaller Budget," *Women's Wear Daily*, 3 June 1942.

71. *Tobé Report*, 20 August 1942, 3.

72. "Navy Wants 'Low Down' on Fashion; Radcliffe Reassure Puzzled Gobs," *Radcliffe News*, 15 February 1946, 3.

73. "Cry Is for Better Grade Even on a Smaller Budget," *Women's Wear Daily*, 3 June 1942.

74. "We, the Women," *Daily Collegian*, 10 January 1942, 6.

75. Elsie M. Murphy, "What's What for Spring," speech to Fashion Group International, 17 November 1941, FGIR, box 144, folder 13.

76. For more on gender norms and sexuality during wartime, see Honey, *Creating Rosie the Riveter*, and Hegarty, *Victory Girls*. For information on wartime rationing, see Delano in "Making Up for War." Wartime rationing did not apply to cosmetics that were deemed crucial to women's morale, such as lipstick. According to Delano, "war paint" both mitigated public fears that women in war industries were too masculine and conveyed an assertive, sexual, air of independence.

77. "Yours Truly—The Public," *Sweet Briar News*, 20 May 1942, 2.

78. "Social Paradox," *Radcliffe News*, 15 November 1935, 2.

79. "Girls Take to Boys Clothes for College Wear This Fall," *Boston Traveler*, 25 July 1940, 23.

80. "Off Campus Entertainment Varies," *Harvard Crimson*, 5 September 1940, 3.

81. Marilyn Whisman, "In the City," *Mademoiselle*, August 1944, 191.

82. "Students Like Slacks at Home—Not in School," *Radcliffe News*, 1 May 1942, 1.

83. Radcliffe College, *Red Book*, 1947–48, 84.

84. Giles's diary entries are published in Florence M. Read's *Story of Spelman College*, 67.

85. "Miscellaneous Suggestions," *Atlanta University Bulletin*, April 1912, 24.

86. Watson and Gregory, *Daring to Educate*, 89.

87. Spelman College, *Fortieth Annual Circular*, 6.

88. Watson and Gregory, *Daring to Educate*, 89. Spelman also had high school students until the late 1920s. A certain degree of the administrators' diligence was due to the ages of these younger students.

89. Margaret Lowe argues that Spelman students "adopted the dress, deportment, and speech of Christian womanhood," they were able to move "beyond the limitations society imposed and to fight for economic and political inclusion" (*Looking Good*, 60).

90. "Do Not Let Your Daughter Wear Them," *Spelman Messenger*, May 1917, 6.

91. Dorothy Kneeland Clark Autobiography, "Around the World in 75 Years," SLH. Wellesley graduate Dorothy Kneeland worked as the assistant to Read and recorded her impressions in this unpublished memoir.

92. "Shoes and Ships and Sealing Wax," *Campus Mirror*, 15 November 1928, 4.

93. Dorothy Kneeland Clark Autobiography, "Around the World in 75 Years," 68, SLH.

94. "A Better School or an Etiquette Library," *Campus Mirror*, 15 October 1928, 3.

95. "That Spelman Look," *Campus Mirror*, April 1947, 6.

96. Spelman College, *Freshman Handbook*, 1946, 6. Melvin Wade explores coronation ceremonies in African American culture in order to show how this culture used dress and religious ceremony as a response to white hegemony in the colonial era: "In their systematic relations with other social systems," he writes, "the black communities of colonial and antebellum New England embodied a model of social adaptation based on cultural creolization" ("'Shining in Borrowed Plumage,'" 217).

97. Manley, *Legacy Continues*, 20.

98. "The Biffer Party," *Campus Mirror*, January 1947, 3.

99. Spelman College, *Freshman Handbook, 1955–1956*, 16. In the chapter on Spelman in her book *Born Colored*, graduate Erin Goseer Mitchell details the dress regulations at the college in the early 1950s.

100. Spelman College, *Student Handbook*, 1959-1960, 14.

101. Mitchell, *Born Colored*, 141.

102. Ibid., 150.

103. Cal students to director of housing services, 16 December 1966, CU Collection 14.2, box 2, Dress Standards folder, UAUCB.

104. "Relax in Slacks of Many Kinds," *Daily Californian*, 20 September 1940, 3.

105. Pennsylvania State University, *College Customs and Co-Ediquette*, 1942, 6. In *Odd Girls and Twilight Lovers*, Lillian Faderman discusses the war as an influence in the acceptance of pants. She argues that in post–World War II culture, pants became a "symbol that allowed women who identified as lesbians to identify each other" (126). On dude ranches as another impetus for the mass acceptance of blue jeans and the marketing of jeans to women, see Wilson, "American Cowboy Dress," and Kaplan, Tigerman, and Adamson, *California Design*, 248.

106. "The Anti-Slack Campaign," *Daily Collegian*, 7 December 1945, 2.

107. "Dates for Slackers to Slacken," *Daily Collegian*, 7 December 1945, 1.

108. "Letters to the Editor," *Daily Collegian*, 14 December 1945, 5. The song "Mademoiselle from Armentiers" was a French army song from the nineteenth century, and the English version (with its well-known "Hinky Dinky Parlez Vous" chorus) was popularized in World War I. During World War II, the song was later incorporated into a routine by comedians Flanagan and Allen, who added additional lyrics to the first English version.

109. Putnam, *Lady Lore*, 17.

110. *Vogue*, 15 August 1940, 76.

111. "Fashion's Fight for Femininity Will be Futile If Campus Queens Wear Shirts and Jeans," *Freelance Star*, 15 August 1951, 4.

112. Pearl O. Weston (dean of women) to "Young Women of Penn State," 13 April 1948, Dean of Women Papers (General Vertical File), PSU.

113. Marjorie Mousley, "We the Women," *Daily Collegian*, 27 April 1948, 4.

114. "Dean Urges Coed Tidiness in Dining Common Dress," *Daily Collegian*, 14 April 1948, 4.

115. Social Policies Suggestions for the Use of Women at University of California, poster, November 1952, CU Collection 14, box 16, folder 15, UAUCB.

116. Sharon Takanoto (president of Cunningham Hall) to Mrs. Donnelly of Housing Services, 24 October 1966, CU Collection 14.2, box 2, Dress Regulations folder, UAUCB.

117. Women of Spens Black dormitory to Dean of Women, 25 October 1966, CU Collection 14, box 16, folder 17, UAUCB.

118. "In Loco Imprisonment," *Daily Collegian*, 27 January 1967, 10. This title was mocking the phrase *in loco parentis*.

119. "Sports Wear May Get Into Offices," *City Herald*, 5 April 1955, 11.


CHAPTER THREE

1. "Talks after Dates, Sunday Teas, Social Baths are 'Bloom of Dormitory Life,'" *Radcliffe News*, 29 April 1938, 3.

2. In her book *College Girls*, Lynn Peril writes, "At the turn of the twentieth century, the college girl was as much an object of public interest as Civil War battlefields or the natural wonders of Yosemite," and images of "dormitory life were sold alongside other, perhaps more august subjects" (311).

3. "An English View of American College Life," *New Student*, 20 December 1924, 15.

4. Marjorie Cherry to her parents, 18 September 1928, Marjorie Cherry Rohfleisch Papers, SLH.

5. Chalmers Alexander to his parents, 14 May 1931, Chalmers Alexander Letters, PUA.

6. Nancy Murray to her parents, 25 September 1942, Anne Nancy Murray Morgan Papers, SLH.

7. Porter Butt, "Some Implications of Housing." For a detailed discussion of the housing dilemma at colleges and universities, see Carman, "Campus Issues and Problems."

8. Office of Housing and Food Services, "Report on Housing," 1979, General Vertical File, Housing and Food Services/General folder, PSU.

9. Penn State University, *La Vie*, 1921, 449.

10. "Cities Rise More Beautifully from Their Ashes," *Maroon Tiger*, October 1935, 5.

11. Edwards Hartshorne. "Undergraduate Society," 321. Hartshorne was the chief U.S. educational officer who was charged with reopening German universities in the zones that the United States occupied after World War II.

12. "Radcliffe Group Life; Fun in the Dormitories for Residents and Other Girls," *Boston Herald*, 21 March 1909, 13.

13. Office of Publicity, "Report on Housing," 26 January 1951, Collection RG10, box 7, folder 66, SLH.

14. Robb Carson to his parents, 1 September 1904, Robb and John Carson Letters, PUA.

15. Stanford University, *Stanford Handbook*, 1951, 20.

16. Eleanor Stabler to Dorothy, 10 November 1910, Eleanor Stabler Brooks Papers, SLH.

17. "Jolly-Ups to Usher in New Social Season Soon," *Radcliffe News*, 26 September 1941, 3.

18. "Harvard Given Sex Pointers," *Boston America*, 8 October 1934, 22. This newspaper article is a summary of a book published by Ralph Cohen, a supposed Harvard student, that was titled *The Harvard Man's Guide-Book*, 1934.

19. Eleanor Stabler to Dorothy, 10 November 1910, Eleanor Stabler Brooks Papers, SLH.

20. Unidentified student to parents, 24 October 1915, College of Health and Human Development Records, box 26, folder unnamed, PSU. It is apparent from the content of the letters that the unidentified student was female and had a brother who attended the college.

21. "Impressions of a Fire Drill Prove Source of Amusement," *Radcliffe News*, 6 October 1927, 4.

22. "Disturbing Experience," *Daily Californian*, 9 March 1948, 2.

23. Entry for 27 September 1929, Bailey Patterson Sweeney Diary, SLH.

24. Dorothy Kneeland Clark Autobiography, "Around the World in 75 Years," SLH.

25. Stone, "College Girl and the Depression."

26. Stanford University, *Stanford Handbook*, 1936, 121.

27. University of Michigan, *Freshman Handbook*, 1930, 14.

28. Students Affairs and Services Committee, memorandum, "Interviews with Campus Administrators," box 30, Social Regulations folder, ODSAR. This memo is undated but is likely from the early 1960s. Catherine Gidney compares administrators' regulation of male and female dorm residents and explains how and why female students policed their dorm mates in "Dating and Gating." This study is one of the few scholarly inquiries into the history of dorm life.

29. "My Freshman Adjustment at Spelman College," *Campus Mirror*, December 1939, 3.

30. "Editorial," *Radcliffe News*, 19 January 1917, 2.

31. Edith Culver to her parents, 15 January 1921, Edith Culver Hagar Papers, SLH. At many dorms, the doors were locked at curfew and women returning late would have to wake up the housemother.

32. Students Affairs and Services Committee, memorandum, "Interviews with Campus Administrators," box 30, Social Regulations folder, ODSAR; Stanford University, *Stanford Handbook*, 1940, 38.

33. "The Ten Commandments: Dormitory Edition," *Jack-O-Lantern*, 1929, 30.

34. "The College Girl's Wardrobe—What Should Go in the Freshman Trunk," *New York Times*, 9 September 1906, 26.

35. "Campus Wearwithal," *Esquire*, September 1947, 105.

36. Pennsylvania State University, *Home Economics Handbook, 1939*, 4.

37. "Regardless of Rain," *Daily Californian*, 26 January 1940, 5.

38. "War Has Caused Refashioning of Nearly All College Clothes," *Radcliffe News*, 16 October 1942, 3.

39. Pennsylvania State University, *Home Economics Handbook, 1943*, 5.

40. Agnes Edwards to her parents, 3 October 1920, Agnes Edwards Partin Papers, UAUCB.

41. Advertisement of Jordan Marsh, *Radcliffe Daily*, 8 May 1931, 4.

42. "Average Budget for Two-Year Period," *Daily Californian*, 20 September 1940, 7.

43. "No Odd Coats," *Daily Princetonian*, 20 February 1941, 2; Chalmers Alexander to his parents, 3 December 1928, Chalmers Alexander Letters, PUA.

44. "Ninon Stresses Simplicity," *Daily Californian*, 15 September 1933, 8. For more on the relationships between mothers and daughters, see an important work by Linda W. Rosenzweig, "The Anchors of My Life." Rosenzweig discusses intergenerational tensions around changes in how and where women consumed.

45. "Clothes Requirements for Radcliffe Are Simple," *Radcliffe News*, September 1938, 1.

46. "Fog and Sun Styles Are on Parade on Wheeler Steps," *Daily Californian*, 19 April 1950, 4.

47. Stanford University, *Stanford Handbook*, 1940, 141.

48. Hazel Hunkins to her mother, 11 January 1913, Hazel Hunkins-Hallinan Papers, SLH.

49. Ibid. Rather than "shamuses," Hunkins most likely meant charmeuse, a satin-finished, drapable fabric usually made of silk and used for formalwear.

50. Ibid.

51. Ibid., 12 April 1913.

52. Chalmers Alexander to his parents, 6 April 1932, Chalmers Alexander Letters, PUA.

53. Ibid., 19 January 1930.

54. Ibid., 16 September 1928.

55. Ibid., 10 February 1932.

56. "The Californiac," *Daily Californian*, 6 September 1927, 2.

57. "Dress by Mary Hampton," *Berkeley Daily Gazette*, 2 August 1938, 14.

58. "The H.C.L in W.K. New Haven," *Harvard Crimson*, 16 April 1920, 3.

59. "Popularity of Home Laundry Is Aid to Baggage Business," *Radcliffe News*, 8 November 1935, 3.

60. Fredrick W. Baker diary, 10 February 1937, Fredrick W. Baker Papers, RSCL.

61. Nancy Murray to her parents, 16 August 1943, Anne Nancy Murray Morgan Papers, SLH.

62. Ibid., 19 August 1943.

63. Ibid., 24 November 1943.

64. Pennsylvania State University, *Home Economics Handbook, 1939*, 6.

65. Chalmers Alexander to his parents, 13 February 1931, Chalmers Alexander Letters, PUA.

66. Ibid., 22 September 1928.

67. Ibid., 13 February 1931.

68. Radcliffe College, *Brochure on Radcliffe*, 1934, 2.

69. In the modern dorms built on campuses such as Radcliffe and Penn State in the mid-1930s, laundry rooms became standard. Universities strove to make campus laundry services an affordable option for students. Notre Dame bragged of its St. Michael's laundry service, the cost of which the university incorporated into boarding fees, and claimed that it was appreciated by the students for its "affordable rates" and "quick sure service . . . an angle much appreciated by returning servicemen who know how difficult it has been to get laundry service anywhere." See Gerald Hoar, "Laundry Services Both School and

Student," *College and University Business*, 9 January 1946. Gerald Hoar was the manager of the Laundry and Dry Cleaning Departments at the University of Notre Dame and regularly wrote for the publication.

70. "Home Laundry Service," *Harvard Crimson*, 18 March 1949, 3. Administrators' decisions relating to dormitories impacted local business. At Penn State, for example, administrators were also accused of dragging their heels in dorm building in order to keep local landlords supplied with tenants.

71. "In the Laundry," *Spelman Messenger*, January 1908, 3.

72. "The Laundry's Soliloquy," *Campus Mirror*, November 1929, 3.

73. For a detailed history of Du Pont's role in the development of the synthetic fiber industry, see Hounshell and Smith's *Science and Corporate Strategy*. For a briefer discussion of the firm's marketing of nylon, see Hounshell and Smith, "Nylon Drama." For a summary of the rayon industry in the 1920s, see Darby, *Rayon and Other Synthetic Fibers*. In "Rayon and Its Impact on the Fashion Industry," Carmen N. Keist discusses the rayon industry's difficulties in selling the fiber to American consumers, which were due, in part, to its use of terms such as "artificial" as descriptors, the consumer's confusion about the fiber's many names, and the perception that cheaper meant lower quality. Jane Schneider conducted a similar study on the public perception of polyester. See "In and Out of Polyester." For a succinct history of polyester, see Brown and Reinhard, "Polyester Fiber."

74. "Regardless of Rain," *Daily Californian*, 26 January 1940, 3.

75. "Gals Wear What They Want," *Daily Collegian*, 13 September 1953, 7.

76. *Tobé Report*, 12 August 1948, 4.

77. Ruth Ayres, "Our Clothing and Textiles Challenge for the Future," speech to National Meeting of College Teachers of Textiles and Clothing, 22 June 1968, UAUM. For more information on the marketing strategies of the natural fiber industry during the 1940s, 1950s, and 1960s, see O'Donnell, "Selling California Cotton"; McNally, "American Wool Problem"; and Jacobson and Smith, *Cotton's Renaissance*.

78. "Home Ec Weekend to Feature Fabrics," *Daily Collegian*, 26 March 1953, 4.

79. "Sauntering with Vi," *Daily Californian*, 9 August 1927, 3.

80. An important work of scholarship on the history of home sewing is Sarah A. Gordon's *Make It Yourself*.

81. Helvenston and Bubolz, "Home Economics and Home Sewing," 311. The authors note that by 1939–40 there were more than 348 home economics programs in the country with 36,521 students in the subject. More than 95 percent of them were women.

82. Unknown student to parents, 7 February 1916, College of Health and Human Development Records, box 26, folder unnamed, PSU.

83. "Information," *Spelman Messenger*, November 1908, 2.

84. Hazel Hunkins to her mother, 25 February 1912, Hazel Hunkins-Hallinan Papers, SLH.

85. Ibid., 7 March 1912.

86. For a discussion of college women, dieting, and clothing, see Lowe, *Looking Good*, chap. 6.

87. Chalmers Alexander to his parents, 10 February 1932, Chalmers Alexander Letters, PUA.

88. Agnes Edwards to her parents, 29 September 1917, Agnes Edwards Partin Papers, UAUCB.

89. Ibid., 28 January 1918.

90. Ibid., 8 October 1917.

91. "Dearie" to Mabel Smith," 10 November 1907, Mabel Kent Smith Papers, SLH.

92. Unknown student to parents, 5 March 1917, College of Health and Human Development Records, box 26, folder unnamed, PSU.

93. "Our Dress," *Spelman Messenger*, March 1912, 3.

94. Edith Culver to her mother, 2 January 1919, Edith Culver Hagar Papers, SLH.

95. Hazel Hunkins to her mother, 23 November 1912, Hazel Hunkins-Hallinan Papers, SLH.

96. Edith Culver to her mother, 16 March 1919, Edith Culver Hagar Papers, SLH.

97. "Radcliffe Auctions Off Lost and Found Goods," *Boston Post*, 20 December 1925, 14.

98. "Lost and Found Auctions Sell Beaver Jackets for Eleven Cents, Pens for Five," *Radcliffe News*, 19 February 1940, 1.

99. The exchange of letters between Chalmers and Thad occurred between early November and early December 1930.

100. Agnes Edwards to her parents, 1 June 1919, Agnes Edwards Partin Papers, UAUCB.

101. Chalmers Alexander to his parents, 1 December 1928, Chalmers Alexander Letters, PUA.

102. "The New Owenites," *Radcliffe News*, 29 November 1919, 2.

103. Edith Culver to her parents, 12 December 1918, Edith Culver Hagar Papers, SLH. A "college ice" was another term for an ice cream sundae.

104. Eldridge, *Co-Ediquette*, 164.

105. Stanford University, *Stanford Handbook*, 1936, 122.

106. Agnes Edwards to her parents, 14 October 1917, Agnes Edwards Partin Papers, UAUCB.

107. Marjorie Cherry to her parents, 12 March 1929, Marjorie Cherry Rohfleisch Papers, SLH.

108. Hazel Hunkins to her mother, 23 November 1912, Hazel Hunkins-Hallinan Papers, SLH.

109. "Radcliffe Promises '52 Varied Year Featuring Teas, Dances, Harvard," *Radcliffe News*, September 1948, 1.

110. Richard Eberhardt to father, 22 April 1924, Richard Eberhardt Papers, RSCL.

111. "Clothes for Double Life Necessary at 'Cliffe; Separates Are Popular," *Radcliffe News*, September 1950, 1.

### CHAPTER FOUR

1. Chalmers Alexander to his parents, 17 May 1932, Chalmers Alexander Letters, PUA.

2. "On Your Toes," *Campus Mirror*, November 1946, 1.

3. In the last decades of the nineteenth century, the tuxedo became a popular alternative to tailcoats worn with striped pants, a waistcoat, and a bow tie. Tailcoats came in a range of cuts, each being the proper for a specific type of event. For example, a black coat featuring tails much longer than the front of the jacket was worn to formal evening affairs, while a morning coat, which was often grey and featured a more tapered cut, was correct clothing for daytime events. Tuxedos had fewer accessories than tailcoats and were generally only worn for evening events.

4. Smith, "Rating and Dating."

5. Bailey, *From Front Porch to Back Seat*, 9.

6. "Urges Franker Discussion of Sex by Men and Women," *Cleveland News*, 1 January 1927, 6.

7. Penn State University, *Penn State Woman's World*, 14.

8. "La Dame Facon," *Froth*, April 1947, 30.

9. "Future of Jr. Prom Termed 'Unlikely,'" *Daily Collegian*, 14 November 1962, 1.

10. "Juniors Anticipate Thrills of First Prom," *Radcliffe News*, 18 February, 1921, 1.

11. "The Prom," *Froth*, April 1921, 13.

12. "School and College," *Boston Evening Transcript*, January 13, 1912, 8.

13. "Taft's Son Ill at Yale," *New York Times*, 27 January 1909, 1.

14. "Notes from the Colleges," *Daily Princetonian*, 6 April 1910, 2.

15. Chalmers Alexander to his parents, 12 March 1929, Chalmers Alexander Letters, PUA.

16. Bishop, "Higher Learning in America," 56.

17. Williams, *Princeton Stories*, 26.

18. Edith Culver to her parents, 6 May 1922, Edith Culver Hagar Papers, SLH.

19. "Feminine Institution," *Harvard Lampoon*, 29 October 1936, 108.

20. "Vassar Seniors Cancel Prom for Lack of Suitable Dates," *Harvard Crimson*, 12 February 1942, 1.

21. Cohen, *Harvard Man's Guide-Book*, 11.

22. "The 'Cliffie Girl: An Instructor's View," *Harvard Crimson*, 18 April 1953, 3.

23. "Perfect Prom Partners and How to Recognize Them," *Radcliffe News*, 10 February 1928, 3.

24. "How to Ask a Man to the Prom," *Radcliffe News*, 10 February 1928, 3.

25. "That Yen against Harvard Boys," *Boston Herald*, 23 October 1938, 15. In the late 1940s, two important books were written by Dartmouth men that give insight into the student culture of the Seven Sisters and the Ivy League. See Jones, Moss, and O'Riley, *For Men Lonely*, and Jones and O'Riley, *Weekend*, which provides women with an insider's take on what to expect—and to wear—on a visit to Harvard, Yale, Princeton, et cetera.

26. Mother to Eleanor Gilbert, 24 October 1914, Eleanor Gilbert Montgomery Papers, SLH.

27. Eleanor Gilbert to her mother, 9 January 1917, Eleanor Gilbert Montgomery Papers, SLH.

28. "Vassar," *Harvard Lampoon*, 26 February 1937, 66.

29. "Marionettes Are Novelty at Wellesley Prom," *Radcliffe News*, 21 May 1926, 2. Tony Sarg was a well-known puppeteer in the 1920s, and such acts, along with well-known musical groups, were hired to perform at elite school's proms.

30. "On Being Hosts," *Daily Princetonian*, 3 March 1921, 2.

31. "The Junior High-Hatters," *Froth*, April 1923, 13.

32. "Editorial," *Froth*, May 1929, 16.

33. Unidentified student to parents, 5 November 1915, College of Health and Human Development Records, box 26, folder unnamed, PSU.

34. "Editorial," *Froth*, May 1929, 16.

35. "On With the Dance!," *Froth*, April 1926, 19.

36. "Spelman Dances," *Maroon Tiger*, January 1935, 4.

37. Mitchell, *Born Colored*, 165.

38. Agnes Edwards to her parents, 3 October 1920, Agnes Edwards Partin Papers, UAUCB.

39. "Report of the International House," 15 May 1935, CU Collection 14.1, box 3, untitled folder, UAUCB.

40. "Students Took Steps Similar to Charleston for Gymnasium Work," *Daily Californian*, 9 February 1925, 4.

41. Assembly Dance Committee, "Minutes from a Meeting," 11 May 1940, CU Collection 14, box 1, folder 26, UAUCB.

42. Entry for 25 October 1928, Bailey Patterson Sweeney Diary, SLH.

43. Burnham Beckwith to his mother, 11 May 1923, Burnham Beckwith Papers, Stanford Student Letters and Memoirs Collection, University Archives, Cecil H. Green Library, Stanford University, Stanford, Calif.

44. "Splitting Tickets," *Daily Collegian*, 10 October 1952, 2.

45. For more information on the social and cultural significance of fraternities on the college campus, see Syrett, *Company He Keeps*. See also Little, "Extra-Curricular Activities," which offers insight into the beginnings of fraternities at black colleges and their role in replacing the literary society as the primary means of social networking.

46. Cooper, *Why Go to College?*, 125.

47. "Are Fraternities Usurping the Morehouse Spirit?," *Maroon Tiger*, May 1935, 2.

48. For more on fraternity men as consumers, see Swiencicki, "Consuming Brotherhood."

49. Waller, "Rating and Dating Complex." Waller's study was one of the first systematic studies of date selection and inspired more than fifty years of scholarship. Samuel Harman Lowrie offers a survey of early literature inspired by Waller in "Dating Theories and Student Responses."

50. College administrators studied the benefits and detriments of Greek life and published their findings in journals for other administrators and for their specific academic discipline. See Deakins, "In Defense of Fraternities," and Vreeland, "Social Relations in the College Fraternity."

51. Dean of Undergraduate Division to Mrs. Raymond, 14 December 1923, CU Collection 14.1, box 3, Fraternities General folder, UAUCB.

52. Memorandum to Dean of Students at University of California at Berkeley, 28 February 1955, CU Collection 14, box 1, folder 10, UAUCB.

53. Richard Eberhardt to father, 2 April 1924, Richard Eberhardt Papers, RSCL.

54. Ernest Martin Hopkins to Jessie Douglas, 18 April 1931, Records of Dartmouth College, Office of the President, Administration of Ernest Martin Hopkins, Papers, 1930–31, RSCL.

55. Agnes Edwards to her mother, 1 September 1917, Agnes Edwards Partin Papers, UAUCB.

56. "How to Get into a Sorority," *Froth*, February 1960, 22.

57. Marjorie Cherry to her parents, 2 October 1930, Marjorie Cherry Rohfleisch Papers, SLH.

58. Eldridge, *Co-Ediquette*, 77.

59. Agnes Edwards to her parents, 20 October 1917, Agnes Edwards Partin Papers, UAUCB.

60. Ibid., 9 February 1919.

61. Ibid., 12 June 1918.

62. Ibid., 3 March 1918. For a history of women hosting social events for servicemen during World War II, see Winchell, *Good Girls*.

63. University of California, Berkeley, *Panhellenic Handbook*, 1942, 6.

64. Ibid., 1948, 12.

65. Kelley, *College Life and the Mores*, 14.

66. "College Sororities: They Pose a Social Problem," *Life*, 17 December 1945, 97.

67. Thorn, "Veterans and Fraternities," 8.

68. "Slams Dink Tradition," *Daily Princetonian*, 22 October 1946, 2.

69. Horowitz. *Campus Life*, 274.

70. Ballou, *Etiquette at College*, 232.

71. Fass, *The Damned and the Beautiful*, 196.

72. Ibid., 127.

73. Koritz, *Culture Makers*, 65. In her chapter on the Charleston, Koritz argues that the dance was part of a larger concern over the interconnectedness of jazz music, rhythm, and sexuality. Popularized by 1923 by an all-black musical called *Runnin' Wild*, "the Charleston," according to Koritz, "moved from the stage to the audience with amazing speed and showed unusual staying power" (66). With it came the necessity for a discussion on art forms crossing social and racial lines, which was a topic of great importance in the culture of the 1920s.

74. Ibid., 71.

75. "This Charleston," *Froth*, October 1925, 17.

76. "Charleston Menace Stalking Colleges," *New Student*, 27 January 1926, 1. The *New Student* was a progressive national student newspaper.

77. Bailey, *Front Porch to Back Seat*, 86.

78. "Co-ed Commandments," 1945, Women's Student Goverment Association and Association of Women Students Records, PSU; entry for 11 November 1929, Bailey Patterson Diary, SLH. Bailey Patterson married Harvard graduate Arthur Sweeney in June 1932. She documented in her diary the first time they had sex: "On Friday, July 8 Arthur actually took me and put an end forever to my virginity! Going the limit is greatly overrated I think, but at least it didn't hurt me a bit. That was because Arthur had been doing it gradually. As a matter of fact, I am enjoying our intercourse more each time as we get more adjusted to each other. I seem to know so pitifully little and Arthur has told me an awful lot about myself. I didn't even know we had really gone the limit until he sat up and said, 'Well darling, how does it feel?' When I asked what, he laughed and kissed me tight and said, 'You're not a virgin any longer, darling, you're a truly married woman!'" (entry for 10 July 1932, Bailey Patterson Sweeney Diary, SLH).

79. Entry for 1 March 1929, Bailey Patterson Sweeney Diary, SLH.

80. For a history and discussion of administrators' policies on student drinking, see Atkinson and Brugger, "Do College Students Drink Too Much?" Atkinson and Brugger were deans of students at the University of California at Los Angeles.

81. Entry for 4 March 1931, Bailey Patterson Sweeney Diary, SLH.

82. Ibid., 6 July 1929. Applejack is a brandy that was very popular among college students in the late 1920s. Chalmers Alexander reported that his friend Bill Priestly commonly drank Apple-Jack. For more on students' opinions on drinking, see Barrett, "College Seniors and the Liquor Problem."

83. Chalmers Alexander to his parents, 14 March 1929, Chalmers Alexander Letters, PUA.

84. The exchange of letters between Hopkins, Bridges, and Bridges' father, is found in the Records of Dartmouth College, Office of the President, Administration of President Ernest Martin Hopkins, Papers, 1930–31, RSCL.

85. "Clothes Requirements for Radcliffe Are Simple," *Radcliffe News*, September 1938, 1.

86. Stratton and Schleman, *Your Best Foot Forward*, 192. Stratton was the former executive director of the Girl Scouts, and Schleman was the dean of women at Purdue University.

87. "Simple Basics Make Best 'Cliffie Costume in Uncertain Climate," *Radcliffe News*, September 1948, 1.

88. Ohio Wesleyan University, *Student Handbook, 1944*, 17.

89. Robb Carson to his parents, 23 November 1907, Robb and John Carson Letters, PUA.

90. "Return of Full Dress Suit Means More Pumps," *Boot and Shoe Recorder*, 5 September 1931, 24.

91. Chalmers Alexander to his parents, 22 March 1931, Chalmers Alexander Letters, PUA.

92. "Prom Promises," *Froth*, April 1924, 15.

93. "Fashion Notes for Gullible Readers," *Pelican*, September 1924, 4.

94. Pennsylvania State College, *College Customs and Co-Etiquette*, 1948, 12.

95. "BMOC's Set to Dazzle Dates with Latest in Campus Fashions," *Daily Collegian*, 4 April 1941, 4.

96. "Ninon Stresses Simplicity for Sophistication in Fall Dresses," *Daily Californian*, 15 September 1933, 8.

97. Women's Executive Board, "Minutes from a Meeting," 10 March 1953, CU Collection 281, box 2, folder 6, UAUCB.

98. "Mad Rush Climaxes Dance Preparations," *Daily Collegian*, 6 November 1951, 1.

99. "Informality Pervades Campus Dress," *Daily Princetonian*, 22 February 1954, 1.

100. "A Look Back," *Town Topics*, 7 April 1957, 14.

101. Spelman College, *College Handbook, 1946–1947*, 20.

102. "Pages from a Co-Ed's Diary," *Campus Mirror*, 2 June 1935, 15. Mousseline is a very sheer fabric much like muslin, used in layers for formalwear.

103. Hazel Hunkins to her mother, 20 January 1913, Hazel Hunkins-Hallinan Papers, SLH. Hunkins most likely meant "charmeuse" not "shamuses." Charmeuse is a satin-weave fabric usually made of silk that is used for draped formalwear.

104. "Junior/Senior Prom," *Spelman Messenger*, May 1951, 29.

105. Eldridge, *Co-Etiquette*, 38.

106. Pennsylvania State College, *College Customs and Co-Etiquette*, 1942, 12.

107. "Fashion Flashes," *Campus Mirror*, December 1944, 4.

108. Agnes Edwards to her parents, 20 October 1917, Agnes Edwards Partin Papers, UAUCB.

109. Ibid.

110. Ibid., 19 October 1918.

111. "Through the Looking Glass," *Daily Collegian*, 20 September 1948, 5.

112. Putnam, *Lady Lore*, 18.

113. "La Dame Facon," *Froth*, April 1947, 30.

114. On the term "look" to describe fashion styles, see Ackerman, "Use of 'Look' in the Language of Fashion."

115. See *Froth*, November 1947.

116. "Girls Don't Like Hobble Skirts," *Harvard Crimson*, 29 September 1947, 1.

117. "Hemlines Headlines," *Froth*, November 1947, 14.

118. Bailey, *Back Seat to Front Porch*, 3. Key elements of what Bailey calls a "national system of culture" are "national systems of communication, transportation, and economy, the extension of education and the forces of urbanization and industrialization." Most significant, she argues, is the emergence of the media, complete with magazines, radio, movies, and television, that provided a common ground for American youth.

119. *Froth*, November 1947, 24.

120. Stratton and Schleman, *Your Best Foot Forward*, 193.

121. Butz, *Unsilent Generation*, 50. This book received much attention upon its release, and its title became a term collegians used to describe themselves. Political journalist James Ridgeway named his popular blog after the book.

122. *Women's Wear Daily*, 7 October 1965, 4.

CHAPTER FIVE

1. "Student Body Endorses Shorts for Daily Wear," *Dartmouth*, 15 May 1930, 1.

2. "Comfort, Not Principle," *Dartmouth*, 15 May 1930, 2.

3. "What College Boys Are Wearing and What to Sell Them," *National Retail Clothier*, 16 August 1928, 62.

4. "Rolled Socks, Short Skirts Are Defended," *San Francisco Call and Post*, 14 February 1922, 14.

5. "Big College Market," *Knitted Outerwear Times*, 9 August 1941, 12.

6. *Tobé Report*, 7 September 1938, 1.

7. "The Accessories of College Life," *Harvard Lampoon*, December 1912, 181.

8. Robert C. Ruark, "Let's Spin a Yarn," *Reading Eagle*, 5 June 1957, 20.

9. Margaret De Mille, "Speech on Fall Fashion," speech to Fashion Group International, 23 June 1955, FGIR, box 76, folder 14.

10. "Male Fashion Board Bans Bustles, Condemns Slacks, Sweaters and Jeans," *Radcliffe News*, 12 November 1948, 1.

11. Peter Curtis, "Critical Coed Coordinates," *Froth*, October 1959, 28.

12. "Radcliffe College Athletes 'Blossom Out' in Shorts," *Boston Post*, 30 October 1938, 15.

13. "Ye Turtle Necke Sweater," *Froth*, October 1932, 21.

14. *Tobé Report*, 9 July 1942, 15.

15. "Safety Valve . . . on Bermuda Shorts," *Daily Collegian*, 29 September 1955, 4.

16. "Short Subjects," *Esquire*, August 1955, 90.

17. In his seminal work, *The Psychology of Clothes*, J. C. Flugel delineates two main "systems" of apparel: costume (fixed) and fashion (modish). Costume is traditional wear for many nonwestern countries and rarely changes. Modish clothing is marked by perpetual change and flourishes in capitalist societies. According to Flugel's definition, knitwear was primarily costume until the twentieth century. Important works on the history of knitting in the United States include Anne L. Macdonald's *No Idle Hands* and Susan M. Strawn's *Knitting America*.

18. "Sweaters and Jewelry and Scarves and Hats Keep Filling in Wardrobes, Aid to Attract," *Harvard Crimson*, 5 September 1940, 4.

19. "Back to School Merchandising to Feature Knits," *Knitted Outerwear Times*, 16 July 1937, 32.

20. "Why College Girls Dress That Way," *New York Times*, 7 April 1946, 104.

21. "Snappy Sweaters Go to Office, Campus or Links," *Atlanta Daily World*, 11 October 1946, 4.

22. Martin and Koda, *Jocks and Nerds*, 139. According to Martin and Koda, the letterman's sweater lost its social clout when high school students began wearing the garment in the 1940s.

23. James Rosenthal to his parents, 9 April 1907, James Max Rosenthal Papers, University Archives, Pusey Library, Harvard University, Cambridge, Mass.

24. Hazel Hunkins to her mother, 19 November 1910, Hazel Hunkins-Hallinan Papers, SLH.

25. Radcliffe College, *Red Book*, 1914, 4.

26. Pennsylvania State University, *La Vie*, 1925, 45. A similar system was set up at Radcliffe. In 1917, the Department of Physical Training awarded active women chevrons to be sewn onto gym uniforms. *Radcliffe News* explained that the "[t]he Honor Point System is a new thing here—it has been found to work very successfully in other colleges—it means that any girl who takes the full work in gymnasium and out-door sports may win honors" (ibid., 29 September 1917). Participation in various sports yielded a certain number of points. When a woman accumulated 10 points, she was given a blue chevron; 15 earned a red one; a star was given for 20 points; and permanent honors were given for 20 points earned in just three semesters.

27. Agnes Edwards to her parents, 2 March 1918, Agnes Edwards Partin Papers, UAUCB.

28. Ibid., 29 September 1917.

29. Ibid. Cretonne is a thick, durable cotton fabric that is usually patterned and used for home furnishing.

30. "News from Other Colleges," *Radcliffe Daily*, 29 March 1929, 2.

31. According to Patricia Campbell Warner (*When the Girls Came Out to Play*), the advent of knitting machines of the 1870s led to the development of jersey, which was first used for tennis dresses late in that decade.

32. Osgerby, *Playboys in Paradise*, 34.

33. "California Knitwear Manufacturers Emerge as Increasingly Important," *Knitted Outwear Times*, 6 May 1937, 12. In his essay "California Casual," William R. Scott discusses the rise of California as a leader in men's fashion and its influence on American style in general. See also "California . . . A Land to Dream On," *Holiday Magazine*, December 1954.

34. Osgerby, *Playboys in Paradise*, 101.

35. "Questionnaires Reveal Oddities of Fashions at Girls' Schools," *Daily Collegian*, 9 October 1934, 1. This study was published in the August issue of *Harper's Bazaar* and summarized in this student newspaper.

36. "Seniors to Wear Sweaters in Year Book Pictures," *Radcliffe News*, 18 November 1938, 1.

37. "Radcliffe Version of Campus Fashions Decrees Snuggly Woolens for Winter Boston Breezes," *Radcliffe News*, 2 September 1941, 2.

38. Spelman College, *Freshman Handbook, 1946–1947*, 19.

39. "College Girls Shun Campus Clothes Group Tell E. T. Slattery Experts," *Boston Herald*, 19 August 1938, 24. The trend for silk scarves was another development on the campuses of the Seven Sisters in the 1930s, and it lasted through the 1960s.

40. "99% Campus Uniform: Sweater, Skirt, Jacket," *Vogue*, 15 August 1939, 156.

41. "Girls Take to Boys Clothes for College Wear This Fall," *Boston Traveler*, 25 June 1940, 23.

42. "Knickers for Fall," *National Retail Clothier*, 17 September 1925, 109.

43. "We Nominate to Oblivion," *Daily Californian*, 16 February 1940, 2.

44. "Ye Turtle Necke Sweater," *Froth*, October 1932, 21.

45. For a concise summary of the report, see "Voice of the Trade," *Boot and Shoe Recorder*, 15 December 1934, 15. For more information on consumerism and the Depression, see McGovern, *Sold American*, chaps. 8 and 9.

46. "Army Provides Coats," *Daily Princetonian*, 19 February 1942, 2.

47. "Charlie Sets Styles, Survey Says," *Daily Princetonian*, 17 February 1950, 1.

48. "Fashion Is Spinach' to the Practical College Girl," *Springfield Massachusetts Republican*, 28 August 1938, 14.

49. Putnam, *Lady Lore*, 18.

50. "Radcliffe Girl Emphasizes Femininity in Switch from 'Sloppy-Joe' Style," *Harvard Crimson*, 3 October 1952, 4.

51. "Caracalla: His Humble Opinions and Particular Views," *Radcliffe News*, 19 November 1937, 5.

52. "Ye Turtle Necke Sweater," *Froth*, October 1932, 21.

53. "Woolknits Get Opinions on Knit Goods from *Mademoiselle*'s College Board," *Knitted Outerwear Times*, 2 August 1941, 1.

54. "Selling 'Slop-On,'" *Knitted Outerwear Times*, 16 August 1941, 4.

55. Dorothy Dix, "Girls Get Good Advice but Follow Other Kinds," *Tuscaloosa News*, 1 September 1943, 3.

56. "College Girls at Slattery's Parade in Campus Fashions," *Boston Herald*, 22 August 1940, 23.

57. Rhea Seeger, "Want Their Co-eds Neat and Natural," *Chicago Daily Tribune*, 26 December 1937, G3.

58. "Why College Girls Dress That Way," *New York Times*, 10 December 1944, SM28.

59. "That Spellman Look," *Campus Mirror*, October 1946, 2.

60. "College Sweater Fashions Make Debut in Shops, Magazines," *Knitted Outerwear Times*, 13 September 1951, 4.

61. "Fashions—Women's," *Froth*, February 1951, 25.

62. "College Shop Offers Lots of Sweaters," *Chicago Tribune*, 23 July 1956, B12.

63. *On & Off the Avenue*, 1965, 25. *On & Off the Avenue* was the title of Barnard's orientation booklet.

64. Mary Jo Kline to her parents, 28 February 1960, Mary Jo Kline Papers, Barnard College Archives, Lehman Hall, Barnard College, New York.

65. "The Liberated Body," speech to Fashion Group International, 15 May 1970, FGIR, box 79, folder 4.

66. *Dartmouth*, 13 May 1930, 2. The D.O.C. House was the Dartmouth Outing Club house, which was built in 1929 on Occorn Pond. The D.O.C. House was a popular place for students and their visitors to ice skate or cross-country ski and to eat. Members of the club ran a restaurant out of the building for decades.

67. "Short Subjects," *Esquire*, August 1955, 90.

68. "The Once Over," *Portsmouth Times*, 25 May 1960, 10.

69. "Colleges for Women Taboo Shorts Except for Sports Wear," *Boston Globe*, 24 May 1935, 14.

70. For more on the influence of the bicycle on women's fashion, see Garvey, "Reframing the Bicycle."

71. "Radcliffe," *Boston Sunday Post*, 13 January 1909, 4.

72. Children's clothing, sportswear, and men's pants were the first kinds of clothing to use zippers. For more information on the evolution of the zipper, see Friedel, *Zipper: An Exploration in Novelty*.

73. "Radcliffe College Athletes 'Blossom Out' in Shorts," *Boston Post*, 30 October 1938, 15.

74. "Radcliffe Athletes Have to Sacrifice Traditional Bloomers—Adopting Pleated Shorts with Zippers," *Harvard Crimson*, 31 May 1938, 1.

75. "Colleges for Women Taboo Shorts Except for Sports Wear," *Boston Globe*, 24 May 1935, 14.

76. "Shorts Are Banned as Attire for Girls By Major of Grafton," *Evening Independent*, 26 June 1930, 1.

77. "Double Dare Ya," *Dartmouth*, 8 May 1930, 2.

78. "Vox Populi," *Dartmouth*, 13 May 1930, 5.

79. Ibid., 15 May 1930, 5.

80. "Shorts Story," *Dartmouth*, 14 May 1930, 1.

81. "Student Body Endorses Shorts for Daily Wear," *Dartmouth*, 15 May 1930, 1.

82. "Double Dare Ya," *Dartmouth*, 8 May 1930, 2.

83. "Vox Populi," *Dartmouth*, 15 May 1930, 4.

84. "Caught Short," *Dartmouth*, 13 May 1930, 1.

85. "Vox Populi," *Dartmouth*, 19 May 1930, 3.

86. "With Other Editors," *Dartmouth*, 15 May 1930, 2.

87. Chalmers Alexander to his parent, 28 February 1932, Chalmers Alexander Letters, PUA.

88. "Comfort Not Principle," *Dartmouth*, 15 May 1930, 2.

89. "Campus Culottes Bode an End to Shorts Story," *New York Times*, 29 April 1960, 35.

90. Ibid.

91. "Long Life for Bermuda Shorts Seen on Near-By Campuses, *New York Times*, 6 August 1955, 8.

92. "On-Campus, Any Campus," *Vogue*, 15 August 1946, 34.

93. "Long Life for Bermuda Shorts Seen on Near-By Campuses," *New York Times*, 6 August 1955, 8.

94. "Fall Fashions for College Freshmen Are in Class by Themselves," *New York Times*, 28 July 1958, 27.

95. "Campus Culottes Bode an End to Shorts Story," *New York Times*, 29 April 1960, 35.

96. "As Others See Us," *Daily Collegian*, 15 November 1955, 4.

97. "Fashion Parade," *Tiger*, January 1959, 15.

98. "Bermuda Shorts: The Unnecessary Stigma," *Daily Collegian*, 8 April 1954, 2.

99. "Standards of Conduct," 1947, Dean of Women Papers (General Vertical File), PSU. This document is a draft of *Standards of Conduct*, which outlined regulations for women. It appears to have been produced by the Dean of Women's Office in 1947 and includes rules made by the Women's Student Government Association.

100. "Bermuda Day Proclaimed by Grove," *Daily Collegian*, 30 April 1954, 8.

101. "Bermuda Shorts: The Unnecessary Stigma," *Daily Collegian*, 8 April 1954, 2.

102. "Dean Releases Men's Bermuda Shorts Rule," *Daily Collegian*, 28 April 1954, 5.

103. Pat Mewborn, "Safety Valve," *Daily Collegian*, 8 May 1957, 4.

104. "Boards Give Penalties to 112 Coeds," *Daily Collegian*, 26 February 1959, 8. There was no mention in the student newspaper or university papers of men receiving punishment for breaking dress codes.

105. "Safety Valve," *Daily Collegian*, 6 September, 1955, 3.

106. "Editorial Opinion," *Daily Collegian*, 4 May 1962, 2.

107. "Women Are Now Wearing Sweaters," *Chicago Daily Tribune*, 6 June 1896, 16.

108. Robert C. Ruark, "School Principal Tries Dress Prohibition," *Victoria Advocate*, 12 February 1957, 4.

109. Unidentified speaker, "How the US Dresses Today" (speech, 10 February 1972), FGIR, box 79, folder 7.

## CONCLUSION

1. Frank, *Conquest of Cool*, 23.

2. "Sometimes You Can't Tell the Shops Without a Score Card," *New York Times*, August 12, 1967, Section Family, 13;

3. David Brass, "The New Breed of Consumer" (speech, 16 August 1973, New York City), FGIR box 80, folder 1.

4. Priscilla Tucker, "Off, Off, Off Seventh Avenue" (speech, 7 October 1975, New York City), FGIR, box 81, folder 5.

5. "Youth Impact Shakes U.S. Stores, Business," *Calgary Herald*, 10 February 1966, 10.

6. Polly Shaine, "Speech" (speech, New York City, April 1965), FGIR, box 96, folder 3,

7. "Report from Campus," *Princeton Alumni Weekly*, 14 May 1968, 9.

8. James Laver, "Speech" (speech, New York City, 10 February 1966), FGIR, box 76, folder 8.

9. "The No Bra Look," *Women's Wear Daily*, 27 August 1969, 12.

10. "Radcliffe Rejects the 'Stringbean Silhouette,'" *Harvard Crimson*, 20 March 1953, 4.

11. "Ex-Marine at Penn State Calls 'Bill of Rights' a 'Good Deal,'" *Penn State Alumni News*, February 1945, 6.

12. "Why College Girls Dress That Way, *New York Times*, 7 April 1946, 104.

13. Peter Curtis, "Critical Coed Coordinates," *Froth*, October 1959.

14. William S. Rukeyser, "Changing American Values about Money" (speech, New York City, 6 October 1976), FGIR, box 81, folder 12.

15. Jeanne Eddy, "Today Is an Age of Options" (speech, New York City, 6 June 1970), FGIR, box 79, folder 1.

16. Laurel Cutler, "Speech" (speech, New York City, 14 February 1969), FGIR, box 79, folder 1.

17. Katherine Murphy, "Speech" (speech, New York City, c. 1974), FGIR, box 80, folder 6.

18. Regina Lee Blaszczyk, "Styling Synthetics: DuPont's Marketing of Fabrics and Fashion in Postwar America," *Business History Review*, Autumn 2006, 519.

19. Ibid., 525.

20. G. Alman, "American Ready-to-Wear Spring 1979" (speech, New York City, November 14, 1978), FGIR, box 83, folder 6.

21. Frances Kotan, "On Travel and Leisure" (speech, New York City, 3 November 1977), FGIR, box 82, folder 2. Kotan provided industry predictions for the growth of the active sportswear market based on the rise of jogging as a form of exercise.

22. Khan et al., *Export Success and Industrial Linkages*, 36.

23. For a readable history of outsourcing apparel production, see Rosen, *Making Sweatshops*, chap. 6. For a look at the role of South Asia in clothing export, see Khan et al., *Export Success and Industrial Linkages*.

24. In her book *The Travels of a T-Shirt in the Global Economy*, Pietra Rivoli details the trade policies that established China as the leader of clothing production.

25. Rosen, *Making Sweatshops,* 115.

26. American Apparel and Footwear Association, *ApparelStats 2012*, 7.

27. Bess Myerson, "Speech" (speech, New York City, 18 April 1975), FGIR, box 82, folder 8.

28. "Rolled Socks, Short Skirts are Defended," *San Francisco Call and Post*, 14 February 1922, 3.

29. Hill, "People Dress So Badly Nowadays," 69.

30. Yves St. Laurent quoted in a speech by fashion editor of *Mademoiselle* magazine Nonnie Moore at the Pret-A-Porter show for the Fashion Group International in New York City on 2 May 1975. It can be found in the FGIR, box 81, folder 1.

31. "The Undergraduate Week," *Princeton Alumni Weekly*, 16 January 1924, 294.

# Bibliography

ARCHIVAL COLLECTIONS

Berkeley, California
    University Archives, Bancroft Library, University of California
        Agnes Edwards Partin Papers
        Record Book of the Women's Student Affairs Committee
        Records of the Associated Women Students, 1912–68
        Records of the Office of Student Activities
Cambridge, Massachusetts
    Radcliffe College Archives, Schlesinger Library, Radcliffe Institute, Harvard
        University
        Eleanor Stabler Brooks Papers
        Mary Hawthorne White Bunker Papers
        Dorothy Kneeland Clark Autobiography: "Around the World in 75 Years"
        Edith Culver Hagar Papers
        Hazel Hunkins-Hallinan Papers
        Eleanor Gilbert Montgomery Papers
        Anne Nancy Murray Morgan Papers
        Office of Public Information Records
        Office of Publicity Papers
        Marjorie Cherry Rohfleisch Papers
        Bailey Patterson Sweeny Diary
    University Archives, Pusey Library, Harvard University
        James Max Rosenthal Papers, 1905–7
Hanover, New Hampshire
    Rauner Special Collections Library, Dartmouth College
        Fredrick W. Baker Papers
        Richard Eberhardt Papers
        Records of Dartmouth College, Office of the President, Administration of Ernest
            Martin Hopkins, 1916–45
Minneapolis, Minnesota
    University Archives, Elmer L. Andersen Library, University of Minnesota, Twin Cities
        Nils and Patricia Hasselmo Papers
New York, New York
    Barnard College Archives, Lehman Hall, Barnard College
        Mary Jo Kline Papers
        Sherry Suttles Papers
    Manuscripts and Archives Division, Humanities and Social Sciences Library,
        New York Public Library
        Fashion Group International Records, ca. 1930–97
        Tobé-Coburn School For Fashion Careers, Records, 1937–96

Princeton, New Jersey
  Princeton University Archives, Seeley G. Mudd Library, Princeton University
    Chalmers W. Alexander Letters
    Robb and John Carson Letters
    Harrington DeGolyer Green Letters
Stanford, California
  University Archives, Cecil H. Green Library, Stanford University
    Burnham P. Beckwith Papers, Stanford Student Letters and Memoirs Collection
    Office of the Dean of Student Affairs Records
State College, Pennsylvania
  University Archives, Special Collections Library, Pennsylvania State University
    Ruth Ayres-Givens Papers
    College of Health and Human Development Records, 1909–2011
    Dean of Women Papers (General Vertical File)
    Women's Student Government Association and Association of Women Students
      Records


## UNIVERSITY PUBLICATIONS

*Atlanta University Bulletin*. Atlanta: Atlanta University, April 1912.
*Atlanta University Bulletin*. Atlanta: Atlanta University, April 1920.
*Atlanta University Bulletin*. Atlanta: Atlanta University, July 1922.
Barnard College. *On & Off the Avenue*. New York: Barnard College, 1965.
Morehouse College. *Annual Catalogue of Morehouse College for 1917–1918*. Atlanta:
  Morehouse College, 1917.
Ohio Wesleyan University. *Student Handbook, 1944*. Delaware: Ohio Wesleyan
  University, 1944.
Pennsylvania State University. *Announcement of Rules*. University Park, Pa.: Organization of
  the Women's Student Government Association of the Pennsylvania State College, 1918.
———. *College Customs and Co-Ediquette at Penn State*. University Park, Pa.: Association
  of Women Students at Pennsylvania State University, 1940–49.
———. *Home Economics Handbook, 1939*. University Park, Pa.: Department of Home
  Economics at Pennsylvania State University, 1939.
———. *Home Economics Handbook, 1942*. University Park, Pa.: Department of Home
  Economics at Pennsylvania State University, 1942.
———. *Home Economics Handbook, 1944*. University Park, Pa.: Department of Home
  Economics at Pennsylvania State University, 1944.
———. *Intramural Athletics Pamphlet*. University Park, Pa.: School of Education and
  Athletics at Pennsylvania State University, 1931.
———. *Introducing Penn State*. University Park, Pa.: Pennsylvania State University, 1955.
———. *La Vie*. University Park, Pa.: Pennsylvania State University, 1921.
———. *La Vie*. University Park, Pa.: Pennsylvania State University, 1925.
———. *The Penn State Woman's World: A Handbook for the Woman Student*. University
  Park, Pa.: Pennsylvania State University, 1958.
———. *Pennsylvania and Its Women: A Statement of Facts Concerning the Housing Needs
  for Women Students at The Pennsylvania State College*. University Park, Pa.: Women's
  Committee at The Pennsylvania State College, 1922.

———. *Report on Enrollment, Department of Public Information*. University Park, Pa.
Pennsylvania State University, 12 September 1961.

———. *Report on Housing, Office of Housing and Food Services*. University Park, Pa.:
Pennsylvania State University, 10 September 1979.

———. *Your Way Around Campus*. University Park, Pa.: Dean of Women's Office at
Pennsylvania State University, 1948.

Radcliffe College. *Alumni Questionnaire*. Office of the President. Cambridge: Radcliffe
College, 9 March 1945.

———. *Brochure on Radcliffe*. Cambridge: Office of Publicity at Radcliffe College, 1934.

———. *The Red Book: Student's Handbook of Radcliffe College, 1914*. Radcliffe Student
Government Association, 1914.

———.*The Red Book: Student's Handbook of Radcliffe College, 1947-1948*. Radcliffe
Student Government Association, 1947.

———. *The Red Book: Student's Handbook of Radcliffe College, 1957-1958*. Radcliffe
Student Government Association, 1957.

———. *Report On Housing, Office of Publicity*. Cambridge: Radcliffe College, 26 January 1951.

———. *Rules for the Halls of Residence*. Cambridge: Student Government Association of
Radcliffe College, 1919.

Spelman College. *College Government Handbook*. Atlanta: Spelman College, 1959

———. *The College Handbook, 1946-1947*. Atlanta: Spelman College, 1946.

———. *Fortieth Annual Circular of Spelman Seminary for Women and Girls*. Atlanta:
Spelman College, 1920.

———. *Freshman Handbook, 1946-1947*. Atlanta: Spelman College, 1946-47.

———. *Freshman Handbook, 1955-1956*. Atlanta: Spelman College, 1955-56.

———. *Promotional Pamphlet*. Atlanta: Spelman College, 1931.

———. *Spelman College Bulletin*. Atlanta: Spelman College, 1931.

———. *Student Handbook, 1946-1947*. Atlanta: Spelman College, 1946.

———. *Student Handbook, 1959-1960*. Atlanta: Spelman College, 1959.

Stanford University. *Stanford Handbook*. Stanford, Calif.: Stanford University, 1936-57.

University of California, Berkeley. *Panhellenic Handbook*. Berkeley: University of
California, 1939.

———. *Panhellenic Handbook*. Berkeley: University of California, 1942.

———. *Panhellenic Handbook*. Berkeley: University of California, 1945.

———. *Panhellenic Handbook*. Berkeley: University of California, 1948.

———. *Student Handbook*. Berkeley: Mortar Board of University of California, 1941.

University of Michigan. *Freshman Handbook*. Ann Arbor: University of Michigan, 1930

STUDENT NEWSPAPERS

*Adelphi College Fortnightly* (Adelphi University)
*Campus Mirror* (Spelman College)
*Carnegie Tartan* (Carnegie Tech)
*Daily Californian* (University of California, Berkeley)
*Daily Collegian* (Pennsylvania State University)
*Daily Princetonian* (Princeton University)
*Dartmouth* (Dartmouth)
*Froth* (Pennsylvania State University)

*Harvard Crimson* (Harvard University)
*Harvard Lampoon* (Harvard University)
*Jack-O-Lantern* (Dartmouth College)
*Maroon Tiger* (Morehouse College)
*Pelican* (University of California, Berkeley)
*Penn State Alumni News* (Pennsylvania State University)
*Princeton Alumni Weekly* (Princeton University)
*Radcliffe Daily* (Radcliffe College)
*Radcliffe Fortnightly* (Radcliffe College)
*Radcliffe News* (Radcliffe College)
*Red and Black* (Washington and Jefferson College)
*Spelman Messenger* (Spelman College)
*Spelman Spotlight* (Spelman College)

## TRADE AND COMMERCIAL MAGAZINES

*Boot and Shoe Recorder*
*Boston America*
*Boston Traveler*
*College and University Business*
*The Emporia Gazette*
*Esquire*
*Good Housekeeping*
*Harper's Monthly*
*Holiday Magazine*
*Knitted Outerwear Times*
*Life*

*Mademoiselle*
*Men's Wear Magazine*
*National Retail Clothier*
*New York Times Magazine*
*Boot and Shoe Recorder*
*Smart Set*
*Tobé Report*
*Town Topics*
*Vanity Fair*
*Vogue*
*Women's Wear Daily*

## NEWSPAPERS

*Berkeley Daily Gazette*
*Boston Evening Transcript*
*Boston Globe*
*Boston Herald*
*Boston Journal*
*Boston Post*
*Centre Daily Times*
*Chicago Daily Tribune*
*Chicago Defender*
*Cleveland News*
*The Emporia Gazette*
*The Evening Independent*
*Gettysburg Times*
*Freelance Star*

*Los Angeles Times*
*New London Evening Day*
*The New Student*
*New York Times*
*The Portsmouth Times*
*Reading Eagle*
*San Francisco Call and Post*
*Saturday Evening Post*
*Springfield Massachusetts Republican*
*St. Joseph News-Press*
*The Sunday Morning Star*
*Sweet Briar News*
*The Tuscaloosa News*
*The Victoria Advocate*

Ackerman, Louise M. "The Use of 'Look' in the Language of Fashion." *American Speech* 34, no. 2 (May 1959): 147–48.

Alexis, Marcus. "The Changing Consumer Market: 1935–1959." *Journal of Marketing* 26, no. 1 (January 1962): 42.

Atkinson, Byron H., and A. T. Brugger. "Do College Students Drink Too Much?: Two Deans Reply to This Perennial Question." *Journal of Higher Education* 30, no. 6 (June 1959): 305–12.

Ballou, Nellie. *Etiquette at College.* Harrisburg, Penn.: Handy Book Company, 1925.

Barnouw, Eric. *Open Collars.* Princeton: Princeton University Press, 1928.

Barrett, J. H. "College Seniors and the Liquor Problem." *Annals of the American Academy of Political and Social Science* 163 (September 1932): 130–46.

Bishop, John Peale. "The Higher Learning in America: Princeton University." *The Smart Set* 66, no. 3 (November 1921): 55–61.

Bjurstedt, Molly, and Samuel Crowther. *Tennis for Women.* New York: Doubleday, Page, 1916.

Boys, Richard C. "The American College in Fiction." *College English* 7 (April 1946): 379–87.

Butt, Porter. "Some Implications of Housing." *Journal of Higher Education* 8, no. 1 (January 1937): 27–32.

Butz, Otto. *The Unsilent Generation: An Anonymous Symposium in Which Eleven College Seniors Look at Themselves and Their World.* New York: Rinehard, 1958.

Darby, W. D. *Rayon and Other Synthetic Fibers: A Brief Account of the Origin, Etc.* New York: Dry Goods Economist, 1929.

Carman, Harry J. "Campus Issues and Problems." *Annals of the American Academy of Political and Social Science* 301 (September 1955): 46–57.

Chivers, Walter R. "Teaching Social Anthropology in a Negro College." *Phylon* 4 (1943): 353–61.

Cohen, Ralph F., ed. *The Harvard Man's Guide-Book.* Boston: E. S. Publishing, 1934.

Comstock, Ada L. "Health and the College Routine." In *The Freshman Girl: A Guide to College Life,* edited by Kate W. Jameson and Frank Lockwood, 146–54. Boston: D.C. Heath, 1925.

Cooper, Clayton Sedwick. *Why Go To College?* New York: The Century, 1912.

Cowley, W. H., and Willard Waller. "A Study of Student Life." *Journal of Higher Education* 6, no. 3 (March 1935): 132–42.

Crowell, Benedict, and Robert Forrest Wilson. *The Armies of Industry: Our Nation's Manufacture of Munitions for a World in Arms, 1917–1918.* New Haven: Yale University Press, 1921.

Deakins, Clarence E. "In Defense of Fraternities: The Fraternity As an Integral Part of the Educational Program." *Journal of Higher Education* 12, no. 5 (May 1941): 259–64.

Denny, Reuel. "American Youth Today: A Bigger Cast, A Wider Screen." *Daedalus* 91, no. 1 (Winter 1962): 124–44.

Editors of Esquire Magazine. *Esquire Etiquette: A Guide to Business, Sports, and Social Conduct.* New York: J. B. Lippincott, 1953.

Eldridge, Elizabeth. *Co-Ediquette: Poise and Popularity for Every Girl.* New York: E. P. Dutton, 1936.

Endelman, Reba Irwell. "Trends in the College Wardrobe." *Journal of Home Economics* 32, no. 5 (May 1940): 315-16.

Fitzgerald, F. Scott. *This Side of Paradise.* New York: Pocket Books, 1995.

Gardner, D. H. "The Student in the Land-Grant College Survey." *Journal of Higher Education* 3, no. 2 (January 1932): 26-30.

Glover, John George, ed. *The Development of American Industries: Their Economic Significance.* New York: Prentice-Hall, 1951.

Hall, Frances Howe. *The Correct Thing to Do in Good Society.* Boston: Dana Estes, 1902.

Harder, Kelsie, and Doris Thompson. "Who or What Is a Junior?" *American Speech* 37, no. 4 (December 1962): 285-88.

Harrison, Mrs. Burton, and Constance Cary Harrison. *Maidens and Matrons in American Society.* Cedar Falls: University of Northern Iowa, 1894.

Hartshorne, Edwards. "Undergraduate Society and the College Culture." *American Sociological Review* 8, no. 3 (June 1943): 321-32.

House of Kuppenheimer, Chicago. *Tempered Clothing; An Investment in Good Appearance.* Chicago: House of Kuppenheimer, 1921.

Hughes, Langston. "Cowards from the Colleges." *Crisis* 4 (1934).

Jaffe, Moe, Nat Bronx, and Dick Konter. *Collegiate.* New York: Shapiro, Bernstein, 1925.

Janney, J. E. "Fad and Fashion Leadership among Undergraduate Women." *Journal of Abnormal Psychology* 36, no. 2 (April 1941): 275-78.

Jones, William Bright, Donald E. Mose, and Richard Henry O'Riley. *For Men Lonely, A Complete Guide to Twelve Women's Colleges, 1947-1948.* Hanover, N.H.: Ripley, 1947.

Jones, William Bright, and Richard Henry O'Riley. *Weekend: A Girl's Guide to the College Weekend.* Boston: Houghton Mifflin, 1948.

Kelley, Janet Agnes. *College Life and the Mores.* New York: Bureau of Publications, Teachers College, Columbia University, 1949.

Kuenstler, Walter. "The Buying Habits of Women Students on the University of Pennsylvania Campus." *Journal of Marketing* 5 no. 2 (October 1940): 166-67.

Lindsey, Ben B., and Wainwright Evans. *The Revolt of Modern Youth.* Garden City, N.Y.: Garden City Publishing, 1925.

Lowrie, Samuel Harman. "Dating Theories and Student Responses." *American Sociological Review* 16, no. 3 (June 1951): 332-40.

McNally, Raymond V. "The American Wool Problem." *American Journal of Economics and Sociology* 7, no. 2 (January 1948): 185-203.

Merrill, Estell, ed. *Cambridge Sketches.* Cambridge, Mass.: Cambridge Christian Young Women's Association, 1896.

Miller, Annie Jenness. *Physical Beauty: How to Obtain and How to Preserve It.* New York: Webster, 1892.

Miller, Kelly. "The Past, Present and Future of the Negro College." *Journal of Negro Education* 2, no. 3 (July 1933): 411-22.

Mitchell, Erin Goseer. *Born Colored: Life Before Bloody Sunday.* Chicago: Ampersand, 2006.

National Center for Education Statistics. *120 Years of American Education: A Statistical Portrait.* Washington, D.C.: Department of Education, 1993.

Newcomer, Mabel. *A Century of Higher Education for American Women.* New York: Harper, 1959.

Nystrom, Paul H. *Fashion Merchandising*. New York: Ronald Press, 1932.

O'Donnell, Cyril. "Selling California Cotton, 1944–1948." *Southern Economic Journal* 17, no. 3 (January 1951): 288–301.

Presbry, Frank, and James Hugh Moffatt. *Athletics at Princeton*. New York: Frank Presbry, 1903.

Putnam, James W. *Lady Lore: A Swingtime Handbook of Etiquette for Girls, Young and Old*. Lawrence: University of Kansas, 1939.

Reader's Digest Association and National Educational Advertising Services (U.S.). *Characteristics of the College Market: A Marplan Research Report*. New York: National Educational Advertising Services, 1966.

Robinson, Dwight E. "The Importance of Fashions in Taste to Business History: An Introductory Essay." *Business History Review* 37, no. 1–2 (Spring–Summer 1963): 5–36.

Sloane, William. *Four American Universities*. New York: Harper and Brothers, 1895.

Smith, William M., Jr. "Rating and Dating." Home Economic Research Publication 110. Unpublished paper, Pennsylvania State University, 1 June 1952.

Sonneborn, Siegmund. "Price Factors in Men's Ready-to-Wear Clothing." *Annals of the American Academy of Political and Social Sciences* 89, no. 1 (May 1920): 61–66.

Stone, Natalia S. "The College Girl and the Depression." *Journal of Educational Sociology* 13, no. 6 (February 1940): 336–51.

Stote, Dorothy. *Men Wear Clothes, Too*. New York: Stotes, 1939.

Stratton, Dorothy, and Helen Schleman. *Your Best Foot Forward: Social Usage for Young Moderns*. New York: McGraw Hill, 1955.

Stuart, Jesse. *The American Fashion Industry*. Boston: Simmons College Prince School Publications in Retailing, 1951.

Thorn, Bob. "Veterans and Fraternities." *Student Veteran Association Journal*, 28 February 1946.

Unger, Art. *Complete Guide to Dating*. Englewood Cliffs, N.J.: Prentice-Hall, 1960.

U.S. Department of Education. *Historical Summary of Faculty, Students, Degrees, and Finances in Degree-Granting Institutions: Selected Years, 1869–70 through 2003–4, July 2005*, http://nces.ed.gov/programs/digest/d05/tables/dt05_169.asp. Accessed 12 July 2013.

Veblen, Thorstein, and Stuart Chase. *The Theory of the Leisure Class; An Economic Study of Institutions*. New York: Modern Library, 1934.

Vreeland, Francis McLennan. "Social Relations in the College Fraternity." *Sociometry* 2, no. 2 (May 1942): 151–62.

Waller, William. "The Rating and Dating Complex." *American Sociological Review* 2, no. 4 (October 1937): 727–34.

SECONDARY SOURCES

Agnew, John A. *The United States in the World-Economy: A Regional Geography*. Cambridge: Cambridge University Press, 1987.

The American Apparel and Footwear Association. *ApparelStats 2012*. Arlington, Va.: American Apparel and Footwear Association, 2012.

Anderson, Fiona. "This Sporting Cloth: Tweed, Gender and Fashion, 1860–1900." *Textile History* 37, no. 2 (November 2006): 166–86.

Arnold, Rebecca. *The American Look: Sportswear, Fashion, and the Image of Women in 1930s and 1940s New York*. London: I. B. Tauris, 2009.

Aron, Cindy S. *Working at Play: A History of Vacations in the United States*. New York: Oxford University Press, 2001.

Axtell, James. *The Making of Princeton University: From Woodrow Wilson to the Present*. Princeton, N.J.: Princeton University Press, 2006.

Bailey, Beth. *From Front Porch to Back Seat: Courtship in Twentieth-Century America*. Baltimore: Johns Hopkins University Press, 1988.

Banks, Jeffrey, and Doria de La Chapelle. *Preppy: Cultivating Ivy Style*. New York: Rizzoli, 2011.

Baudrillard, Jean. *Symbolic Exchange and Death*. London: Sage Publications, 1993.

Belasco, Warren, and Philip Scranton, eds. *Food Nations: Selling Taste in Consumer Societies*. New York: Routledge, 2002

Bentley, Amy. *Eating for Victory: Food Rationing and the Politics of Domesticity*. Urbana: University of Illinois Press, 1998.

Berry, Sarah. *Screen Style: Fashion and Femininity in 1930s Hollywood*. Minneapolis: University of Minnesota Press, 2000.

Blaszczyk, Regina Lee, ed. *Producing Fashion: Commerce, Culture, and Consumers*. Philadelphia: University of Pennsylvania Press, 2009.

Bledstein, Burton. *The Culture of Professionalism: The Middle Class and the Development of Higher Education in America*. New York: W. W. Norton, 1978.

Bledstein, Burton, and Robert D. Johnston. *The Middling Sorts: Explorations in the History of the American Middle Class*. New York: Routledge, 2001.

Blumer, Herbert. "Fashion: From Class Differentiation to Collective Selection." *Sociological Quarterly* 10, no. 3 (Summer 1969): 275–91.

Bradley, Stefan. *Harlem vs. Columbia University: Black Student Power in the late 1960s*. Urbana: University of Illinois Press, 2009.

Brander, Joseph. *The Middle Class in America: Perspectives and Trends*. New York: Nova, 2001.

Breward, Christopher, and Caroline Evans, eds. *Fashion and Modernity*. New York: Berg, 2005.

Brown, Alfred E., and Kenneth A. Reinhard. "Polyester Fiber: From Its Invention to Its Present Position." *Science* 173, no. 3994 (July 1971): 287–93.

Carter, Lawrence Edward. *Walking Integrity: Benjamin Elijah Mays, Mentor to Martin Luther King, Jr.* Macon, Ga.: Mercer University Press, 1998.

Chudacoff, Howard P. *The Age of the Bachelor: Creating an American Subculture*. Princeton, N.J.: Princeton University Press, 1999.

Clark, Daniel A. *Creating the College Man: American Mass Magazines and Middle-Class Manhood, 1890–1915*. Madison: University of Wisconsin Press, 2010.

Clarke, Allison J. *Tupperware: The Promise of Plastic in 1950s America*. Washington, D.C.: Smithsonian Books, 1990.

Clemente, Deirdre. "The Evolution of Collegiate Clothing, 1900–1930." *Journal of American Culture* 31, no. 1 (March 2008): 20–33.

———. "Made in Miami: The Development of the Sportswear Industry in South Florida, 1900–1960." *Journal of Social History* 41, no. 1 (Fall 2007): 127–48.

———. "Prettier Than They Used to Be: Femininity, Fashion and the Recasting of Radcliffe's Reputation, 1900–1950." *New England Quarterly* 82, no. 4 (December 2009): 637–66.

———. "Student Culture and Clothing on the Princeton Campus, 1910-1933." *Princeton University Library Chronicle* 71, no. 3 (Spring 2009): 237-64.

Cockerham, William, Thomas Abel, and Gunther Luschen. "Max Weber, Formal Rationality, and Health Lifestyles." *Sociological Quarterly* 34, no. 3 (August 1993): 413-28.

Cole, Johnetta Betsch, and Beverly Guy-Sheftall. *Gender Talk: The Struggle for Women's Equality in African American Communities*. New York: Ballantine Books, 2003.

Collins, Alicia C. "Black Women in the Academy: An Historical Overview." In *Sisters of the Academy: Emergent Black Women Scholars in Higher Education*, edited by Anna L. Green and Reitumetse Mabokela, 29-42. Sterling, Va.: Stylus, 2001.

Comstock, Susan. "The Making of an American Icon: The Transformation of Blue Jeans during the Great Depression." In *Global Denim,* edited by Daniel Miller and Sophie Woodward, 23-50. New York: Berg, 2011.

Cooke, John William. *Brooks Brothers: Generations of Style: It's All about the Clothing.* New York: Brooks Brothers, 2003.

Corrigan, Peter. *The Dressed Society: Clothing, the Body, and Some Meanings of the World.* London: Sage Publications, 2008.

Cowan, Ruth Schwartz. *More Work for Mother: The Ironies of Household Technology from the Open Hearth to the Microwave.* New York: Basic Books, 1983.

Craik, Jennifer. *The Face of Fashion: Cultural Studies in Fashion*. New York: Routledge, 1994.

Cromwell, Benedict, and Robert Forrest Wilson. *The Arms of Industry II: How America Went to War: An Account from Official Sources of the Nation's War Activities, 1917-1920.* New Haven: Yale University Press, 1921.Cunningham, Patricia. *Reforming Women's Fashion, 1850-1920*. Kent, Ohio: Kent State University Press, 2003.

Cunningham, Patricia A., and Susan Voso Lab, eds. *Dress in American Culture*. Bowling Green, Ohio: Bowling Green State University Popular Press, 1993.

Davis, Fred. *Fashion, Culture, and Identity*. Chicago: University of Chicago Press, 1992.

Delano, Page Dougherty, "Making Up for War: Sexuality and Citizenship in Wartime Culture." *Feminist Studies* 26, no. 1 (Spring 2000): 33-68.

Desser, David, and Garth Jowett. *Hollywood Goes Shopping*. Minneapolis: University of Minnesota Press, 2000.

Diner, Hasia. *Hungering for America: Italian, Irish, and Jewish Foodways in the Age of Migration*. Cambridge: Harvard University Press, 2003.

Douglas, Susan J. *Where the Girls Are: Growing Up Female in the Mass Media*. Pittsburgh: Three Rivers Press, 1995.

Dumas, Carrie M., and Julie Hunter. *Benjamin Elijah Mays: A Pictorial Life and Times*. Macon, Ga.: Mercer University Press, 2006.

Edwards, Caroline. *Fashion at the Edge: Spectacle, Modernity, and Deathliness*. New Haven: Yale University Press, 2003.

Eisenmann, Linda. *Higher Education for Women in Postwar America, 1945-1965*. Baltimore: Johns Hopkins University Press, 2006.

Enstad, Nan. *Ladies of Labor, Girls of Adventure: Working Women, Popular Culture, and Labor Politics at the Turn of the Twentieth Century*. New York: Columbia University Press, 1999.

Faderman, Lillian. *Odd Girls and Twilight Lovers: A History of Lesbian Life in Twentieth-Century America*. New York: Columbia University Press, 1991.

Farrell, James. *One Nation Under Goods: Malls and the Seductions of American Shopping.* Washington, D.C.: Smithsonian Books, 2003.

Farrell-Beck, Jane, and Colleen Gau. *Uplift: The Bra in America.* Philadelphia: University of Pennsylvania Press, 2002.

Fass, Paula S. *The Damned and the Beautiful: American Youth in the 1920s.* New York: Oxford University Press, 1979.

Featherstone, Mike. *Consumer Culture and Postmodernism.* London: Sage Publications, 2007.

Feldman, Christine Jacqueline. *"We Are the Mods": A Transnational History of a Youth Subculture.* New York: Peter Lang, 2009.

Fine, Ben, and Ellen Leopold. *The World of Consumption.* New York: Routledge, 1993.

Flugel, J. C. *The Psychology of Clothes.* London: Hogarth, 1932.

Frank, Thomas. *The Conquest of Cool: Business Culture, Counterculture, and the Rise of Hip Consumerism.* Chicago: University of Chicago Press, 1997.

Friedel, Robert D. *Zipper: An Exploration in Novelty.* New York: W. W. Norton, 1996.

Garvey, Ellen Gruber. "Reframing the Bicycle: Advertising-Supported Magazines and Scorching Women." *American Quarterly* 47, no. 1 (March 1995): 66–101.

Gasman, Marybeth. "Swept Under the Rug? A Historiography of Gender and Black Colleges." *American Educational Research Journal* 44, no. 4 (December 2007): 760–805.

Gerber, Ellen. "The Controlled Development of Collegiate Sport for Women, 1923–1936." *Journal of Sports History* 2, no. 1 (Spring 1975): 1–28.

Gidney, Catherine. "Dating and Gating: The Moral Regulation of Men and Women at Victoria and University Colleges, University of Toronto, 1920–1960." *Journal of Canadian Studies* 41 (Spring 2007): 138–40.

Gilman, Charlotte Perkins, Michael R. Hill, and Mary Jo Deegan. *The Dress of Women: A Critical Introduction to the Symbolism and Sociology of Clothing.* Westport, Conn.: Greenwood Press, 2002.

Gordon, Lynn. "The Gibson Girl Goes to College: Popular Culture and Women's Higher Education in the Progressive Era, 1890–1920." *American Quarterly* 39, no. 2 (Summer 1987): 211–30.

Gordon, Sarah A. "'Any Desired Length': Negotiating Gender Through Sports Clothing, 1870–1925." In *Beauty and Business: Commerce, Gender, and Culture in Modern America,* edited by Philip Scranton, 24–51. New York: Routledge, 2001.

———. *Make It Yourself: Home Sewing, Gender, and Culture, 1890–1930.* New York: Columbia University Press, 2009.

Grafton, Anthony. "The Precept System: Myth and Reality of a Princeton Institution." *Princeton University Library Chronicle* 64, no. 3 (Spring 2003): 467–503.

Hale, Grace Elizabeth. *A Nation of Outsiders: How the White Middle Class Fell in Love with Rebellion in Postwar America.* New York: Oxford University Press, 2011.

Handley, Susannah. *Nylon: The Story of a Fashion Revolution: A Celebration of Design from Art Silk to Nylon and Thinking Fibres.* Baltimore: Johns Hopkins University Press, 1999.

Harwarth, Irene, Mindi S. Maline, and Elizabeth DeBra. *Women's Colleges in the United States: History, Issues, and Challenges.* Washington, D.C.: National Institute on Postsecondary Education, Libraries, and Lifelong Learning, U.S. Dept. of Education, 1997.

Hayes, Elizabeth Joy. "White Noise: Performing the White Middle-Class Family on 1930s Radio." *Cinema Journal* 51, no 3 (Spring 2012): 97–119.

Hebdige, Dick. *Subculture: The Meaning of Style*. New York: Routledge, 2002.

Hegarty, Marilyn E. *Victory Girls, Khaki-Wackies, and Patriotutes: The Regulation of Female Sexuality during World War II*. New York: New York University Press, 2008.

Helvenston Sally I., and Margaret M. Bubolz. "Home Economics and Home Sewing in the United States, 1870-1940." In *The Culture of Sewing: Gender, Consumption, and Home Dressmaking*, edited by Barbara Burman, 303–25. New York: Berg, 1999.

Hill, Andrew. "People Dress So Badly Nowadays." In *Fashion and Modernity*, edited by Christopher Breward and Caroline Evans, 67–78. New York: Berg, 2005.

Hollander, Anne. *Sex and Suits: The Evolution of Modern Dress*. New York: Knopf, 1994.

Hollander, S. C., ed. *Marketing*. Vol. 2. Aldershot: Ashgate Publishing, 1993.

Honey, Maureen. *Creating Rosie the Riveter: Class, Gender, and Propaganda during World War II*. Amherst: University of Massachusetts Press, 1984.

Hornstein, Jeffrey. *A Nation of Realtors: A Cultural History of the American Middle Class*. Durham, N.C.: Duke University Press, 2005.

Horowitz, Helen Lefkowitz. *Campus Life: Undergraduate Cultures from the End of the Eighteenth Century to the Present*. Chicago: Chicago University Press, 1987.

Hounshell, David A., and John K. Smith. "The Nylon Drama." *American Heritage of Invention and Technology* 4 (Winter 1988): 40–55.

———. *Science and Corporate Strategy: Du Pont R&D, 1902–1980*. Cambridge: Cambridge University Press, 1988.

Hunter, Tera. *To 'Joy My Freedom: Southern Black Women's Lives and Labors after the Civil War*. Cambridge: Harvard University Press, 1997.

Iverson, Stephanie D. "'Early' Bonnie Cashin, before Bonnie Cashin Designs, Inc." *Studies of the Decorative Arts*, 8, no. 1 (Fall-Winter 2000-2001): 108–142.

Jacobson, Lisa. *Children and Consumer Culture in America Society: A Historical Handbook and Guide*. Westport, Conn.: Praeger, 2008.

Jacobson, Timothy Curtis, and George David Smith. *Cotton's Renaissance: A Study in Market Innovation*. Cambridge: Cambridge University Press, 2001.

Kaplan, Wendy, Bobby Tigerman, and Glenn Adamson. *California Design, 1930–1965: Living in a Modern Way*. Los Angeles: Los Angeles County Museum of Art, 2011.

Keist, Carmen N. "Rayon and Its Impact on the Fashion Industry at Its Introduction, 1910-1924." Master's thesis, Iowa State University, 2009.

Khan, Shahrukh Rafi, et al. *Export Success and Industrial Linkages: The Case of Readymade Garments in South Asia*. New York: Palgrave Macmillan, 2009.

Kimbrough, Walter M. *Black Greek 101: The Culture, Customs, and Challenges of Black Fraternities and Sororities*. Madison Teaneck, N.J.: Fairleigh Dickinson University Press, 2003.

Koritz, Amy. *Culture Makers: Urban Performance and Literature in the 1920s*. Chicago: University of Illinois Press, 2009.

Kuchta, David. *The Three-Piece Suit and Modern Masculinity England, 1550–1850*. Berkeley: University of California Press, 2002.

Leach, William. *Land of Desire: Merchants, Power, and the Rise of a New American Culture*. New York: Pantheon Books, 1993.

Leipzig, Sheryl, et al. "It's a Profession That Is New, Unlimited, and Rich: Promotion of the American Designer in the 1930s." *Dress* 35 (2008): 25–56.

Lewis, Guy. "Sport, Youth Culture and Conventionality, 1920–1970." *Journal of Sports History* 4, no. 2 (Summer 1977): 129–50.

Lipovetsky, Gilles. *The Empire of Fashion: Dressing Modern Democracy*. Princeton, N.J.: Princeton University Press, 1994.

Little, Monroe H. "The Extra-Curricular Activities of Black College Students, 1868–1940." *Journal of African American History* 87 (Winter 2002): 43–55.

Lowe, Margaret. *Looking Good: College Women and Body Image, 1875–1930*. Baltimore: Johns Hopkins University Press, 2006.

Lurie, Alison. *The Language of Clothes*. New York: Random House, 1981.

Macdonald, Anne L. *No Idle Hands: The Social History of American Knitting*. New York: Ballantine Books, 1990.

Maglio, Diane Marie. "From the Gilded Age to the Jazz Age: The Influence of Social Sports on American Men's Casual Dress, 1895–1930." Master's thesis, Fashion Institute of Technology, 1999.

Manley, Albert E. *A Legacy Continues: The Manley Years at Spelman College, 1953–1976*. Lanham, Md.: University Press of America, 1995.

Martin, Richard. "The Great War and the Great Image: J. C. Leyendecker's World War I Covers for *The Saturday Evening Post*." *Journal of American Culture* 20, no. 1 (June 2004): 55–74.

Martin, Richard, and Harold Koda. *Jocks and Nerds: Men's Styles in the Twentieth Century*. New York: Rizzoli Books, 1989.

Maynard, Margaret. *Dress and Globalisation*. Manchester: Manchester University Press, 2004.

McGovern, Charles. *Sold American: Consumption and Citizenship, 1890–1945*. Chapel Hill: University of North Carolina Press, 2006.

Mears, Patricia. *Ivy Style: Radical Conformist*. New Haven: Yale University Press, 2012.

Mettler, Suzanne. *Soldiers to Citizens: The G.I. Bill and the Making of the Greatest Generation*. New York: Oxford University Press, 2007.

Mintz, Steven. *Huck's Raft: A History of American Childhood*. Cambridge: Belknap Press of Harvard University Press, 2004.

Mohun, Arwen P. *Steam Laundries: Gender, Technology, and Work in the United States and Great Britain, 1880–1940*. Baltimore: Johns Hopkins University Press, 1999.

Moskowitz, Marina. *Standard of Living: The Measure of the Middle Class in Modern America*. Baltimore: Johns Hopkins University Press, 2004.

Munich, Adrienne. *Fashion in Film*. Bloomington: Indiana University Press, 2011.

Newman, Kathy. *Radio Active: Advertising and Consumer Activism, 1935–1947*. Berkeley: University of California Press, 2004.

Osgerby, Bill. "The Bachelor Pad as Cultural Icon: Masculinity, Consumption and Interior Design in American Men's Magazines." *Journal of Design History* 81, no. 1 (Spring 2005): 99–113.

———. *Playboys in Paradise: Masculinity, Youth, and Leisure-Style in Modern America*. New York: Berg, 2001.

———. "Understanding the 'Jackpot Market': Media, Marketing, and the Rise of the American Teenager." In *The Changing Portrayal of Adolescents in the Media Since*

*1950*, edited by Patrick E. Jamieson and Daniel Romer, 27–58. New York: Oxford University Press, 2008.

Pendergast, Thomas. *Creating the Modern Man: American Magazines and Consumer Culture, 1900–1950*. Columbia: University of Missouri Press, 2000.

Peril, Lynn. *College Girls: Bluestockings, Sex Kittens, and Coeds, Then and Now*. New York: W.W. Norton, 2006.

"The Politics of Consumption/The Consumption of Politics." *Annals of the American Academy of Political and Social Science* 611 (May 2007): 21.

Read, Florence M. *The Story of Spelman College*. Ann Arbor: University of Michigan, 1961.

Richardson, Joe Martin. *A History of Fisk University, 1865–1946*. Tuscaloosa: University of Alabama Press, 2002.

Riesman, David, Nathan Glazer, and Reuel Denney. *The Lonely Crowd*. New Haven: Yale University Press, 1961.

Rivoli, Pietra. *The Travels of a T-Shirt in the Global Economy: An Economist Examines Markets, Power, and the Politics of World Trade*. Hoboken, N.J.: John Wiley & Sons, 2005.

Robinson, Rebecca J. "American Sportswear: A Study of the Origins and Women Designers from the 1930's to the 1960's. Cincinnati, Ohio: University of Cincinnati, 2003." Master's thesis: University of Cincinnati, 2003.

Rosen, Ellen Israel. *Making Sweatshops: The Globalization of the U.S. Apparel Industry*. Berkeley: University of California Press, 2002.

Rosenzweig, Linda W. "'The Anchors of My Life': Middle-Class American Mothers and College-Educated Daughters, 1880–1920." *Journal of Social History* 25, no. 1 (Autumn 1991): 5–25.

Ross, Dorothy. *G. Stanley Hall: The Psychologist as Prophet*. Chicago: University of Chicago Press, 1972.

Rotundo, Anthony. *American Manhood: Transformations in Masculinity from the Revolution to the Modern Era*. New York: Basic Books, 1993.

Ryan, Susan. "The Architecture of James Gamble Rogers at Yale University." *Perspecta* 18 (1982): 25–41.

Samuel, Lawrence R. *The American Middle Class: A Cultural History*. New York: Routledge, 2014.

Savran, David. *Highbrow/Lowdown: Theater, Jazz and the Making of the New Middle Class*. Ann Arbor: University of Michigan Press, 2010.

Schneider, Eric. *Vampires, Dragons, and Egyptian Kings: Youth Gangs in Postwar New York*. Princeton, N.J.: Princeton University Press, 2001.

Schneider, Jane. "In and Out of Polyester: Desire, Disdain and Global Fibre Competitions." *Anthropology Today* 10, no. 4 (August 1994): 2–10.

Schor, Juliet. "In Defense of Consumer Critique: Revisiting the Consumption Debates of the 20th Century." *Annals of the American Academy of Political and Social Science* 611, no. 1 (May 2007): 16–30.

Schrum, Kelly. *Some Wore Bobby Sox: The Emergence of Teenage Girls' Culture, 1920–1945*. New York: Palgrave Macmillan, 2004.

Schwartz, Robert A. "Reconceptualizing the Leadership Roles of Women in Higher Education: A Brief History of the Importance of Deans of Women." *Journal of Higher Education* 68, no. 5 (September–October 1997): 502–22.

———. "The Rise and Demise of Deans of Men." *Review of Higher Education* 26, no. 2 (Winter 2003): 217–39.

Scott, Joan. "Gender: A Useful Category of Historical Analysis." *American Historical Review* 91, no. 5 (December 1986): 1053–75.

Scott, William R. "California Casual: Lifestyle Marketing and Men's Leisurewear, 1930–1960." In *Producing Fashion: Commerce, Culture, and Consumers*, edited by Regina Lee Blaszczyk, 169–86. Philadelphia: University of Pennsylvania Press, 2008.

Segal, Eric J. "Normal Rockwell and the Fashioning of American Masculinity." *Art Bulletin* 78, no. 4 (December 1996): 633–46.

Sequin, Robert. *Around Quitting Time: Work and Middle-Class Fantasy in American Fiction*. Durham, N.C.: Duke University Press, 2001.

Simmel, Georg. *On Individuality and Social Forms; Selected Writings*. Chicago: University of Chicago Press, 1971.

———. "Philosophy of Fashion." In *Simmel on Culture: Selected Writings,* edited by David Frisby and Mike Featherstone, 187–206. London: Sage Publications, 1997.

Solomon, Barbara Miller. *In the Company of Educated Women: A History of Women and Higher Education in America*. New Haven: Yale University Press, 1985.

Steele, Valerie. *The Corset: A Cultural History*. New Haven: Yale University Press, 2003.

Strasser, Susan. *Satisfaction Guaranteed: The Making of the American Mass Market*. New York: Pantheon Books, 1989.

———. *Waste and Want: A Social History of Trash*. New York: Henry Holt, 1999.

Strawn, Susan M. *Knitting America: A Glorious Heritage from Warm Socks to High Art*. New York: Voyager Books, 2007.

Sullivan, James. *Jeans: A Cultural History of an American Icon*. New York: Gotham Books, 2006.

Summers, Martin. *Manliness and Its Discontents: The Black dle Class and the Transformation of Masculinity, 1900-1930*. Chapel Hill: University of North Carolina Press, 2004.

Swiencicki, Mark A. "Consuming Brotherhood: Men's Culture, Style and Recreation as Consumer Culture, 1880-1930." *Journal of Social History* 31, no. 4 (Summer 1998): 773–808.

Syrett, Nicholas L. *The Company He Keeps: A History of White College Fraternities*. Chapel Hill: University of North Carolina Press, 2009.

Thelin, John R. *The History of American Higher Education*. Baltimore: Johns Hopkins University Press, 2004.

Tomlinson, Mark. "Lifestyle and Social Class." *European Sociological Review* 19, no. 1 (February 2003): 97–111.

Trigg, Andrew. "Veblen, Bourdieu, and Conspicuous Consumption." *Journal of Economic Issues* 35, no. 1 (March 2001): 99–115.

Turbin, Carole. "Fashioning the American Man: The Arrow Collar Man, 1907-1931." *Gender & History* 14, no. 3 (February 2003): 470–91.

Ulrich, Laurel Thatcher. *A Midwife's Tale: The Life of Martha Ballard, Based on Her Diary, 1785-1812*. New York: Vintage Books, 1991.

Veysey, Laurence R. *The Emergence of the American University*. Chicago: University of Chicago Press, 1965.

Wade, Melvin. "'Shining in Borrowed Plumage': Affirmation of Community in the Black Coronation Festivals of New England (c. 1750–c. 1850)." *Western Folklore* 40, no. 3 (July 1981): 211–31.

Wagner, Ann. *Adversaries of Dance: From the Puritans to the Present*. Urbana: University of Illinois Press, 1997.

Walker, Susannah. *Style and Status: Selling Beauty to African American Women, 1920–1975*. Lexington: University Press of Kentucky, 2007.

Ward, Cynthia L. "Vanity Fair Magazine and the Modern Style, 1914–1936." Ph.D. diss., State University of New York at Stony Brook, 1983.

Warner, Patricia Campbell. "Clothing the American Woman for Sport and Physical Education, 1860–1940: Public and Private." Ph.D. diss., University of Minnesota, 1986.

———. *When the Girls Came Out to Play: The Birth of American Sportswear*. Amherst: University of Massachusetts Press, 2006.

Watson, Yolanda, and Sheila Gregory. *Daring to Educate: The Legacy of the Early Spelman College Presidents*. Sterling: Stylus, 2005.

Webber-Hanchett, Tiffany. "Dorothy Shaver: Promoter of 'The American Look.'" *Dress* 30 (2003): 80–90.

Williams, Jesse Lynch. *Princeton Stories*. Freeport, N.Y.: Books for Libraries Press, 1969.

Wilson, Elizabeth. *Adorned in Dreams: Fashion and Modernity*. Berkeley: University of California Press, 1987.

Wilson, Laurel. "American Cowboy Dress: Function to Fashion." *Dress* 28 (2001): 40–52.

Winchell, Meghan K. *Good Girls, Good Food, Good Fun: The Story of USO Hostesses during World War II*. Chapel Hill: University of North Carolina Press, 2008.

Wouters, Cas. *Informalization: Manners and Emotions Since 1890*. Los Angeles: Sage Publications, 2007.

Yellis, Kenneth V. "Prosperity's Child: Some Thoughts on the Flapper." *American Quarterly* 21, no. 1 (Spring 1969): 44–64.

Yohannan, Kohle. *Claire McCardell: Redefining Modernism*. New York: Harry N. Abrams, 1998.

Zakim, Michael. *Ready-Made Democracy: A History of Men's Dress in the American Republic, 1760–1860*. Chicago: University of Chicago Press, 2006.

# Index

38, 40; history of, 3, 30, 39–40; influence on choice, 34, 39; interaction with collegians, 14, 27–28, 30, 34; Lord & Taylor, 28, 30, 32, 36, 40; Saks Fifth Avenue, 36–37, 40. *See also* Consumerism

Depression, 3, 13, 125

Dress codes, 6, 8, 37, 44–45, 50, 55–66, 58–59, 60–62, 64, 67–69, 134–35

Drinking, 21, 71, 73, 88, 90, 99, 100–101, 105–6, 113

Edward, Agnes, 77, 86–88, 90, 98, 101, 112–13, 123–24

Fabrics: flannel, 7, 34, 46, 48, 76; jersey, 2, 77, 123, 129, 142; tweed, 116, 118, 124, 144–45

Fiber: industry, 81, 84–85, 118, 142; man-made, 3, 9, 72, 76, 81, 85, 91, 118, 142; natural, 72, 128

Fitzgerald, F. Scott, 7, 13, 26–27, 48, 144. *See also* Princeton

Flapper culture, 21, 24–25, 108

Food, 10, 50, 54, 72–73, 89

Formal dress, 3, 5–6, 8–10, 18, 24, 29, 33, 46, 49, 51, 54, 69, 92–94, 98–115, 117, 140

Fraternities. *See* Greek life

Freshmen, 5, 29, 30, 39, 62, 64, 72, 78, 82, 91, 94, 102–3, 125

Fur, 21, 24, 27, 79, 88–89, 90, 97; raccoon, 21–23, 88, 102, 145

Gender: and administrative policy, 16, 37, 49, 60, 64, 67–69, 74, 135; black femininity, 6, 18, 24–25, 55, 61–62, 98, 118; black masculinity, 16, 19, 50, 118; blurred lines between, 13, 127, 139–40; tension between men and women on clothes, 34, 38–39, 65, 126–27, 133–34, 140; white femininity, 11, 19, 24, 54, 60, 101, 118, 122, 127, 130; white masculinity, 16, 44, 46–47, 101, 118, 122. *See also* African Americans; Consumerism; Magazines

Geography: city versus country, 6, 8, 24, 55, 57–58, 60; East Coast versus West Coast, 5–6, 32, 109, 124; influence on practicality of garments, 37, 43

Greek life, 102–3; fraternities, 67, 92, 99–103; sororities, 27, 68, 92, 101–2

Harvard, 7, 8, 23–24, 26, 34, 38–39, 55, 60, 72, 81, 83, 90, 95–96, 111, 121–22, 129, 132; Radcliffe women on men's dress, 34; students' comments on Radcliffe women, 72; student publications, 23, 46, 81, 113, 118, 126

Hats, 24, 34, 87

Home economics, 37, 76, 84–86, 113

Hosiery, 21, 29, 35, 85, 91, 125, 143; bare legs versus, 127; garters, 3–4, 21; industry, 35, 143; socks, 10, 21, 30, 38–40, 79, 81, 86, 91, 109, 119, 121, 133–34

Hunkins, Hazel, 27, 78–79, 86, 88, 90, 111, 122

Individuality in dress: rise of, 10, 13, 36, 41, 11, 115

Jeans, 6, 8, 39, 55, 57, 59–60, 66, 69, 134, 140; and dress codes, 56, 60, 62, 64, 67; men's jeans, 51, 54, 121, 139; and wartime, 36–37, 58

Knitting, 36, 59, 118, 121, 123–24

Laundry, 9, 55, 72, 81–84, 91

Leyendecker, J. C., 15–16. *See also* Arrow Collars

Lifestyle: rise of, 13, 137–38, 140, 143

Magazines, 12, 14, 23, 47; college humor, 4, 18, 23, 47, 75, 89, 94, 101, 108–9, 125, 134; contests sponsored by, 29, 33; editors of, 8, 12, 13–14, 28–29, 33, 35–36, 38–39, 65, 122, 124, 138, 140–41; *Esquire*, 8, 12, 34, 121, 128; guest editors of, 30, 32–34, 60; interactions with collegians, 1, 12, 18, 33–34, 38–39, 41, 47, 54, 56, 60, 65, 121–22; interactions with fashion industry, 8, 13, 32–34, 38; *Mademoiselle*, 1, 9, 12–13, 30, 32–33, 35, 133; *Vogue*, 1, 9, 27, 34, 39, 65, 124, 133

Marketing, 13, 29–30, 33, 36, 39, 41, 118

Middle class, 2, 4–7, 10–11, 13, 18, 25, 109, 115; consumerism of, 3, 9–10, 16, 18, 29, 34, 37, 41, 122, 137; education of, 4–7, 13, 17, 25; historiography of, 2, 4, 138; influence of middle-class youth, 13, 32, 25, 28, 39, 40–41, 47, 69, 114–15, 118, 121, 125, 132, 137; and suburbanization, 3, 10–11, 69, 85, 118, 137–39

Morality, 5, 24, 35, 50, 61, 106

Morehouse College: administration, 43, 50; athletics, 16, 50; masculinity, 43, 50, 64, 97; religion, 50, 98. *See also* African Americans; Gender; Spelman College

Mothers: adoption of casual dress, 35, 41, 69, 118, 122, 129; as inhibitors to casual dress, 5, 29, 35, 80, 112; influence of, on choices, 5, 11, 13, 18, 28, 30, 37–38, 64, 75, 77–80, 86–91, 102, 111, 114. *See also* Laundry

Murray, Anne Nancy, 13, 15, 37–38, 54, 70, 81

Nationalization of collegiate culture, 23, 25, 47, 103

Pajamas, 30, 67, 73, 77

Pants: Anti-Slacks Campaign, 65; college women in, 8, 11, 28, 34–36, 38–39, 54–69, 142; Committee to Wear Pants to Dinner, 1, 68; men's and editors' dislike of, 8, 38–39, 65; nonmatching jackets and, on men, 44, 47, 50–51, 54; World War II origins of, 36–37, 57–59, 65. *See also* Appropriation of menswear, women's; Gender; Jeans

Patterson, Bailey, 28, 74, 104–5

Penn State: administration dress codes, 8, 36, 54–55, 58, 64, 67–69, 132–36, 140; curriculum influence on clothing, 7, 44, 49, 50–51; daily life, 17, 64–65, 72, 76–77, 80, 82, 87, 92–94, 103–4; female enrollment, 5, 71, 97; middle-class students, 2, 5, 7, 26, 50, 71, 107–10; suits on campus, 44, 49, 51

Princeton: administration, 43, 54, 106; as trendsetter, 16, 22, 25, 47, 107; beer

suits, 79; campus life, 70–71, 82, 97, 144; and Fitzgerald, 26–27; public image of, 7, 12, 23–25, 27, 48, 96–97, 106; social hierarchy, 5, 11, 21–23, 27, 77, 122, 125. *See also* Alexander, Chalmers

Prohibition, 23, 105–6

Radcliffe College: city location as influence on dress, 8, 24, 55, 60; daily life, 19, 24, 28, 54, 60, 70, 72–73, 83, 88, 90, 104, 124; rejection of editors' and men's opinions, 1, 33–34, 38, 78, 96, 113–14; reputation of students, 24, 71, 95; self-regulation at, 1, 5, 35, 45, 58, 60, 74–75, 91. *See also* Culver, Edith; Gender; Murray, Nancy; Patterson, Bailey; Seven Sisters schools

Retailing, 27, 29–32, 34, 125, 139

Self-regulation, 1, 45, 54–55, 60, 134–36

Seven Sisters schools, 6, 27, 33, 55–56, 60, 95–97; women at, as slobs, 8, 37, 57, 124; Barnard, 6, 8, 24, 60, 128, 133; Ivy League men's opinions of women at, 96; Smith, 8, 24, 27, 35, 55–58, 60, 92, 95, 104, 124, 133, 135; Vassar, 24, 27, 30, 32, 35, 43, 55, 57–58, 78–79, 86, 95, 124, 133, 135; Wellesley, 8, 35, 45, 54, 56–58, 60, 74, 95–96, 127, 130

Sewing, 19, 33, 85–88, 98, 111, 113

Sex: in cars, 104, 114; changing standards of practice, 21, 24, 73–74, 103–4; and drinking, 42, 73, 99, 105–6

Shopping, 27–29, 32, 36, 63–64, 89, 111, 134, 139

Sizes, 35, 39–40, 126, 137

Sloppy dress, 5, 21, 34–35, 38, 66, 121; accusation of, from old guard, 5, 9, 21, 42, 118, 121, 126–27, 140; dirty clothes, 38, 57, 66; Harvard and, 24, 38; oversized clothes, 9, 12, 21, 38, 57, 66, 121, 126–27, 140

Sloppy joe sweater, 35, 41, 120, 126–28

Smoking, 21, 97, 103

Sororities. *See* Greek life

Spelman College: administration, 6, 18,